ASIAN HISTORICAL DICTIONARIES
Edited by Jon Woronoff

1. *Vietnam,* by William J. Duiker. 1989
2. *Bangladesh,* by Craig Baxter and Syedur Rahman. 1989
3. *Pakistan,* by Shahid Javed Burki. 1991
4. *Jordan,* by Peter Gubser. 1991
5. *Afghanistan,* by Ludwig W. Adamec. 1991
6. *Laos,* by Martin Stuart-Fox and Mary Kooyman. 1992
7. *Singapore,* by K. Mulliner and Lian The-Mulliner. 1991
8. *Israel,* by Bernard Reich. 1992
9. *Indonesia,* by Robert Cribb. 1992
10. *Hong Kong and Macau,* by Elfed Vaughan Roberts, Sum Ngai Ling, and Peter Bradshaw. 1992
11. *Korea,* by Andrew C. Nahm. 1993
12. *Taiwan,* by John F. Copper. 1993
13. *Malaysia,* by Amarjit Kaur. 1993

Historical Dictionary
of
MALAYSIA

by

AMARJIT KAUR

Asian Historical Dictionaries, No. 13

The Scarecrow Press, Inc.
Metuchen, N.J., & London
1993

British Library Cataloguing-in-Publication data available

Library of Congress Cataloging-in-Publication Data

Kaur, Amarjit
Historical dictionary of Malaysia / by Amarjit Kaur.
p. cm.—(Asian historical dictionaries ; no. 13)
Includes bibliographical references.
ISBN 0–8108–2629–1 (alk. paper)
1. Malaysia—History—Dictionaries. I. Title. II. Series: Asian historical dictionaries ; no. 13.
DS596.K36 1993
959.5′003—dc20 92–37427

Manufactured in the United States of America

Printed on acid-free paper

for IAN, NOREEN, and DAVID

CONTENTS

FOREWORD

Malaysia is usually regarded as one of Asia's success stories. By most measures, it certainly deserves that reputation. The country has achieved strong economic growth, gradually shifting from an agricultural and commodity-based economy to a newly industrialized one. Great social and cultural gaps have been overcome in forging the new nation of Malaysia. Politically, it has done better than most in maintaining a working democracy. Despite some remaining flaws, enough has been accomplished to make it a model of sorts and a country outsiders should know more about.

Understanding Malaysia, however, is not that easy as it is a very complex country. Various racial and religious groups from diverse regions have been brought together into what is often regarded as a model multi-ethnic, multi-religious society. The political situation is frequently complicated, if not confusing, and today's events are harder to grasp if one is unaware of the earlier colonial and pre-colonial periods. Finally, individuals play an important role so it is essential to know who is who.

We are therefore pleased that this Malaysia Dictionary delves into so many aspects and sheds light on so many people, places and events that outsiders (and Malaysians) should know more about. It helps us follow history and current events with numerous entries, tables and a chronology. The comprehensive bibliography points the reader in the right direction for further information.

This volume was written by someone who knows Malaysia well. Herself a Malaysian and formerly Associate Professor of History at the University of Malaya, Dr. Amarjit Kaur is presently teaching at the University of New England in Australia. Aside from this book, she has written extensively on economic history, particularly transport, and issues relating to women and human rights during the colonial and modern periods.

Jon Woronoff
Series Editor

ACKNOWLEDGEMENTS

In the preparation of this Dictionary, I especially wish to thank my husband, Ian Metcalfe for his encouragement and valuable assistance. I also wish to thank a number of my former colleagues at the Faculty of Arts and Social Sciences, University of Malaya, who discussed specific aspects of the bibliography and made useful suggestions. Thanks also go to Gerda van Houtert of the University of New England, who typed the final draft and gave much assistance. My thanks are also due to Kiranjit, Manjit, Manmeet and Pauline Lee who helped in many ways. The libraries of the History Department and the University of Malaya (Kuala Lumpur); Queen Elizabeth House and Rhodes House (Oxford); and the School of Oriental and African Studies (London) gave me facilities and assistance which contributed to the accomplishment of this project.

Amarjit Kaur
University of New England
July 1991

ABBREVIATIONS AND ACRONYMS

ABIM	Angkatan Belia Islam Malaysia
ALIRAN	Persatuan Aliran Kesedaran Negara
AMIPF/IPF	All-Malaysian Indian Progressive Front
APU	Angkatan Perpaduan Ummah/Umah
ASA	Association of Southeast Asia
ASEAN	Association of Southeast Asian Nations
ASN	Amanah Saham Nasional
BERJASA	Barisan Jama'ah Islamiah Se Malaysia
BERJAYA	Bersatu Rakyat Jelata Sabah
BERSEPADU	Parti Bersatu Rakyat Bumiputera Sabah
BN	Barisan Nasional
BNBCC	British North Borneo Chartered Company
CPM	Communist Party of Malaya
DAP	Democratic Action Party
EIC	English East India Company
FELDA	Federal Land Development Authority
FMS	Federated Malay States
GERAKAN	Gerakan Rakyat Malaysia
HAMIM	Parti Hisbul Muslimin Malaysia
ICA	Industrial Co-ordination Act
ICU	Implementation Coordination Unit
IMP	Independence of Malaya Party
ISA	Internal Security Act
KADA	Kedah Regional Development Authority
KIMMA	Kongres India Muslim Malaysia
KITA	Kesatuan Insaf Tanah Air
KMM	Kesatuan Melayu Muda
KRIS	Kekuatan Rakyat Istimewa
MADA	Muda Agricultural Development Authority
MARA	Majlis Amanah Rakyat
MCA	Malaysian Chinese Association
MIC	Malaysian Indian Congress
MPAJA	Malayan People's Anti-Japanese Army
MTUC	Malaysian Trades Union Congress
NCC	National Consultative Committee

NECC	National Economic Consultative Committee
NEP	New Economic Policy
NOC	National Operations Council
NSP	National Security Council
PAP	People's Action Party
PAPERI	Parti Persaudaraan Islam
PAS	Parti Islam Se Malaysia
PASOK	Pertubuhan Kebangsaan Pasok Nunukragang Bersatu
PBDS	Parti Bansa Dayak Sarawak
PBS	Parti Bersatu Sabah
PEKEMAS	Parti Keadilan Masyarakat Melayu
PERNAS	Perbadanan Nasional Berhad
PMIP	Pan-Malayan Islamic Party
PPBB	Parti Pesaka Bumiputera Bersatu
PPP	People's Progressive Party
PSRM	Parti Sosiolis Rakyat Melayu
PUTERA	Pusat Tenaga Ra'ayat
SB	Special Branch
SCCP	Sabah Chinese Consolidated Party
SCP	Sabah Chinese Party
SDP	Socialist Democratic Party
SEDC	State Economic Development Corporation
SNAP	Sarawak National Party
SS	Straits Settlements
SUPP	Sarawak United People's Party
UDP	United Democratic Party
UMNO	United Malays National Organization
UMS	Unfederated Malay States
UNKO	United National Kadazan Organization
UPKO	United Pasok-Momogun Kadazan Organization
USNO	United Sabah National Organization
ZOPFAN	Zone of Peace, Freedom and Neutrality

CHRONOLOGY

PREHISTORY UP TO AROUND 500 BC

BC	38,000	earliest remains of man in area: Niah, Sarawak
	8,000	local prehistoric cultures (Hoabinhion and Neolithic)
	300	earliest signs of Bronze and Iron Age cultures in Malaysia Dong Son
	200	start of trading contacts with India and China

EARLY POLITIES IN THE MALAYA PENINSULA BC 500–1400 AD

BC	100–200 AD	emergence of trading kingdoms in the Isthmus of Kra
AD	500–800	development of local trading polities with Hindu-Buddhist orientation in Bujang Valley and in North Perak
	600–1000	west coast of Peninsular Malaysia under influence of Sri Vijaya
	1290	first Muslim states in north Sumatra
	1300–1400	area of Straits of Melaka under influence of Majapahit Kingdom

THE MELAKA SULTANATE 1400–1511

1400	foundation of Melaka
1403–1410	the Ming voyages: Melaka under protection of China
1445	Melaka becomes a sultanate
1450	expansion of Melakan 'empire'
1509	the first Portuguese at Melaka
1511	the fall of Melaka to the Portuguese

THE COMING OF THE WEST AND THE RISE OF OTHER MALAY KINGDOMS 1511–1800

1511–1640	triangular war between Aceh, Johor and Portuguese Melaka
1511–1699	empire of Johor under the Melaka line
1528	Sultan Muzaffar Syah establishes Perak Kingdom
1641	the Dutch capture Melaka from the Portuguese; start of Dutch dominance in area
1699	assassination of Sultan Mahmud of Johor at Kota Tinggi
1699–1819	empire of Johor, mostly at Riau, under Bendahara line
1699–1784	period of Menangkabau-Bugis struggle for domination of Straits of Melaka
1722	first Ruler of Trengganu Kingdom installed

1740–1779	reign of Sultan Muhammed Jiwa in Kedah
1745	formation of Bugis sultanate of Selangor
1770s	Trengganu faction in control of Kelantan
1773	establishment of confederacy of Negeri Sembilan
1784	death of Raja Haji at Melaka: Dutch break Bugis power in area
1786	British occupy Penang
1800	Sultan Muhammed I (of Kelantan descent) assumes control in Kelantan
1812	death of Sultan Mahmud Syah, last ruler of united Johor-Riau kingdom

THE COLONIAL PERIOD

1819	British occupy Singapore
1824	Anglo-Dutch Treaty dividing Malay world into Dutch and British spheres of influence: Melaka taken over by British
1826	British treaty with Bangkok (Burney's Treaty) limiting spread of Thai influence in Peninsula, but Kedah under the Thais (1821)
1831–1832	the Naning War
1840s	increase of importance of tin; influx of Chinese tin miners in west coast tin states
1841	James Brooke established as 'Raja' of Sarawak
1842	Thais establish Perlis as a separate state

1846	British annex Labuan
1858–1868	civil war in Pahang
1860s	Larut wars (*kongsi* wars in Perak) and Perak succession dispute
1866	start of Selangor civil war
1874	start of British intervention and control in Perak, Selangor and Sungei Ujung
1875–1876	the Perak War
1874–1896	period of the Residential System in Perak, Selangor and Sungei Ujung
1881	British North Borneo Chartered Company establishes center in North Borneo (Sabah)
1888	Pahang comes under the Residential System; Sarawak and North Borneo granted protectorate status by British government
1891–1895	Pahang Rebellion (To' Bahaman)
1896	Treaty of Federation: formation of FMS; Anglo-French agreement giving British free hand in northern Thai-protected Malay States
1909	Treaty of Bangkok: four northern Malay states transferred from Thai to British overlordship
1914	Johor brought under British control
1914–1918	First World War
1915	To' Janggut rebellion in Kelantan
1920–1941	British adopt decentralization policy in FMS; early signs of Malay nationalism

1929–1932	the Great Depression
1931	free immigration into Malay Peninsula ended
1937+	start of sporadic but quite serious labour unrest in Malaya and Singapore
1941–1945	Japanese conquest and occupation
1945	return of British to Malaya, North Borneo and Sarawak
1946	Malayan Union Scheme introduced and anti Malayan Union Movement; formation of UMNO; formation of MIC; Sarawak and British North Borneo become Crown Colonies
1948	Malayan Union Scheme abandoned; Federation of Malaya inaugurated
1948–1960	the Emergency
1951–1957	development of struggle for Malayan independence
1951	formation of MCA-UMNO alliance in Kuala Lumpur municipal elections
1955	MIC joins Alliance; first federal elections; Alliance triumphs in elections

POST–INDEPENDENCE PERIOD 1957–

1957	Malaya becomes Independent
1960	formation of the Association of Southeast Asia (ASA) with the Philippines and Thailand

1961	Tunku Abdul Rahman proposes formation of Malaysia
1963	creation of Malaysia
1963–1966	confrontation with Indonesia
1965	Singapore leaves Malaysia
1967	formation of the Association of Southeast Asia Nations (ASEAN) with Singapore, Indonesia, the Philippines and Thailand
1969	13 May Riots in Kuala Lumpur; constitution suspended
1969–1971	Malaysia ruled by National Operations Council (NOC); start of the New Economic Policy
1981	Start of the Mahathir era
1983	constitutional crisis involving the position of Malaysia's hereditary rulers
1985–1986	constitutional crisis in Sabah results in ***Berjaya*** being ousted and ***Parti Bersatu Sabah*** comes into power
1987	UMNO racked by power struggle between Mahathir Mohamad and Tengku Razaleigh Hamzah; "Operation Lallang" carried out by the Mahathir administration resulting in the detention of prominent opposition politicians, trade unionists, educationalists, environmentalists and church and community leaders
1988	deregistration of UMNO; formation of UMNO ***Baru*** by Mahathir Mohamad

1989 — ***Semangat*** '46, led by Tengku Razaleigh Hamzah, registered as a new political party;
formation of the ***Angkatan Perpaduan Ummah*** (APU) (comprising ***Semangat*** '46, PAS, ***Berjasa*** and ***Hamim***);
Malaysia hosts the Commonwealth Heads of Government Meeting in Kuala Lumpur;
peace accord signed by Malaysia, Thailand and the outlawed Communist Party of Malaya. The CPM under Chin Peng abandons its 41-year armed struggle to overthrow the Malaysian government.

1990 — formation of ***Gagasan Rakyat*** (comprising ***Semangat*** '46, DAP, ***Parti Rakyat Malaysia***, All Malaysian Indian Progressive Front and Malaysian Solidarity Party);
electoral coalition between the ***Angkatan Perpaduan Ummah*** and the ***Gagasan Rakyat***, forged by Tengku Razaleigh Hamzah;
Parti Persatu Sabah withdraws from the ***Barisan Nasional*** coalition;
Eighth General Elections. Ruling coalition—the ***Barisan Nasional*** retains its two-third majority in Parliament. Kelantan and Sabah won by the Opposition.

MAP 1 MALAYSIA

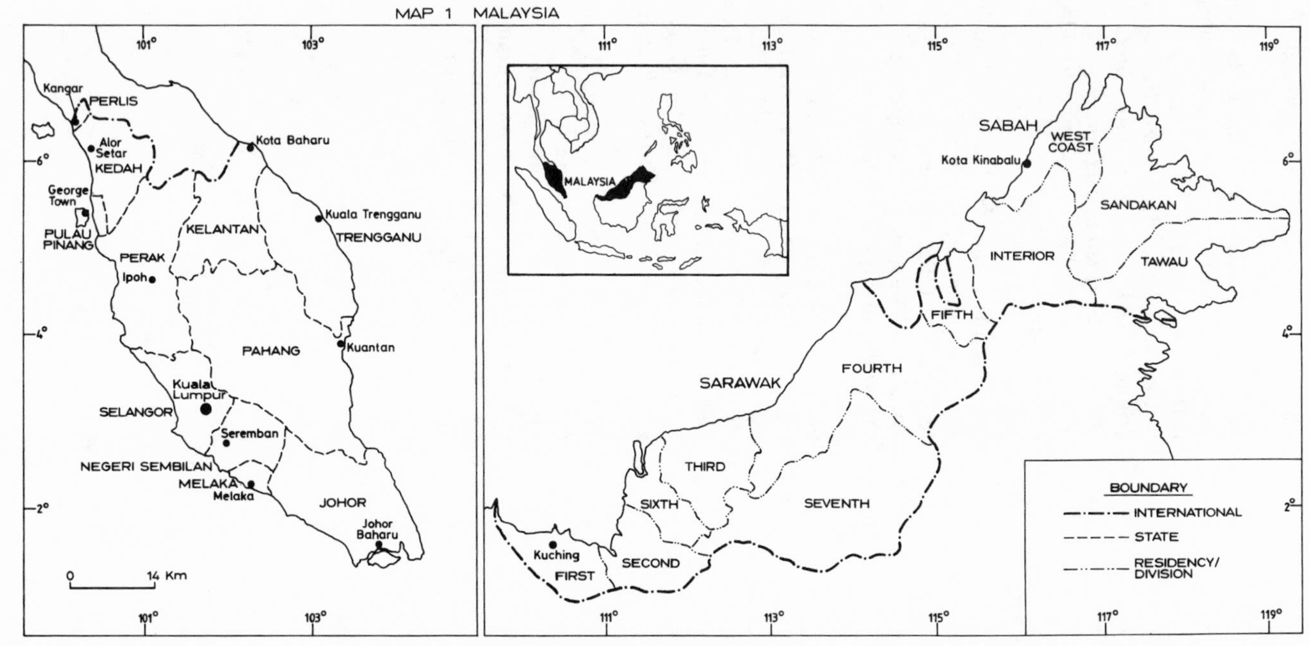

MAP 2 MALAYSIA RELIEF

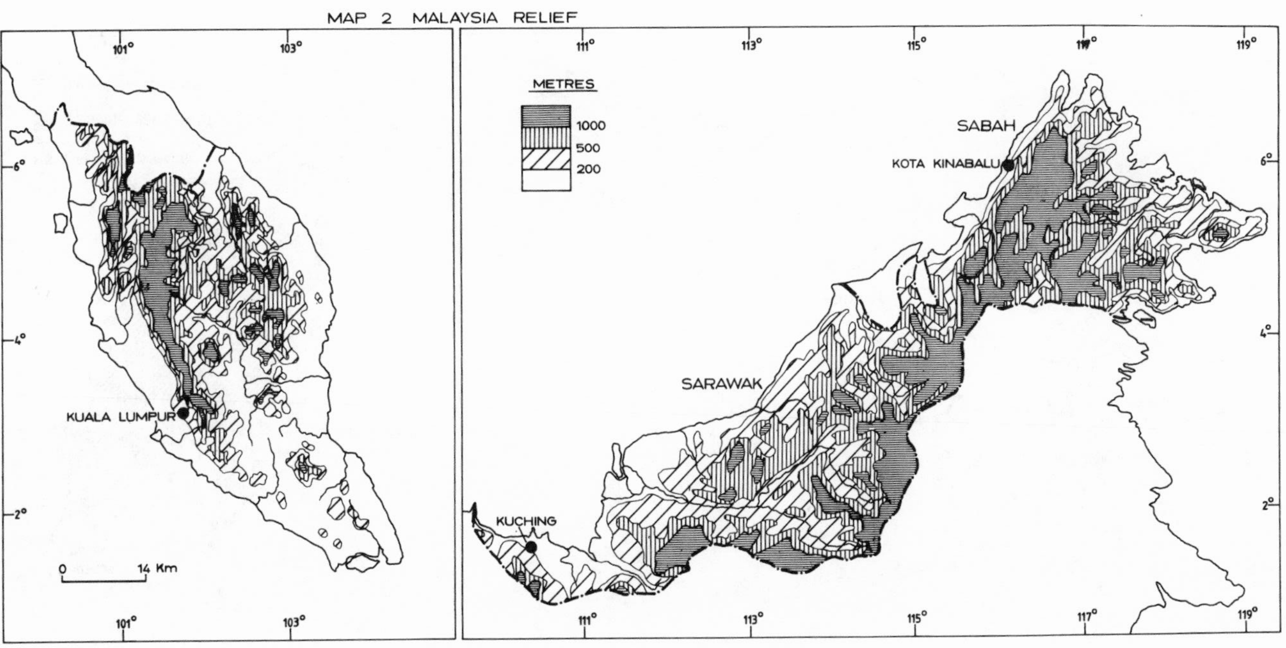

MAP 3 HISTORICAL MAP OF MALAYSIA

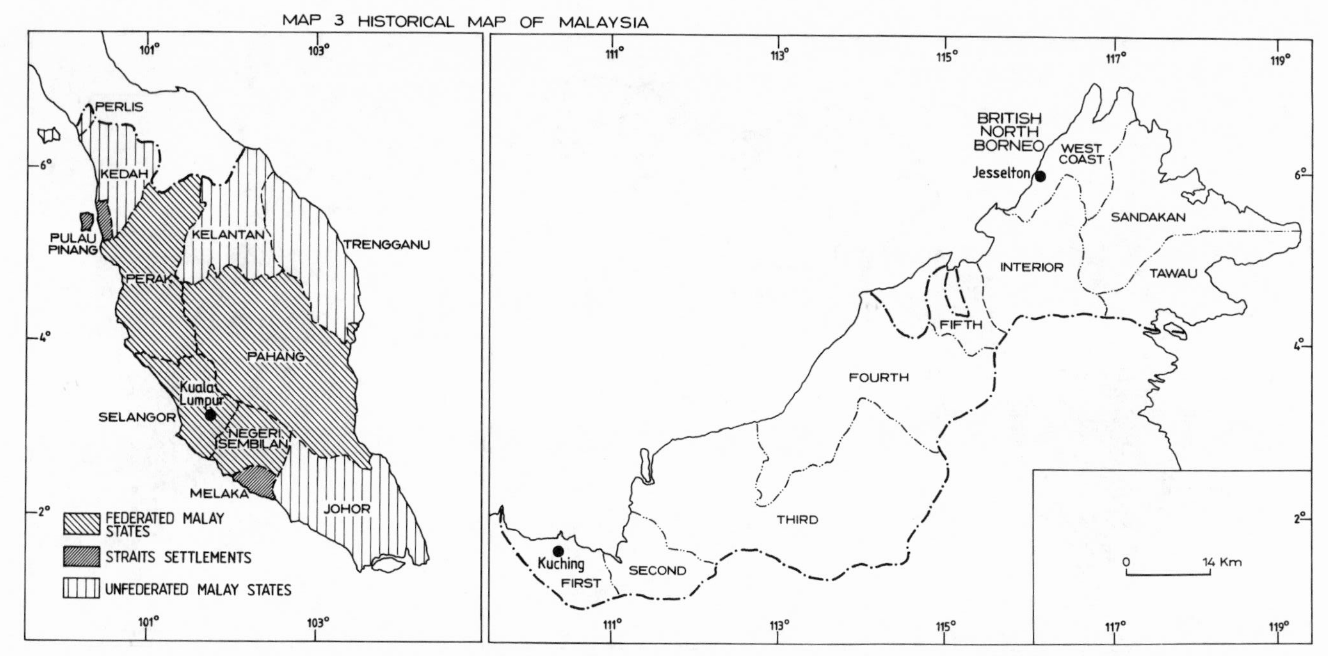

MAP 4 MALAYSIA ECONOMY

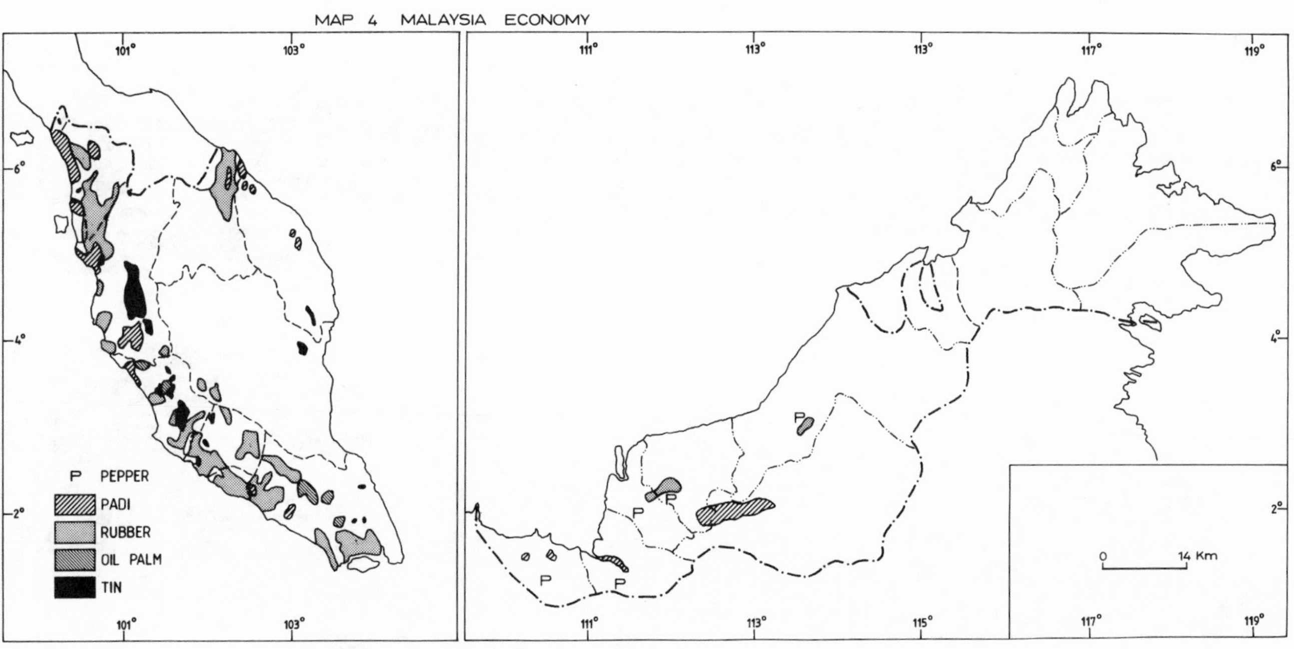

MAP 5 MALAYSIA POPULATION

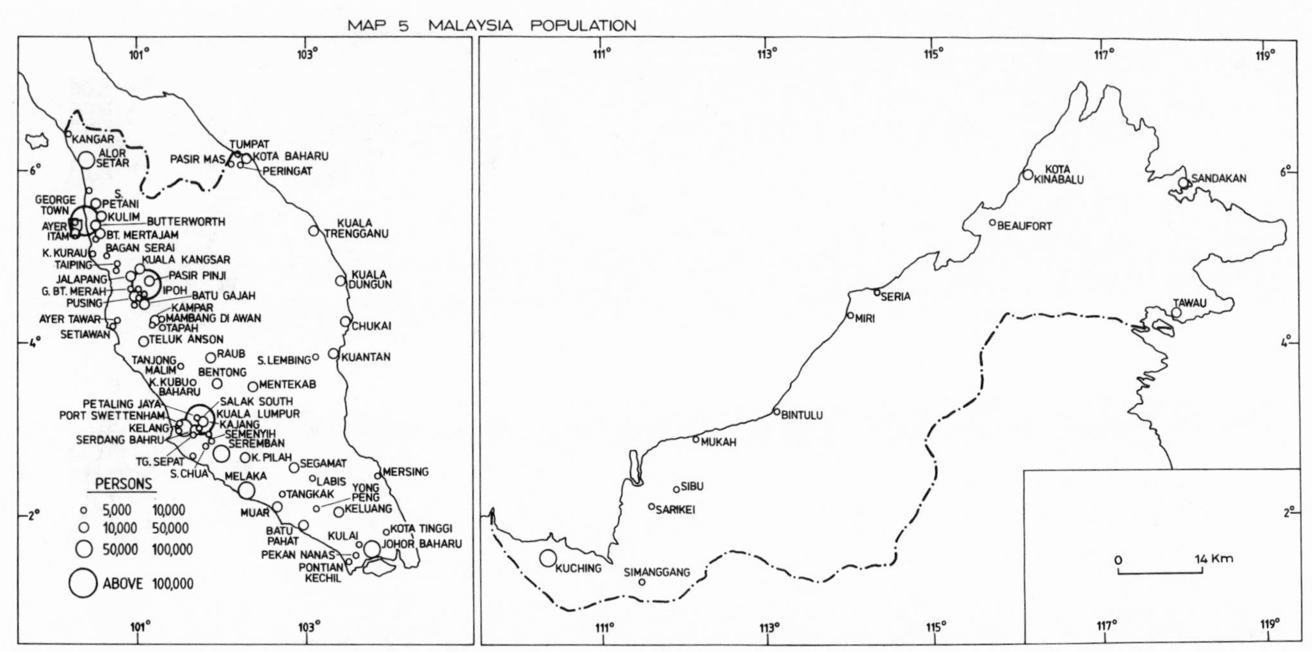

INTRODUCTION

The modern state of Malaysia was formed in 1963 by the union of the Federation of Malaya which had achieved independence from Britain in August 1957, the island of Singapore which had been given internal self-government by Britain in 1958 and the territories of North Borneo (Sabah) and Sarawak, which had been British crown colonies from July 1946. On 9 August 1965, Singapore was expelled from the new Federation and became a separate independent state. Present day Malaysia therefore comprises two territories separated by the South China Sea; West Malaysia (Peninsular Malaysia) and East Malaysia (Sabah and Sarawak). It is a parliamentary democracy which functions within the framework of ancient kingdoms adapted and federated to become constitutional monarchies. In its constitution and its economic and social systems, Malaysia bears the mark of British colonial rule to which every part of the country was subject for a long period of years.

Geographic Location West Malaysia (Peninsular Malaysia) forms part of the southern projection from the Asian mainland, with Thailand immediately to its north and the island of Singapore to the south. It has an area of 131,794 square kilometers and consists of eleven states: Perlis, Kedah, Penang, Perak, Selangor (with the Federal Capital Territory of Kuala Lumpur), Melaka, Johor, Negeri Sembilan, Pahang, Trengganu and Kelantan. East Malaysia occupying the northern part of the island of Borneo has an area of roughly 198,000 square kilometers.

Climate and Rainfall Both West and East Malaysia, located between 1° and 7° north of the equator, have a uniformly warm and humid climate with temperatures ranging from 25.5°C to 33°C, except at high altitudes where the nights are considerably cooler.

Seasonal changes are marked not by variations in temperature but by changes in rainfall, which in turn are related to the cycle of the monsoonal winds. The northeast monsoon, which sweeps down across the South China Sea, is the dominating air stream during November–January. It then gradually decreases in force with a transitional period in April–May followed by the southwest monsoon. Another transitional period occurs in October–November and the whole cycle repeats. Throughout most of Malaysia the rainfall ranges from 2,000 mm to 4,000 mm per annum, although there is considerable variation between different regions. Nowhere is there a true dry season, but most areas receive more rainfall during certain periods in the year. The wettest season coincides with the northeast monsoon.

The Physical Environment The landform of both the peninsula and Borneo is characterized by coastal plains giving way to a rugged mountainous interior. The spine of the peninsula is the Main Range, and there is a further block of highland covering most of upper Kelantan, inland Trengganu and Pahang. The peninsula's highest peak is Gunung Tahan (2,207 meters). The interior mountains have always posed a formidable barrier to trans-peninsular movement and the focus of settlement has been the coastal lowlands. From early times, political centers were established on the rivers which have their headwaters in the inland ranges. Most peninsular states derive their name from the principal rivers. In Borneo, lowlands, often swampy alluvial plains, also form a belt along the coast. Behind these plains are the foothills leading inland up to a mountainous mass through which runs the border between Malaysian and Indonesian Borneo. The highest mountain in Borneo, and also Southeast Asia, is Mount Kinabalu (4,500 meters). The great rivers of Borneo, like in the peninsula, were the original sites of settlement. The heavy rainfall and warm temperatures have resulted in Malaysia being covered by equatorial forests. About seventy per cent of the land is still covered with some form of forestation. In East Malaysia, the forests are a source of rich hardwoods, which represent a major export trade item of both Sarawak and Sabah. Along the plains, most of the original forest cover has been removed to make way for settlements, physical infrastructure and commercial agriculture and industries.

Population In 1980, Malaysia's population was about 13.75 million (revised figures), of which about 11.43 million live on the peninsula. In West Malaysia the dominant ethnic group are the Malays, who according to the 1980 revised census figures, comprised 55.3 per cent of Peninsular Malaysia population. The contemporary definition of a Malay—one who habitually speaks Malay and is a Muslim, has readily permitted the inclusion of migrants from the Indonesian Archipelago as well as those with an admixture of non-Malay blood. The Malays are largely involved in the bureaucracy and rural agriculture. There are also numerically small but important indigenous groups in the peninsular—the *orang asli* (literally, original people) aborigines, who number around 53,000, less than 1 per cent of the population. Most of them live in the jungle. The *orang asli* are commonly divided into three broad groups: the nomadic hunting and gathering Negritos (estimated at 2,000) in the northern and central regions; the semi-nomadic Senoi of the central area, who practise a form of shifting cultivation; and the Jakun of the southern part of the peninsular, often termed proto-Malays, who are increasingly adopting a sedentary farming life. The other main communities are the Chinese (33.8 per cent) and the Indians (including persons from Pakistan, Bangladesh and Sri Lanka) (10.2 per cent). The Chinese and the Indians are descendants from migrants who arrived in Malaya especially after the establishment of British rule in the peninsula in the last quarter of the nineteenth century. The Chinese came to work in the tin mines and were also involved in rural trade. They live mainly in the urban areas and predominate in the commercial sector. The Indians came as labourers to build the roads and railways and as agricultural workers to work in the coffee, rubber and later oil palm plantations. There is also a range of different groups such as the Arabs, Armenians and Eurasians. In Sabah and Sarawak, the categorization of the local peoples has been a difficult task and the resulting classification conceals considerable variation in language and life style. In the early period, there were at least thirty-eight different groups in Sabah but in the 1980 census, only three categories are listed: *Pribumi/bumiputera* (literally 'sons of the soil' or indigenous peoples), Chinese and others. The population of Sabah in 1980 was 1.01 million. The Kadazan (formerly termed Dusun) comprise about 30 per cent and include several different language groupings. The Bajaus form the largest Muslim group (total Muslims—38 per cent). Other people of the interior include the Muruts. The Chinese comprise 16.2 per cent. In Sarawak, more than three categories are listed. The population, according to the 1980 census was 1.13 million. The indigenous groups include the Ibans (Sea Dayaks), the Bidayuh (Land Dayaks), the Kayan, the Kenyah, Melanau and Kedayan. The Muslim figure is given as 25.4 per cent and non-Muslims indigenes account for approximately 44 per cent of the population. The Chinese population of Sarawak accounts for 30 per cent. In East Malaysia, the urban Chinese are predominantly merchants and middlemen while the rural Chinese are involved in agriculture. Thus no single group in Malaysia has a total majority. These percentages at present appear stable and although the population growth is rapid (2.7 per cent per annum), no major shifts are predicted in the foreseeable future.

Language The national language is Malay which is seen as an important means of uniting the Malaysian nation. It is also the medium of instruction in schools, colleges and universities and there are plans to make it the language of the courts. English is widely used and taught as a second language and it is also the language of the elite. There are numerous Chinese dialects notably from South China (Hakka, Teochew, Hokkien, Cantonese and Hailam) as well as Mandarin. Among the Indians, Tamil is most common, but numerous other regional languages from the sub-continent are also spoken. About fifteen different languages can be found among peninsular *orang asli*, while the language diversity in East Malaysia is complex and rich. Mandarin and Tamil are also offered in the West Malaysian school system while Kadazan is offered in Sabah.

Religion The diversity and complexity in language is also evident in religion and cultural tradition. The state religion is Islam and virtually all Malays are Muslims. The Chinese are mainly Christian, Buddhist, Confucianist, Taoist or a combination of these, and Muslim. The Indians are principally Hindus, Christians or Muslims. In East Malaysia, the various indigenous groups are often Christian, Muslim or animist.

Political Structure Malaysia's racial composition has contributed to a political structure which seeks to combine some of the main features of the parliamentary system with the practical realities of the local structures. The head of state, the *Yang diPertuan Agung*, is a position which rotates among the nine Sultans of the peninsular states. The governing party, the *Barisan Nasional* (National Front) is a coalition of parties, the most important of which claim to represent the interests of specific ethnic groups. Occasionally the assumptions and compromises underlying this structure have been questioned, as in May 1969, when ethnic disturbances broke out. In general, however, Malaysia has successfully held the balance between its different ethnic communities while maintaining a stable economic front. In terms of history, there are considerable differences between West and East Malaysia and this introduction will therefore consider these separately.

WEST MALAYSIA

Historically, West Malaysia was first a land-bridge by which migrant peoples of the prehistoric period moved southwards from the Asian landmass to Indonesia and Australasia. In the central jungles or along the fringe there are still some 53,000 aborigines, many of whom are descended from those earliest migrants. They were followed by the Malays who reached Malaya and Sumatra about 2000 B.C. using the same overland route from the north.

Henceforth the peninsula was occupied by a number of distinct states of varying territorial extent and political influence and trade was an important factor in shaping the region's history. The peninsula, situated in the Malay archipelago, was part of a complex trading network stretching from Africa to China. There were in antiquity two main routes between Europe and the Far East. One was the overland route, which many travellers avoided because of the incessant wars which made it dangerous, and the other was the sea route, which began at the Red Sea or in the Persian Gulf and went by way of India to the region of Malaya. The voyagers then sailed round Malaya, using either the Straits of Melaka between Sumatra and Malaya or passing west of Sumatra to enter the Straits of Sunda between Sumatra and Java. From here, they made their way to China or to the Spice Islands of Eastern Indonesia. There was also traffic by the same routes from east to west.

The geographic position of the Malay archipelago was fundamental in bringing together traders and sailors from India, the Arab lands, China and the archipelago in a close-knit commercial relationship. Until steam replaced sail as the motive power for ships, the prevailing wind was the all-important factor and the Malay archipelago, located at the convergence of the sea routes between China and India, was linked to these countries by the annual monsoon wind systems. With the north-east monsoon, ships could sail westwards from China or Indonesia as far as Malaya and also from Malaya to India. The southwest monsoon carried them in a reverse direction. Few merchants made complete journeys between India and China or vice versa. Instead they made a crossing to Malaya where they could exchange cargoes with traders coming in the opposite direction. In this way, various ports in the region of the Straits of Melaka became trade centers for the transshipment of cargoes from distant lands and also for the collection of local produce and the distribution of imported goods within the Straits region. The most prominent of these in the pre-colonial period was Melaka (Malacca). Founded in c.1400, Melaka rapidly rose to become the dominant entrepôt in the archipelago, as well as an important center of Malay culture. In the early fifteenth century, the rulers of Melaka embraced Islam, as Muslim traders brought their religion into the region. This added to the prosperity of Melaka because the patronage of Muslim Indian cloth merchants attracted other merchants since Indian textiles were the basic item of trade.

As a collecting center for the valuable spices of the Moloccus, Melaka became a prime target of Portuguese expansionist policies in the early sixteenth century. The Portuguese were determined to divert the Asian spice trade away from the Muslims by establishing a new spice route around the Cape of Good Hope. In 1511, the Melaka Sultanate fell to the Portuguese. This led to a temporary dislocation of Malay power but it reconstituted itself under a new name in another part of its territories. However, no Malay state rose to match the former commercial strength and cultural splendour of Melaka. In the late seventeenth century, the Kingdom of

Johor emerged as the most powerful Malay polity in the area. Its position was secured in part through its alliance with the Dutch who had captured Melaka from the Portuguese in 1641. Both the Portuguese and the Dutch sought political and commercial hegemony in the peninsula but neither power was able to monopolize trade in the area. Furthermore, neither the Europeans nor the indigenous states could achieve sustained pre-eminence over the other. Johor's decline towards the end of the seventeenth century led to the rise of a number of newly independent states, several of which had once been part of the old Johor empire. But no kingdom emerged as a dominant force able to maintain a hold on regional politics and trade. A shift in power occurred with the acquisition of Penang by the British in 1786, the taking over of Melaka in 1795 and the founding of Singapore by Sir Stamford Raffles in 1819. These three acquisitions were formed into one administrative unit, the Straits Settlements, in 1826 and thereafter, the political structures, and the economic and social character of the peninsula were increasingly determined by the British presence.

By the middle of the nineteenth century, Singapore had emerged as the pre-eminent entrepôt in Southeast Asia and one of the major trading ports in the East. Inevitably, the Malay states, particularly on the western side of the peninsula, became drawn into an increasingly dependent commercial relationship with the Straits Settlements. This relationship was based primarily on the exploitation of tin deposits, particularly in Perak. World demand for tin exceeded Malay capacity to produce it by simple methods. Immigrant groups of Chinese miners, financed in larger part by Chinese Straits merchants, moved into the Malay states and went inland along the rivers into the interior. The Straits merchants also financed mining operations and the extracted tin ore was exported principally through Penang and Singapore. By the 1860s, the exploitation of tin had begun to seriously undermine the political structures and social order of the western Malay states. As rival factions within the Malay political elite, frequently in alliance with rival Chinese secret societies, fought for control of tin resources, a severe breakdown in the established order was imminent. In these circumstances, the pressure for formal British intervention increased. The precise reasons which led Britain to extend its political authorities into the Malay states has long been the subject of academic controversy and will not be dealt with here. Suffice it to say that the two crucial considerations were a determination to protect Britain's domination of the more strategically important Straits of Melaka, and a desire to secure for Britain access to markets and sources of raw materials at a time when rival European powers were capable of restricting commercial opportunities in other parts of Southeast Asia.

By the terms of the Pangkor Treaty of January 1874, the Sultan of Perak agreed to accept a British Resident, whose advice "must be asked and acted upon on all questions other than those touching Malay religion and custom". Later in the same year, British authority was extended to Selangor and Sungei Ujung, and in 1888 to Pahang. In 1896 these four states (with Sungei Ujung part of a wider confederacy of Negeri Sembilan) were brought into a Federation of Malay States (FMS) with the federal capital at Kuala Lumpur. In 1909, the four northern states of Kedah, Perlis, Kelantan and Trengganu, long within Siamese suzerainty, were transferred to British authority. Subsequently, in 1914, the southern state of Johor agreed to accept a British Adviser. These five states, however, declined to enter the Federation and were collectively known thereafter as the Unfederated Malay States [UMS]. Briefly, therefore by 1914, Britain had extended its authority throughout the peninsula, but it was exercised through three distinct constitutional arrangements—the Federated Malay States, the Unfederated Malay States and the Straits Settlements. Although there was a move towards constitutional reform during the inter-war years, it was not until the 1940s that the British moved towards the creation of a single unified administration.

British rule in the peninsula had important implications for present day Malaysia. Firstly, the cooperation of the Malay ruling class was essential for the success of British policy. Government was conducted in the name of the Sultans acting on the advice of the British Residents. The appearance of indirect rule of British advice to a ruler and his court was maintained by the institution of a State Council which became the sole legislative body. However, real power ultimately resided with the British. In order to sustain the fiction of government by the Malay Sultans, the British in Malaya took meticulous care to treat the former with the full deference and ceremony due to royalty. In addition, junior members of the Malay ruling houses and aristocracy, after acquiring an elite English language education, were recruited into a distinct Malay administration service. Thus the new regime in effect enhanced the political and social authority of the traditional Malay elite and fostered a major cultural cleavage between the Malay elite and the peasants. The Malay elite therefore succeeded in maintaining a powerful position in the Malay community well into the independence period. Furthermore, British policy in this respect laid the basis for a political tenet which has had a most powerful influence on the political, economic and social structures of the peninsula through to the present—the principle that the Malays occupy a privileged position in the country.

Second, Malaya emerged as the world's leading producer of tin and rubber during the colonial period. Tin dominated the economy from the second half of the nineteenth century. Since the tin deposits were concentrated in the western half of the peninsula, it was only natural that the economic infrastructure, transport and communication facilities, ports, financial and trading agencies were also located in the western part. When rubber planting became widespread during the first two decades of the twentieth century, the planters inevitably selected land that had been made accessible by the transportation system. Consequently, economic development was concentrated on the western side of the Malay peninsula. To this day, this unequal development has resulted in the emergence of two economic systems and two types of settlement. In the north-eastern and north-western regions, are large and fairly compact areas of Malay settlement based on subsistence agriculture and fishing. The western part of the peninsula, on the other hand, is more urbanized, has a large non-Malay population and its economy is export-oriented. The development of oil palm cultivation and manufacturing industry has also occurred in the west coast region.

Finally, it was during the colonial period, too, that the Malay peninsula experienced a major immigration of Chinese, and to a lesser extent, Indians and saw the emergence of a distinct division of economic roles, occupational patterns and settlement types along ethnic lines. Generally, Chinese immigrants were found in tin mining, Indians on plantations whilst the Malays remained predominantly subsistence padi (rice) cultivators. As a result, the Malays found that their numerical superiority was threatened and in the west coast states, Chinese outnumbered Malays. Economic power was largely concentrated in non-Malay hands. The near balance between the size of the Malay and non-Malay communities, together with the serious imbalance in the relative economic strengths of these groups remain the fundamental issues for the contemporary Malaysian polity.

A major turning point in Malayan history occurred with the invasion of Malaya by Japanese forces on 8 December 1941 which led to Singapore's surrender in mid-February 1942 and the occupation of the peninsula by the Japanese until August 1945. Britain's defeat by the Japanese destroyed the myth of white superiority which had been important in sustaining colonial rule in Malaya. The Malay Sultans collaborated with the Japanese but the Chinese community offered strong resistance and the Indians were not treated as well as the Malays by the Japanese—all of which heightened political awareness and communal antagonisms among the people. Soon after the British returned to Malaya in September 1945, they proposed major constitutional reforms that inadvertently raised political and communal sensibilities. These reforms reversed the previous policy of maintaining the primacy of the Malays over the other Asian communities in Malaya and reflected the dilemma faced by the British. While acknowledging the privileged political power of the Malays, the British also realized the major contribution of the Chinese and the Indians to the economic development of the country. These attitudes contributed to the formulation of a plan to incorporate the Federated Malay States, the Unfederated Malay States, Penang and Melaka into a Malayan Union, a unitary state, with a central government, a governor, and legislative and executive councils. Singapore was to be a separate colony. The Malay Sultans were to retain their positions but sovereignty was to be transferred to the British Crown. All citizens of the Malayan Union would have equal rights, including admission to the administrative civil service. Citizenship was to be extended to all without discriminating as to race or creed.

These provisions led to strong opposition by the Malays, the formation of a major Malay political party, the United Malays National Organization (UMNO) in 1946 and a coordinated campaign against the Malayan Union. The British were thus forced to revoke the Malayan Union Plan and in its place, inaugurated an alternative constitutional arrangement, the Federation of Malaya in February 1948. In the Federation, the sovereignty of the Sultans, the individuality of the States, and Malay special privileges were upheld. A strong unitary central government was established with legislative powers, though the states were assured jurisdiction over a number of important fields. Singapore was withdrawn from the Straits Settlements to form a separate Crown Colony. Citizenship was made more restrictive for the non-Malays than in the earlier Malayan Union scheme requiring residence of at least fifteen during the previous twenty-five years, a declaration of permanent settlement and a certain competence in Malay or English. A High Commissioner was appointed rather than a Governor. This new constitutional arrangement provoked discontent among the other ethnic groups and some of the discontented Chinese felt betrayed by the British and turned to the Communist Party of Malaya (CPM).

Almost immediately after the inauguration of the Federation, there was an armed insurrection, known to Malayan history as 'the Emergency', which was a serious threat to the new regime until the mid 1950s (the formal state of emergency was not ended until 1960). The Emergency was a struggle for control of power between the Anglo-Malay group and the CPM and its supporters. Its origin can be traced back to the pre-war period. Formally organized in 1930, the CPM had established itself by penetration of the Malayan labor movement in the 1930s and had provided the leadership to the resistance movement during the Japanese Occupation. The end of the war and of the Japanese Occupation was followed by a period of labor militancy. The CPM decided against seizing power in the interim between the Japanese surrender and the return of the British because it was insufficiently prepared and armed to seize and hold power by force. However, by the first half of 1948, strongly restrictive trade union legislation introduced by the British to weaken the CPM's authority over the labor movement, tied to a change in international communist strategy led the Party to embark on an armed revolt.

The struggle began in June 1948 with attacks on the rubber and tin industries, which were the two pillars of the Malayan economy. The ultimate object was to seize permanent control of areas which were to be used as bases for further advances. Initially the insurrection taxed the resources of British and Commonwealth forces which had been brought into Malaya. Then the Government evolved military, administrative and political counter-measures which gradually wore down the numerically inferior guerillas. The main strategy, used from 1950 was the resettlement of the Chinese squatter communities which had supplied the guerillas with food, information and recruits into militarily enclosed 'New Villages'. A total of 573,000 people (of whom 300,000 were squatters) were moved into New Villages over the decade 1950–60 and thousands of labourers were 'regrouped'. The CPM was also disadvantaged by lack of support from the Malays and wealthy Chinese. By the mid 1950s, the communist insurrection had been effectively broken. Although the Emergency was not officially ended until July 1960, in December 1989 the CPM signed a peace accord with Malaysia and Thailand and abandoned its 41-year armed struggle to overthrow the Malaysian government.

The communist insurrection was also undermined when the British announced their intention to grant independence to Malaya. Earlier, the British had encouraged discussion between the Malay, Chinese and Indian elites because they stressed the need for a united 'Malayan' nation. Political developments in the country however revealed that non-communal parties could not dominate political life and that communal parties were basic to 'Malayan' politics. The three main parties were UMNO, the Malayan Chinese Association (MCA) formed in 1949 and the Malayan Indian Congress (MIC) established in 1946. In the Kuala Lumpur municipal elections of February 1952, the Selangor branches of the UMNO and the MCA successfully contested the elections as a united front. From this local political alignment of Malay interests and non-Malay aspirations grew a national alliance in which both parties retained their separate identities and political objectives while acting as one body in determining the candidates and the party to contest a particular seat. In 1954, the MIC was incorporated into the Alliance as a full-fledged partner. Subsequently, in the federal elections of July 1955, the Alliance demonstrated its overwhelming support by obtaining 81 per cent of the vote and fifty-one of the fifty-two contested seats.

The colonial administration then turned to framing a constitution for an independent Malaya. The most controversial features of this constitution were those dealing with citizenship and the special privileges of the Malays. This was resolved by first, providing for a single Malayan nationality in which all persons in the Federation could qualify as citizens either by birth or by fulfilling requirements of residence, language and loyalty; and second, by charging the Paramount Ruler (*Yang diPertuan Agung*) with responsibility for protecting the privileged position of the Malays as well as the 'legitimate interests' of the other races. This independence constitution also provided for a Paramount Ruler to be chosen by the Conference of Rulers (*Durbar*) on the basis of seniority for a term of five years; a parliament composed of a wholly elected House of Representatives (*Dewan Rakyat*) and an appointed Senate (*Dewan Negara*); an allocation of power designated in subjects under a Federal List, State List and Concurrent List; and a guarantee of civil rights and of judicial review. With the ratification of the constitution, the independence of the Federation of Malaya was proclaimed on 31 August 1957.

British rule was now limited to Singapore only and in 1958, the island was given internal self-government under an interim constitution that was to expire in 1963. It was expected that Singapore would then demand and obtain full independence with total charge of its own affairs. Such prospects were regarded with some apprehension in Malaya because it was feared that the left-wing elements then dominant in Singapore's politics would use their independent base to aid their compatriots in Malaya. One way of preventing this was to incorporate Singapore into some federation with Malaya, where more moderate forces could counteract the left-wing elements in Singapore. This merger would also secure the economic and commercial ties between the mainland and the island which had developed during the colonial period. Fears among UMNO members that Singapore's inclusion would threaten the numerical superiority of the Malays on the mainland were allayed by the proposal that North Borneo and Sarawak also join and thus restore the ethnic balance. Despite initial reluctance, North Borneo (Sabah) and Sarawak joined with Singapore and the Federation of Malaya in the creation of the Federation of Malaysia inaugurated on 16 September 1963.

The Malaysian Federation was soon under strain, from both foreign and domestic forces. Foreign opposition came from Indonesia and the Philippines. However, with Sukarno's fall from power in 1965, Indonesian opposition to the Federation faded. The Philippines extended recognition to the Federation in 1966, without resolving its claim to Sabah. The domestic strain arose from the ambitions of Singapore's Peoples Action Party (PAP) under Lee Kuan Yew to extend its political influence onto the mainland and to secure representation in the Kuala Lumpur parliament. The PAP also attempted to undermine the Malaysian Chinese Association's (MCA) claims to speak for the Chinese and consequently was a threat to the Alliance. For its part, the PAP came to regard various economic and political measures taken by the Malaysian government not only as detrimental to their interests but as Alliance attempts to dislodge it from power. As the political conflict between the Alliance and the PAP threatened to provoke serious communal violence, in August 1965 Singapore was, in effect, expelled from the Federation. At the same time, an assertion of state autonomy by the Sabah and Sarawak leaders led to their 'removal' from office and their replacement by leaders more amenable to directives from Kuala Lumpur. On the international level, Malaysia joined with the Philippines, Indonesia, Singapore and Thailand to form the Association of Southeast Asian Nations (ASEAN) in August 1967.

Although Malaysia survived these foreign and domestic strains, the problem of ethnicity within Malaysian society remained. It reared its head during the federal elections of May 1969 when the two issues of education and language were highlighted by opposition groups. The election results were a blow to the Alliance which was left with less than 50 per cent of the popular vote and a substantially reduced majority in the federal parliament. Electoral support had swung dramatically in favour of Chinese-dominated opposition parties notably the Gerakan and the Democratic Action Party (DAP). The day following the elections, 13 May, Gerakan and DAP supporters held victory celebrations in Kuala Lumpur. A counter-rally that evening by UMNO supporters led to racial violence in the city. The constitution was suspended and a national emergency declared. All administrative powers were centralized in a National Operations Council headed by the Deputy Prime Minister, Tun Razak. It was four days before civil order was restored to the city but inter-communal violence persisted for two months after the 13 May riots. The May 1969 elections and their immediate aftermath have proved to be a crucial turning point in the history of independent Malaysia because the consequences of those events continue to dominate the character of the modern Malaysian state.

Subsequently, a refashioning of Malaysian political life and economic structures was undertaken by the emergency government. This was done through the formulation of a national ideology, the removal from open public discussion of major contentious issues thought likely to incite communal discord, and the implementation of new social and economic programmes to protect and advance Malay rights. The National Ideology, *Rukunegara*, promulgated in August 1970, was an attempt to promote national unity by the adoption of five principles, universal and acceptable to all citizens, regardless of ethnic origin or religion. The five principles are: Belief in God; Loyalty to King and Country; The Supremacy of the Constitution; The Rule of Law, and Mutual Respect and Good Social Behaviour. The principle of supremacy of the Constitution ensured that the powers and position of the Malay rulers and the privileged rights of the Malays were inviolable. Additionally, the sedition ordinance was introduced which prohibited any public questioning or criticism of those sections of the Constitution covered by the *Rukunegara*.

In the area of political restructuring, the UMNO, beginning in 1971 secured the expansion of the Alliance coalition into the much broader alignment of the National Front or Barisan Nasional within which were included former opposition parties as well as political parties from East Malaysia. This move was carried out with the intention of reducing divisive politicking and bringing the processes of communal bargaining within the confines of government. The UMNO had a clear domination of the coalition and UMNO ministers came to hold an increasingly large majority of important government portfolios.

In the area of economic and social restructuring, in 1971, the government inaugurated long-term economic planning with the introduction of the New Economic Policy (NEP) to be implemented over the period to 1990. The two principal objectives of the NEP were the reduction and eventual eradication of poverty irrespective of race and the reduction and elimination of the identification of race with economic function. This second objective primarily implied increased Malay proportions of the modern rural and urban sectors of the economy and of industrial and commercial share capital. This restructuring was to be secured through the proceeds of sustained economic growth rather than redistribution of existing resources. In essence, the NEP was a major program of positive discrimination (or affirmative action) in favor of the Malay population. It involved the creation of a number of public enterprises which would provide assistance to Malay entrepreneurs, establish business concerns which in time could be transferred to private Malay interests, and purchase shares in established companies on behalf of the Malay community; the introduction of Malay as the medium of instruction at all levels of education, and the formalization of privileged access for Malays in such crucial areas as the allocation of public sector housing, university entrance, civil service employment, and in the allocation of commercial licences.

The NEP's end in 1990 has prompted a policy debate which is taking place at a time when past racial scars show signs of reopening. In order to have a degree of consensus, the government in late 1988 set up an all-party body, the National Economic Consultative Council (NECC) whose 150 members—drawn from the whole range of political parties, opinion groups and bodies of expertise—have been charged with the task of formulating the NEP's successor. Many political analysts fear that the NECC has been set up to contain and even stifle debate. They fear that the process is a charade and that at some stage, UMNO will present its own proposals with no real opportunity to challenge or modify them. The current opinion among senior politicians and economists is that a second NEP will be adopted which will be at least a 10-year plan, emphasizing high economic growth and trying to raise the quality of Malay-dominated institutions.

In the political arena, tensions over the past two years suggest a continuing vulnerability to political manipulation of racial fears. In October 1987, open bickering between the UMNO and the MCA culminated in UMNO planning a massive rally in Kuala Lumpur which panicked city residents into stockpiling food. The tension was only broken by the use of detention powers by the government. 119 people were detained without trial in October and November 1987 under Malaysia's Internal Security Act (ISA) in what the authorities called 'Operation Lallang'. Those detained included prominent politicians, trade unionists, Chinese educationalists, environmentalists, and church and community workers. Since then, most of them have been released but a racially charged atmosphere remains.

In addition, the competition for the Malay voter by factions within UMNO has resulted in a divided UMNO—new UMNO (UMNO ***Baru***) and ***Semangat*** '46 (Spirit of '46). ***Semangat*** '46 which was registered in May 1989 as a political party, is headed unofficially by Mahathir's chief rival Tengku Razaleigh Hamzah. It has joined forces with the Barisan's opponent: the fundamentalist ***Parti Islam Se-Malaysia*** (PAS), and ***Berjasa***, and ***Hamim***, former minor members of ***Barison Nasional***, to forge an opposition coalition called the ***Angkatan Perpaduan Ummah*** (APU) (United Movement of Muslim People).

In 1990, another opposition coalition was formed, the ***Gagasan Rakyat*** comprising ***Semangat*** '46, DAP, ***Parti Rakyat Malaysia***, All Malaysian Indian Progressive Front and Malaysian Solidarity Party. Under Tengku Razaleigh's leadership, ***Semangat*** '46 made a bold brave attempt to overcome ethnic polarization within the opposition by forging the two coalitions. The manifestos of these coalitions were issue-oriented and contained concrete proposals for change. The joint opposition meant that there were straight fights in more than 90 per cent of the constituencies between the BN and the newly formed ***Gagasan Rakyat*** and APU in the 1990 General Elections. The BN consequently launched a big campaign through its control of the media to denigrate and demean the opposition and its leaders. The weapons at the disposal of the mass media were ethnic fanaticism, religious bigotry, especially against Christians, and fears of a repetition of the May 13 tragedy. A siege mentality was created within days amongst a substantial segment of Malay society. The BN retained its two-thirds majority but lost two states to the opposition, namely Kelantan and Sabah. The BN also had 52 per cent of the popular vote while the opposition won 46 per cent.

In summary, therefore, increasing dominance by UMNO and the related characterization of open discussion of 'sensitive issues' as sedition, has clearly placed a major strain on the non-Malay communities and on the non-Malay components of the Barisan Nasional. These developments point to a steady breakdown of consensus politics in Malaysia in favor of rule by the strongest. The formation of the APU coalition and its decision to work with opposition parties may very likely alter Malaysia's political landscape.

EAST MALAYSIA

East Malaysia contrasts strongly with West Malaysia in terms of historical experience, and ethnic composition. Archaeological excavations in the Niah Caves of Sarawak resulted in the discovery of one of the oldest finds of modern man, dating from around 40,000 years ago. Archaeological excavations also indicate important trading polities in this area dating from the early centuries of the second millennium A.D. However, the early history of the area is still a matter of conjecture due to the lack of indigenous texts or foreign records. The history of the area comes more fully into focus with the establishment of European administration in Northwest Borneo in the middle of the nineteenth century.

Sarawak, until the mid-nineteenth century a dependency of Brunei (then the dominant polity in that area), owes its founding as a state to an English adventurer, James Brooke. In 1840, Brooke came to the aid of the Raja Muda of Brunei in his suppression of an uprising of Malay chiefs in the area of the Sarawak river. In return for this assistance and for a modest annual payment, Brooke was granted territory in the western extremity of present-day Sarawak. Brooke was bestowed the title Rajah of Sarawak in 1841, and established his capital at Kuching, a small Malay village and became the first of a dynasty of 'white Rajahs' which was to rule Sarawak until World War II. After a consolidation of his authority, Brooke rapidly moved to extend the territory under Sarawak control, going still further into areas nominally under the authority of Brunei. This involved Brooke in military campaigns against, and political intrigues among, the Iban communities. He classified virtually all Iban raiding as piracy, and hence was able to justify the extension of his control into Iban territory. In the 1850s and 1860s, the weak Brunei Sultanate accepted, in return for further annual payments, major Brooke annexations into the principal Iban-occupied districts. Charles Brooke, James Brooke's nephew, became Rajah on the death of his uncle in 1868 and continued the expansion of Sarawak territory. By 1890, Sarawak occupied the largest territory in north-west Borneo.

The conventional view is that the Brookes were averse to foreign investment and did not actively encourage commercial enterprise in Sarawak in order that Sarawak could flourish "on traditional native lines tempered by British idealism". This view of the Brookes' attitude to economic change is hardly accurate. Indeed, Brooke administration resulted in the opening up of the country to the interests of western capital and the economy was geared to the exploitation of Sarawak's mineral and other natural resources. The Borneo Company, which was the principal foreign concessionaire, was given a virtual monopoly over all mineral and trading rights in the country. Foreign capital also dominated the exploitation of the petroleum and forest resources (especially timber). Although rubber cultivation was mainly a smallholder activity, the interests of the smallholders were sacrificed to the interests of western capital. Thus Brooke policy led to the emergence of an export-oriented economy in Sarawak, heavily specialized in rubber, petroleum and timber and dependent on imported food supplies. In this respect, Sarawak was no different from neighbouring British Malaya. Additionally, the Brookes maintained a strongly exclusive personal authority over their territory and the three main ethnic groups played roles deemed appropriate to their cultural attributes. The Malay role was political, the Chinese role economic while the Iban role was military. Although the Brooke administration did not train the local peoples for self-government, it did foster some notion of allegiance to a central authority alongside the traditional identification with a longhouse, a kin group or a river system.

The northern part of Borneo, Sabah, came under European rule at a later date than Sarawak. It was then under the nominal sovereignty of the Sultan of Sulu. Towards the end of the 1870s, a consortium including an influential London businessman, Alfred Dent, and supported by the governor of the British Colony of Labuan, William Treacher, negotiated major territorial concessions in North Borneo from first the Sultan of Brunei and then the Sultan of Sulu. Having established their position in the territory, in 1881 the concessionaires secured the formation of a chartered company in London, the British North Borneo Chartered Company. In 1888, North Borneo, as well as Sarawak and Brunei, was granted protectorate status, under which responsibility for foreign policy was surrendered to the British government in return for assured protection from external attack. An agreement between Britain and the Netherlands in 1891 settled disputed border claims, although the boundary between Dutch and British Borneo was not surveyed until 1912. This became the frontier between modern Malaysia and Indonesia.

Under chartered company rule, North Borneo experienced significant economic growth—in the export of timber and tobacco from the 1890s and of rubber from the beginning of the twentieth century. In contrast to Sarawak, however, the company developed no real administrative policy and consequently had less success than the Brookes in fostering a general recognition of the white overlord and any significant feeling of loyalty to a greater political unit beyond individual groupings.

Following the Japanese Occupation of North Borneo and Sarawak (1941–45), an effective re-establishment of the Company and Brooke administration proved impossible due to lack of resources for economic reconstruction. In July 1946, Sarawak and North Borneo became crown colonies, ending a century of 'white Rajah' rule and of chartered company administration. During the following short period of colonial administration, there was little advancement towards a responsible and representative government. Consequently, in 1961, when the Prime Minister of Malaya, Tunku Abdul Rahman proposed the incorporation of the independent Borneo territories with Malaya and Singapore to form a Malaysian Federation, there was considerable apprehension in Sabah and Sarawak. This resulted in a spurt of political parties, structured along communal lines, in both the Borneo states. Nevertheless, early opposition to Federation on the part of the principal political leaders of North Borneo and Sarawak soon faded. This was largely because Malaya was prepared to make a number of important concessions to Bornean autonomy in order to draw them into Federation and also because both states were concerned over the aggressive stance adopted towards them by Indonesia and the Philippines. In state elections held in the first half of 1963, pro-Malaysia alliances in both North Borneo and Sarawak won decisively. In September 1963, the two states became independent and merged with Malaya to form Malaysia.

Although there has never been a serious East Malaysian challenge to the unity of the Federation, there has been an underlying tension in the relations between the federal government in Kuala Lumpur and the state governments of Sabah and Sarawak since 1963. In essence, this tension has derived from the notably lower level of economic development and political sophistication in Sabah and Sarawak. The people of these two states are preoccupied with trying to catch up to the social and economic progress of Malaya. Additionally, the continuing search for identity has resulted in numerous changes of party alliances as individual groups move into or out of a coalition. However, smooth federal-state relations had been guaranteed because Kuala Lumpur had ensured the supremacy of those political leaders who co-operated more fully with it. A new dimension has since appeared in East Malaysian politics arising from ethnic Kadazan (Sabah) and Iban (Sarawak) political awareness. In 1985–86, a wave of ethnic Kadazan nationalism ousted Berjaya, the National Front component party and catapulted the newly-formed ***Parti Bersatu Sabah*** (PBS) led by a Kadazan into power. The PBS was subsequently admitted into the National Front coalition.

Throughout the four years of PBS rule between 1986–1990, relations between the Federal and State Government had not been altogether cordial. Issues that caused tensions pertained to the federal civil services in Sabah, Sabah's share of oil revenue, the return of Labuan, the control of illegal immigration and corruption cases initiated by the Internal Revenue Department and the Anti-Corruption Agency against senior PBS leaders. In July 1990, Sabahans once again gave the PBS another five-year mandate to administer the state. The strained relations with Kuala Lumpur led to the PBS withdrawal from the BN after nomination day for the 1990 General Elections. Mahathir counter-attacked and within 24 hours, turned the PBS' withdrawal into a major communal issue. Despite Mahathir's unscrupulous manipulation of the withdrawal, the PBS secured a comfortable majority in Sabah's state assembly. Subsequently, Mahathir launched a politically-inspired crackdown against PBS leaders to settle political scores. In Sarawak, Mahathir has been reading the signs of emerging Iban nationalism (the Ibans represent the largest group) and has taken steps to gather Iban support in order to avoid political complications. Generally, in its attempt to enhance its control over Sabah and Sarawak, the Federal Government has been accommodating, to some extent, to ethnic nationalism. Recent events have nonetheless heightened the perception in these states that Kuala Lumpur is prepared to go to any lengths to keep them reigned in. Thus the East Malaysian leaders are aware that no one who is confrontational to Kuala Lumpur will last long and this has led to a symbiotic relationship between the Federal Government and the East Malaysian states.

THE DICTIONARY

ABDUL DAIM BIN HAJI ZAINUDDIN, DATUK PADUKA (1941–), was born in Alor Setar in Kedah (q.v.). He was educated in Kedah, the United Kingdom and the U.S.A. He has had a varied career—teaching, judicial service, business and property development. Where his political career was concerned, he was appointed Senator in 1980 and in 1983 was appointed Minister of Finance in the Malaysian Government, a post he held until 1991. He has also held important positions in state corporations.

ABDUL GHAFAR BIN BABA was born in Kuala Pilah, Negeri Sembilan (q.v.). He was trained as a teacher at the Sultan Idris Training College and taught in Melaka (q.v.) where he was active in the Malay Teachers' Association. He was also active in business. In 1945, he joined the UMNO (q.v.) Melaka Division and became the Secretary of the Division in 1952. From 1959–67, he served as the Chairman of the Melaka State Alliance (q.v.) and was appointed Chief Minister (q.v.) of Melaka from 1959–67. Since then, he has held a variety of government posts and served as cabinet minister. He is currently Deputy Prime Minister and Minister of National and Rural Development.

ABDUL RAHMAN PUTERA AL-HAJ IBNI AL-MARHUM SULTAN ABDUL HAMID HALIM SHAH, TUNKU (1903–1990) was a leading statesman and the first Prime Minister of Malaya/Malaysia. He was born in Kedah (q.v.) and educated there and in the United Kingdom where he qualified as a Barrister-at-Law. He joined the Kedah Civil Service and served as district officer in various districts in the state. He was a founder member of UMNO (q.v.) and a nationalist who demanded that the British grant independence to Malaya.

When Onn Jaafar (q.v.) resigned as president of UMNO on the issue of the admission of non-Malays, Tunku Abdul Rahman became the president and leader of the Malays. He realized that cooperation among the various racial groups was an important criterion in the achievement of independence and consequently formed an alliance first with the MCA (q.v.) and then the MIC (q.v.). The Alliance (q.v.) won in the 1955 elections and Abdul Rahman became Chief Minister and Minister for Home Affairs. As leader of the Alliance, he led the *Merdeka* (q.v.) mission to London in January, 1956 to seek independence. He was also involved in the negotiations on the Malayan constitution. He became the first Prime Minister of independent Malaya in 1957. In 1962–63, he strove for the formation of Malaysia (q.v.) and was rewarded when Malaysia was inaugurated in 1963. After the Thirteenth May Incident of 1969 (q.v.) he was forced to step down as Prime Minister. Apart from his political career, he was active in Islamic Missionary work and served as the Secretary-General of the International Islamic Secretariat. He wrote widely on Malayan/Malaysian affairs and was a regular contributor to the press. In recent years he became highly critical of the present government and despite failing health campaigned on behalf of ***Semangat*** '46. He also spoke out on the erosion of fundamental liberties in the country and on the Prime Minister's 'assault on the Judiciary'. For his role in the independence movement, he is popularly known as *Bapa Malaysia* (q.v.) and was a greatly loved Malaysian leader.

ABDUL RAHMAN, TUANKU, SIR (1895–1960) was the first paramount ruler (*Yang diPertuan Agung*) of Malaya. He was born in Sri Menanti, Negeri Sembilan (q.v.) and was the son of the first paramount ruler (*Yam Tuan*) of Negeri Sembilan after the nine states formed a Confederation. He was educated in Negeri Sembilan and at the Malay College in Kuala Kangsar. He then joined the Malay Administrative Service and was appointed district officer. As district officer, he served in Seremban, Klang and Ulu Selangor. He then started law studies in the United Kingdom and was called to the Bar at the Inner Temple in 1928. On his return to Malaya, he joined the Legal Service and was appointed Second Magistrate in 1930 and rose to become Assistant Registrar at the Supreme Court in Ipoh. He was appointed district officer again but he left his post to become the *Yang diPertuan Besar* of Negeri Sembilan in 1934 upon the death of his father. In 1957, he was elected the first Paramount Ruler of the Federation of Malaya, a post he held until his death in 1960.

ABDUL RAZAK, TUN (1922–1976), was a prominent Malay politician and Prime Minister of Malaysia from 1970–76. He was born in Pekan, Pahang (q.v.) and educated there and at the Malay College, Kuala Kangsar. In 1939, he joined the Malay Administrative Service. During the Japanese Occupation of Malaya, he fought with the Malay resistance movement and when this was disbanded in 1945, was appointed an assistant district officer in Raub, Pahang. He was then awarded a scholarship to pursue law studies in the United Kingdom and was called to the Bar in 1950. Upon his return to Malaya, he joined the Malayan Civil Service and held important administrative posts in Pahang, including that of *Menteri Besar* (Chief Minister). He joined UMNO (q.v.) and was elected leader of the Youth Section in 1950. A year later, he was elected deputy president of UMNO. In 1955, he was appointed Minister of Education. Under his direction a national educational policy with a common content syllabus was formulated for the country. Malay became the national language of the country. He was a member of the *Merdeka* (q.v.) mission to London in 1956. He held a number of important positions, including that of Chairman of the Alliance Political Sub-Committee which drew up the recommendations of the Alliance Party (q.v.) on the new constitution for the Federation of Malaya. Upon independence, he was appointed Deputy Prime Minister and also held the defence portfolio. In 1969, immediately following the May Thirteenth Incident (q.v.), he took over power in the country, and established the National Operations Council (q.v.), with himself as head, to run the country. He also created a Department of National Unity to formulate a national ideology, *Rukunegara* (q.v.) and new social and economic programs. In 1970, the New Economic Policy (q.v.) was launched with the aim of restructuring the economy and society and creating a genuine unity among Malaysians. The

New Economic Policy resulted in the establishment of various government enterprises to ensure greater Malay participation in commerce and industry. In the same year, Abdul Razak became the Prime Minister of Malaysia. UMNO maintained its dominant position in the Alliance which was expanded to form the National Front or ***Barisan Nasional*** (q.v.). Abdul Razak also invited former UMNO members to rejoin the party. During his tenure as Prime Minister he strengthened the position of the Malays and introduced constitutional amendments which disallowed any public discussion of topics dealing with the power and status of the Malay rulers, Malay special privileges, citizenship, Malay as the National Language (q.v.) and the status of Islam as the official religion. The government was thus free to pursue its policies with a greater degree of freedom than before. His efforts were rewarded when the National Front won a decisive victory in the 1974 elections, which encouraged the government to continue its social and economic policies. In 1975, he had trouble with the powerful Chief Minister of Sabah, Tun Mustapha (q.v.). He sought to undermine the latter's position by appointing a Chief of Police and a head of the armed forces in Sabah, who were loyal to Kuala Lumpur. When the opposition party ***Berjaya*** (q.v.) arose in 1975, Abdul Razak quickly accepted it as a member of the National Front. Abdul Razak was a decisive leader who successfully asserted federal domination over Sabah and enhanced his image and that of his National Front Government in Malaysia. He died in January 1976.

ABDUL TAIB BIN MAHMUD, DATUK PATINGGI HAJI (1936–), the Chief Minister of Sarawak since 1981, was born in Miri, Sarawak (q.v.). He was educated in Sarawak and Australia where he obtained a law degree. Upon his return, he served in the State Legal Department from 1961–1963. He also served on the State and Supreme Councils. He then joined the ***Barisan Rakyat Jati Sarawak*** and became vice-chairman. From 1963–70 he served in the Sarawak government administration in a variety of posts. In 1970, he was appointed first as deputy minister and later became a full minister in the federal government. He held a number of different portfolios, including that of defence. Following a crisis in the Sarawak government, he returned there and assumed the presidency of the ***Parti Pesaka Bumiputera Bersatu*** (PBB) (q.v.) which was a merger between his own party, the Muslim-based ***Parti Bumiputera*** and the Iban-based ***Parti Pesaka***. The PBB won the state elections and he became Chief Minister of Sarawak in 1981, a post he has held since then.

ABDULLAH BIN HAJI AHMAD BADAWI, DATO' (1939–) is a leading Malay politician and UMNO (q.v.) Supreme Council Member. He was born in Province Wellesly, Penang (q.v.) and educated in Bukit Mertajam. He graduated with a B.A. degree from the University of Malaya in 1964. He joined the civil service and held various positions including those of Assistant Secretary in the Public Services Department, Director of Youth and Deputy Chief Director in the Ministry of Culture, Youth and Sports. He then entered politics and won a seat in Penang which paved the way for his political career. In 1980, he was appointed first, Deputy Minister of the Federal Territory and subsequently, Minister in the Prime Minister's Department, a post he held until 1984. In 1984 he became Minister of Education and in 1986, Minister of Defence. In 1987, arising out of political differences with the Prime Minister, he was removed from his cabinet position. He chose to join UMNO Baru (q.v.) and is currently a member of the UMNO Supreme Council. In March 1991, he was appointed Minister of Foreign Affairs.

ACTS OF PARLIAMENT Federal Laws are called Acts and State Laws Enactments, except those made by Sarawak (q.v.) which are called Ordinances. Laws enacted by the Federal Legislative Council before Malayan independence, and not repealed, and laws promulgated under clause (2) of Article 150 by the *Yang diPertuan Agung* (q.v.) when Parliament is not sitting during an Emergency proclaimed under that Article are also known as Ordinances. All legislation (at both federal and state level) must be in the national language (q.v.) and in English.

AHMAD BOESTAMAM ABDULLAH SANI RAJA KECIL (1920–1983) was a prominent Malay politician and journalist.

He was born in Perak (q.v.) and educated there. At the age of eighteen, he became a journalist and soon became involved in politics and anti-colonial activities. He was a founder member of the Malay Nationalist Party and leader of the ***Angkatan Pemuda Insaf***, a left-wing youth section of the party. He was detained by the British in 1941 and was released in 1942 when Malaya fell to the Japanese. After the war, the Malay parties united to oppose the Malayan Union (q.v.) but Ahmad Boestamam was dissatisfied with UMNO's handling of the situation and left the group. For his left-wing activities, he was detained under the Emergency (q.v.) regulations from 1948 to 1955. Upon his release, he resumed his journalistic career and became involved with the issue of poverty. He was the president of the ***Parti Rakyat*** (q.v.) from its inception in 1955. In 1959, he was elected member of parliament. Because of his support for the Brunei rebels and Indonesia during the Confrontation (q.v.) he was detained under the ISA (q.v.). He later joined the ***Pekemas*** (the Social Justice Party) (q.v.) and became president in 1976. He retired from politics in 1978. Ahmad Boestamam is best known for his role in the nationalist struggle, for arousing political awareness through his writings, his concern for the poor and his literary contribution.

ALIRAN The ***Persatuan Aliran Kesedaran Negara*** (National Consciousness Society, commonly known as ***Aliran***) was founded in 1977 by a small multi-ethnic group of Penang intellectuals led by Dr. Chandra Muzaffar (q.v.). ***Aliran*** saw itself as a major Malaysian multi-ethnic social reform group and viewed its principal task as that of raising the level of popular consciousness. ***Aliran***'s activities have included a monthly publication, a number of studies and booklets, the organization of seminars, issuing of press releases and lectures to groups such as trade unions and clubs. Memoranda on a number of issues have also been sent to the government. While ***Aliran*** has been careful to stress its support for constitutional channels of political participation and has actually supported government policy on issues such as the national language, its activities sometimes have not been welcomed by sections of the government. During the 1987 'Operation Lallang', a few ***Aliran*** members, including Dr. Chandra were detained under the Internal Security Act. All were subsequently released. The government has also amended the Societies Act with the aim of imposing tighter controls on ***Aliran*** and other social interest groups. ***Aliran***, however, continues to play a prominent role as one of Malaysia's foremost sources of intellectual comment on contemporary social, economic and political issues.

ALL MALAYSIAN INDIAN PROGRESSIVE FRONT/ INDIAN PROGRESSIVE FRONT (AMIPF/IPF) The All Malaysian Indian Progressive Front was formed in 1990 by MIC (q.v.) dissidents unhappy with its present leadership. The AMIPF was a member of an opposition ***Gagasan Rakyat*** (q.v.) coalition in the 1990 General Elections. The President is M.G. Pandithan.

THE ALLIANCE The Alliance Party developed from a pragmatic electoral pact between the United Malay National Organization (UMNO) (q.v.) and the Malayan Chinese Association (MCA) (q.v.), at the 1952 Kuala Lumpur municipal elections. The success of this arrangement led to a more permanent coalition, and by the time Malaya (q.v.) had its first elections for the Federal Legislative Council in 1955 the Alliance Party, which the Malayan Indian Congress (MIC) (q.v.) had joined, won all but one of the seats. As the only political party with proven trans-communal support and a national basis of organization, it was the Alliance which played a major role in the negotiations for independence. The Alliance formed the first government of independent Malaya, under the leadership of Tunku Abdul Rahman (q.v.). It was essentially a conservative and 'establishment' political entity, reflecting in its leaderships the principal power elite of each community. The Malay (q.v.) bureaucracy and aristocracy played a dominant role in UMNO as did Chinese businessmen in the MCA. The 'Alliance System' was characterized by the tripartite trans-communal arrangement which was based upon a commitment to communal power-sharing with due recognition to Malay political ascendancy, and underpinned by the 'racial bargain' between the leaders of its communal elites. At the 1969 general elections, this system came under political strains which it could not withstand. The MCA was rejected by the majority of the Chinese voters and the party was decimated at the polls. It subsequently withdrew temporarily from the Alliance. After a period of emergency rule, the UMNO leadership sought to restore and strengthen the 'Alliance System' by expanding the Alliance into the ***Barisan Nasional*** (q.v.) through a series of coalitions with various non-Malay opposition parties. The UMNO also emerged as the dominant partner in the coalition. See also: UNITED MALAY NATIONAL ORGANIZATION; MALAYSIAN CHINESE ASSOCIATION; MALAYSIAN INDIAN CONGRESS; BARISAN NASIONAL

ANGKATAN BELIA ISLAM MALAYSIA (ABIM) The ***Angkatan Belia Islam Malaysia*** (Muslim Youth Movement of Malaysia, commonly known as ABIM) was formed in 1970 by a group of Malay university graduates with a background of involvement both in Islamic societies and in university politics. ABIM came to public attention in 1974 when its recently elected President, Anwar Ibrahim (q.v.) was detained under the provisions of the Internal Security Act (q.v.) for his part in the Baling (q.v.) demonstrations. ABIM has focussed on *dakwah* (q.v.) activities to raise the level of Islamic consciousness in the Muslim community. ABIM regards its political participation in a number of areas as legitimate since it rejects the idea of any division between religion and politics. ABIM's rise to prominence as a force within Malay society occurred in the late 1970s and it played an important part in the Islamic revival in Malaysia. It also had significant links with Islamic organizations overseas. After developing a personal following among young Malays, Anwar Ibrahim sought to cultivate a moderate stance towards non-Malay organizations through establishing dialogue sessions between them and ABIM. Anwar Ibrahim's standing amongst Malay youth, and his capacity to mobilize them, coupled with his links to radical Islamic movements, was perceived by many UMNO leaders as a political threat. ABIM's political challenge was, however, successfully neutralized by UMNO when Mahathir co-opted Anwar Ibrahim into the ranks of the Malaysian government. (He subsequently became a minister in the Mahathir administration.)
See also: DAKWAH; ISLAMIC REVIVAL

ANGKATAN DEMOKRATIK LIBERAL SABAH (Sabah Liberal Democratic Front—ADIL) The ***Angkatan Demokratik Liberal Sabah*** (Sabah Liberal Democratic Front) formed in July 1989, bases its acronym ***Adil*** on the Bahasa Malaysia word for justice. Although ***Adil*** is open to all Malaysian citizens, its founders intend to attract Malay–Muslim Sabah residents who were once members or supporters of USNO (q.v.) or the now almost defunct ***Berjaya*** (q.v.). While pro-term committee members who applied for the registration of the party are unknown outside Sabah, there are strong hints that Datuk Harris Salleh (q.v.), a businessman since he lost the state election in 1985, is behind the party.
See also: USNO; BERJAYA

ANGKATAN KEADILAN RAKYAT SABAH (AKAR) A ***Parti Bersatu Sabah (PBS)*** (q.v.) splinter group, it is led by Senator Pandikar Amin Haji Mulia, Kalakau Untol and Mark Koding and was formed in September 1989 in anticipation of general elections within the next 12 months. The party, whose acronym 'Akar' means 'roots' in Bahasa Malaysia, represents Sabah's Dusun ethnic group. The Dusun and the Kadazan (led by Sabah Chief Minister Datuk Seri Joseph Pairin Kitingan (q.v.) are from the same indigenous stock but their languages evolved along slightly different lines. This had led to a linguistic battle between the two groups which marks deeper strains between Pairin and Koding who represents the Dusun. Koding's spearheading of a new Dusun assertiveness and his long-standing differences and personal rivalry with Pairin led to his sacking from his post as Deputy Chief Minister and subsequent expulsion from the PBS. Koding then recontested his seat in December 1989 on an AKAR ticket, hoping a victory would tempt a clutch of Sabah's small opposition parties to band together with AKAR to oust the PBS and more specifically Pairin. Instead the contest petered out with the PBS beating the AKAR.
See also: PARTI BERSATU SABAH

ANGKATAN PERPADUAN UMMAH (APU) (Movement for the Unity of the Muslim People/Congregation) The ***Angkatan Perpaduan Ummah*** is a movement born out of the

pact of 'cooperation and understanding' forged between PAS (q.v.) and ***Semangat*** '46 (q.v.). This pact concentrates on the common goal of unity of Malays and Muslims. The pact was formed to challenge the ***Barisan Nasional*** (q.v.) coalition at recent by-elections, and to unseat the ***Barisan Nasional*** (q.v.) at the eighth general elections, albeit unsuccessfully. Two former component parties of the ***Barisan Nasional, Berjasa*** (q.v.) and ***Hamim*** (q.v.) also joined the APU coalition. In 1990, KIMMA (q.v.) joined the coalition as well.
See also: SEMANGAT '46; PAS

ANGLO-DUTCH TREATY OF 1824 The Anglo-Dutch Treaty was signed between Britain and the Netherlands in 1824. By this treaty, the two powers agreed to partition the Malay world through the Melaka Straits, thus carving out separate 'spheres of influence'. By so doing, they irrevocably divided the Riau-Johor kingdom and arbitrarily severed the cultural unity of east coast Sumatra and the Malay peninsula. The terms of the treaty were:

(1) The Netherlands ceded all its 'factories' in India and the town and fort of Melaka to Britain; withdrew its objections to the occupation of Singapore and agreed to restrict its activities to islands south of Singapore, including Java and Sumatra.
(2) The British ceded Bencoolen and all the English East India Company's possessions in Sumatra to the Dutch and agreed to restrict their activities to the Malay Peninsula and the Straits ports.

Other treaty provisions included trading rights and joint operations against piracy.

ANGLO-MALAYAN DEFENCE AGREEMENT—AMDA The Anglo-Malayan Defence Agreement of 1957 was the cornerstone of Malaya's defence policy after independence. Britain and Malaya agreed to provide each other with mutual aid in the event of an armed attack on either Malayan or British possessions in the Far East. The two governments were also to consult each other if the peace of their territories was threatened. Where Britain was concerned, AMDA was a means to protect its interests in the region. AMDA also denoted the pro-West bias and anti-communist posture of Malaya.

ANTI-NATIONAL ELEMENTS A general term applied to those individuals involved in activities considered 'undesirable' by the authorities. The term has been applied to Communist subversives, those professing 'extremist' communal or religious views and those involved in gangsterism or drug-peddling.

ANWAR BIN IBRAHIM (1947–), a rising Malay politician, was born in Penang (q.v.). He was educated in Perak and obtained a Bachelor of Arts degree from the University of Malaya. He was an active student leader and became president of ABIM (q.v.) in 1974. For his involvement in student protests in the Baling (q.v.) affair, he was detained under the Internal Security Act (q.v.) from 1974–76. He was elected head of UMNO Youth in 1982 and 1984 and since then has served as a deputy government minister in the Prime Minister's Department and Minister of Youth, Culture and Sports (1983–84), Minister of Agriculture (1984–86), Minister of Education (1986–91) and is currently Minister of Finance. He has also served on Islamic bodies such as the UN Advisory Group on Youth and the World Council of Mosques.

ASEAN ASEAN, the Association of Southeast Asian Nations, was formed in 1967. Its original founding members were Malaysia, Singapore, Indonesia, Thailand and the Philippines. They were joined by Brunei in 1984. At the time of its formation the ASEAN Declaration laid down seven aims. The first referred to the acceleration of economic growth, social progress and cultural development in the region. The second was to "promote regional peace and stability" through abiding respect for justice and the rule of law in the relationships among communities of the region and adherence to the principles of the United Nations Charter. The remaining aims, like the first, were predominantly economic, social and cultural. The greatest progress made by ASEAN was political—the promotion of the neutralization issue. ASEAN has also sought to reduce tensions among its members and promote collaboration among them. ASEAN has consequently marked a new era in regional relations for Malaysia and is a cornerstone of Malaysian foreign policy.

ASSOCIATION OF SOUTHEAST ASIA (ASA) In 1960, Malaya, the Philippines and Thailand agreed to set up an association which would be non-political, not concerned with security and would not be identified with any ideological bloc. The association took the name 'The Association of Southeast Asia' (ASA) and the first meeting of foreign ministers was held in Bangkok in July and August 1961. Arrangements were made for future meetings and for the setting up of national secretariats. The severance of diplomatic relations between Malaya and the Philippines in 1963 put an end to joint projects. In 1966, ASA meetings began again, leading to the formation of a wider regional grouping, the Association of Southeast Asian Nations (ASEAN) (q.v.).

AZLAN SHAH IBNI AL-MARHUM SULTAN YUSUFF IZZUDIIN SHAH, SULTAN (1928–) is the reigning Paramount Ruler (*Yang diPertuan Agung*) (q.v.) of Malaysia. He was born in Batu Gajah, Perak (q.v.) and educated in Perak and the United Kingdom, where he qualified as a Barrister-at-Law in 1954. On his return to Malaya, he became the assistant state secretary of Perak. In 1955, he joined the legal service and rose to become the top legal officer. From being a First Class Magistrate (1955–56), he became the President of the Sessions Court (1957–59), Federal Council and Deputy Public Prosecutor (1959), State Legal Advisor, Johor (1961–62), Registrar, High Court, Kuala Lumpur (1962–63), Chief Registrar, Federal Court (1963–65), High Court Judge (1965–73), Judge, Federal Court (1973–78), Chief Justice of the High Court (1979–82) and Lord President, the Chief Judicial Officer (1982–89). In 1984, he was elected by the Conference of Rulers (q.v.) as the Deputy *Yang diPertuan Agung* and in 1989 was elected the Paramount Ruler or *Yang diPertuan Agung* by the same body. He has considerable legal and judicial experience and currently serves as the Chancellor of the University of Malaya.

B

BABA/NONYA The term *Baba* is used to describe those communities (found principally in Melaka (q.v.), Penang (q.v.) and Singapore) whose members are descended from Chinese immigrants who intermarried with the local group. The *Baba* speak a language or patois using their own derivative mixture of Chinese dialects and Malay, known as Baba Malay. In dress and cuisine, they have been heavily influenced by Malay culture, but they are not Muslims.

BALING Baling is a town in the northern West Malaysian state of Kedah (q.v.). Its importance lies in the fact that in 1955, the Chief Minister of Malaya, Tunku Abdul Rahman (q.v.), held negotiations with Chin Peng (q.v.), the leader of the Communist Party of Malaya (q.v.) there. The negotiations, which aimed at ending the Communist insurgency, ended without agreement. In 1974, Baling once more came into national prominence when protests by local villagers over rural poverty led to widespread student demonstrations in Kuala Lumpur, Penang and Ipoh. In 1985, at Kampong Memali in the Baling area, a violent clash occurred between the Federal Reserve Unit and the Police Field Force and some villagers who had come under the influence of a local deviant religious leader. When police moved in on the village, they were met by violent resistance from the villagers. According to official reports, fourteen villagers (regarded as 'martyrs' by locals) and four police officers were killed.

BANGSA The term *bangsa* can refer to 'people' or 'race' depending on the context. It also refers to nation and that sense equates the Malay race with the nation.

BAPA MALAYSIA An honorific, meaning literally, 'Father of Malaysia' by which the First Prime Minister of Malaysia, Tunku Abdul Rahman (q.v.), is popularly known. This title acknowledges both his role in obtaining Merdeka (q.v.) and his part in negotiating the inclusion of Sabah and Sarawak into the

Federation of Malaysia. The Tunku has also been known as *Bapa Merdeka* (Father of Independence).

BARISAN NASIONAL/NATIONAL FRONT The ***Barisan Nasional*** (BN) originated in the coalition building activities of Tun Abdul Razak (q.v.) in the years following the electoral reverses suffered by the Alliance (q.v.) in 1969. Anxious to reduce politicking and establish lasting political stability, Tun Abdul Razak chose to expand the Alliance in order to accommodate opposition parties and increase the non-Malay support base of the Alliance System. Between 1970 and 1972, coalitions were formed with the Sarawak-based SUPP (q.v.), the Gerakan (q.v.), PPP (q.v.) and the Pan Malaysian Islamic Party (PAS) (q.v.) in 1973. By 1973, this new political arrangement was being commonly referred to as the ***Barisan Nasional*** and on 1 June 1974 it was officially registered as a political party. Since then, a number of other parties have joined the BN. The BN contains representatives from almost all of Malaysia's ethnic groups spanning both East and West Malaysia. In electoral terms it is overwhelmingly Malaysia's dominant party having easily won the 1974, 1978, 1982 and 1986 general elections. The dominant party is UMNO (q.v.) and the Prime Minister from the UMNO has considerable powers within the BN. For example, he may veto the candidates for election proposed by any constituent party, is empowered to allocate seats between the various parties, and retains the right to nominate the Chief Minister or *Menteri Besar* (q.v.) in any state controlled by a component party. The BN is not a coalition formed only for electoral purposes, nor are the ministerial portfolios within the BN distributed in accordance with the electoral strength of its component parties. Of late UMNO has asserted its domination of the coalition and UMNO ministers have come to hold an increasingly large majority of important government portfolios.
The present membership of the BN comprises:

In Peninsular Malaysia

United Malay National Organization	UMNO (q.v.)
Malaysian Chinese Association	MCA (q.v.)
Malaysian Indian Congress	MIC (q.v.)

Gerakan Rakyat Malaysia	Gerakan (q.v.)
People's Progressive Party	PPP (q.v.)
East Malaysia	
Berjaya (q.v.)	
Parti Pesaka Bumiputra Bersatu	PPBB (q.v.)
Sarawak National Party	SNAP (q.v.)
Sarawak United People's Party	SUPP (q.v.)
Parti Bansa Dayak Sarawak	PBDS (q.v.)
United Sabah National Organization	USNO (q.v.)

Five other parties PAS (q.v.), ***Berjasa*** (q.v.), ***Hamim*** (q.v.), ***Parti Bersatu Sabah*** (q.v.) and the United Sarawak National Organization (q.v.) were once members for short periods.

BARISAN RAKYAT Following the 1978 general elections, a few minor opposition parties, including ***KITA*** (q.v.), the Workers' Party (q.v.), the SDP (q.v.) and ***Pekemas*** (q.v.) held negotiations with the aim of forming an opposition coalition, to be known as the ***Barisan Rakyat*** (People's Front). None of these parties was represented in any legislature. In 1979, a provisional constitution was formulated, but it came to nothing, following the disintegration of ***Pekemas***. However, shortly before the 1982 general elections, some former ***Pekemas*** members registered a new party, under the name of the ***Barisan Rakyat***. The new party failed to win a single seat in the 1982 general elections.

BATU PAHAT The town of Batu Pahat in the southern West Malaysian state of Johor (q.v.) is identified with several significant political events. UMNO (q.v.) had its origins here in 1946 as a coalition of Malay organizations opposed to the Malayan Union (q.v.) scheme proposed by the colonial authorities and endorsed by the hereditary rulers. Batu Pahat also came into prominence in 1980 when a group of about twenty men, clad in white robes and shouting Islamic slogans attacked the local police headquarters. A number of policemen and civilians were injured and a few of the attackers were shot dead by the police. The leader of the attackers had proclaimed himself the *Imam Mahadi* (Messiah) and had declared a *jihad* (holy war). During the 1983 Constitutional Crisis, Dato' Seri

Dr. Mahathir Mohamad (q.v.), the Prime Minister, held a mass rally at Batu Pahat to protest against the position taken by the hereditary rulers. He urged the people to assert their constitutional rights by supporting him as their elected leader. The choice of Batu Pahat symbolized the Prime Minister's determination to mobilize UMNO against the hereditary rulers and also served to remind them of UMNO's role in reversing their original acquiescence to the Malayan Union Scheme.

BERJASA (Barisan Jama'ah Islamiah Se-Malaysia) The ***Barisan Jama'ah Islamiah Se-Malaysia*** (Malaysian Islamic People's Front or ***Berjasa***) was founded in 1977 by a former PAS (q.v.) Menteri Besar of Kelantan, Datuk Haji Mohamad Nasir, following his rift with PAS. ***Berjasa***'s formation was related to attempts to curb the influence of PAS. It adopted a constitution and aims almost identical to those of PAS. At the 1978 state elections, UMNO (q.v.) and ***Berjasa*** cooperated against PAS. Following the elections, a state-level coalition was formed between ***Berjasa*** and the ***Barisan Nasional*** (q.v.) (which had won a majority of the seats). Datuk Haji Mohamed Nasir was appointed to the *Dewan Negara* (q.v.) and to the Federal Cabinet. Some months later, ***Berjasa*** formally joined the ***Barisan Nasional***. In 1983, Datuk Haji Mohamed Nasir resigned as president. The new leader is Haji Wan Hashim bin Wan Ahmad, a Kelantan executive committee member. Since 1977, ***Berjasa***'s political importance has waned. Its limited electoral support is confined to the state of Kelantan (q.v.). In mid 1989, ***Berjasa*** quit the ***Barisan Nasional*** coalition and formed a pact of 'cooperation and understanding' with PAS and ***Semangat*** '46 (q.v.) called the ***Angkatan Perpaduan Ummah*** (APU) (q.v.). It has therefore joined the opposition.

BERJAYA The ***Bersatu Rakyat Jelata Sabah*** (Sabah People's Union, commonly known as ***Berjaya***) was founded in 1975 by veteran Sabahan politicians, including Tun Mohammed Fuad Stephens (q.v.), as an alternative to the United Sabah National Organisation [USNO] (q.v.) led by Tun Mustapha Harun (q.v.). ***Berjaya*** defeated USNO at the 1976 state elections. Tun Fuad Stephens' death in a plane crash in 1976 left Datuk Harris Mohd. Salleh (q.v.) as undisputed party leader and new

Chief Minister (q.v.). Shortly after ***Berjaya***'s success, both ***Berjaya*** and USNO were accepted into the ***Barisan Nasional*** (q.v.), although USNO remained in opposition at the State level. ***Berjaya***, like USNO, had a strong Muslim following and initially also received significant support from the Chinese and Kadazan communities. However, by the early 1980s, the latter groups had become disenchanted with the ***Berjaya*** state government. At the 1985 state elections, ***Berjaya*** was severely trounced by the new ***Parti Bersatu Sabah*** (PBS) (q.v.) led by Joseph Pairin Kitingan (q.v.) which had strong Kadazan and Chinese support. In July 1985, Datuk Harris Salleh resigned as President of ***Berjaya*** and his place was taken by Datuk Haji Mohamed Noor Mansur. In the 1986 state elections, the party suffered further electoral reverses and for all practical purposes is no longer a significant political force in Sabah. In subsequent years, more leaders have resigned from the party. In early 1989, some of these leaders, under the leadership of Datuk Dr. James Ongkili formed the ***Parti Rakyak Sabah*** (PRS) (q.v.).

BERNAMA ***Bernama***, Malaysia's national news agency was inaugurated in 1968. It provides services to newspapers, news agencies, embassies, banks, universities, industrial firms and various organizations through its news as well as economic and feature services. It also provides telecommunication facilities to subscribers for the distribution of news and other services such as economic and commodity news, share market and financial services, photographs and features. ***Bernama*** distributes the services of the following news agencies:

- Agence France-Presse (AFP), France
- Agenzia Nazionale Stampa Associate (ANSA), Italy
- Agerpress, Romania
- Antara News Agency, Indonesia
- Associated Press (AP), USA
- Deutsche Press Agentur (DPA), Germany
- International Islamic News Agency (IINA), Jeddah
- Kyodo News Service, Japan
- Los Angeles Times—Washington Post Service (LAT-WP)
- Non-Aligned Newspool
- Organisation of Asia-Pacific News Agencies (OANA)

- Philippines News Agency (PNA), Philippines
- Press Trust of India (PTI), India
- Qatar News Agency (QNA), Qatar
- Reuters
- Saudi Press Agency, Saudi Arabia
- Tanjug News Agency, Yugoslavia
- Thai News Agency (TNA), Thailand
- UNICOM, USA
- UNIQUOTE, USA
- United Arab Emirates News Agency (WAM), UAE
- United Press International (UPI)
- Yonhap, South Korea

BRITISH NORTH BORNEO CHARTERED COMPANY Until the 1870s, there had seemed no necessity for the British to assert their position along the far northern coast of Borneo, which had remained under the nominal control of the Sultan of Sulu. By the last quarter of the nineteenth century, however, Britain's interest in the area grew because the passage between Sulu and North Borneo provided a trading route between Australia and China. It was therefore necessary to ensure that it would not fall under the control of a rival European power. In 1877 an Englishman, Alfred Dent, advanced capital enabling the Austrian Consul-General in Hong Kong, Baron Von Overbeck, to purchase the unexploited American concessions in North Borneo soon due to expire. With the active support of William Treacher, the acting governor of the British colony of Labuan, Von Overbeck negotiated a new cession of 17,252,000 hectares from the Sultan of Brunei for an annual payment of $15,000. North Borneo was to be independent of Brunei. Shortly afterwards, followed by Treacher, Von Overbeck went to Jolo where the Sultan of Sulu also ceded his rights in North Borneo for a rent of $5,000 yearly and made Von Overbeck 'supreme and independent'. Under Treacher's supervision, a treaty was drafted with Sulu stipulating that this territory could not be alienated to any other nation without Britain's acquiescence. In February 1878, a Resident was appointed in the Port of Sandakan. Subsequently, other representatives of the Dent-Von Overbeck partnership were landed along the west coast. Dent soon bought out Von Overbeck's share in the venture and with his London connections set about to form a company under government auspices. In 1881, a British North Borneo Company was chartered in London and thus gained a degree of protection from the British Crown. The Company was bound to remain 'British in character', to relinquish foreign relations to Britain and to submit the names of proposed governors for London's approval. In 1888, North Borneo was granted protectorate status under which responsibility for foreign policy was surrendered to the British government in return for assured protection from external attack. The Company expanded its territories and by 1901, Company territory included most of the modern state of Sabah (q.v.). The Company ventured into timber and rubber and was also involved in the export of jungle and sea products. Gradually, the Company assumed the vestiges of a colonial government. In 1946, North Borneo became a British Colony.

BROOKE, JAMES, RAJAH (1803–1868), was an English adventurer who founded the modern state of Sarawak (q.v.) in East Malaysia and established a benevolent English administration under a dynasty of 'white Rajahs' which was to rule Sarawak until World War II. He was born in Benares, India, the son of an East India Company (EIC) (q.v.) official. He was sent for education to England but ran away from school and returned to India. At the age of 16, he became a cadet in the Bengal Army and was promoted to lieutenant two years later. He fought in the first Burmese War. With a legacy inherited from his father, he bought a schooner, *The Royalist*, and sailed to the East in 1838. He was influenced by the Rafflesian idea of a strong British presence in the Indonesian archipelago and went to Sarawak after having learned that the Brunei prince in charge of Sarawak was favourably disposed to the British and that the district had valuable antimony ore. He found the Brunei prince struggling to preserve a semblance of authority over Malay chiefs in the Sarawak river basin. He helped the Brunei prince suppress the uprising and in return for this assistance, and a modest annual payment, was bestowed the title Rajah of Sarawak in 1841. He established his capital at Kuching in the Sarawak river basin. After consolidating his authority, he rapidly moved to extend the territory under his control, going still further to areas nominally under the authority of Brunei.

He tried to establish a British colonial presence in the region but was unsuccessful. Nonetheless, he survived the initial military campaigns against him and the political intrigues principally because of British naval support, his co-option of the local Malay elite and his use of voluntary Iban warriors to suppress opposition. In the 1850s and 1860s the weak Brunei sultanate accepted, in return for further annual payments, major Brooke annexations into the principal Iban-occupied districts. James Brooke died in 1868, leaving an expanded state to his nephew Charles. Charles continued the expansion of Sarawak territory and by 1890 Sarawak occupied the largest area in north-west Borneo. In the meantime, in 1888 Sarawak had acquired protectorate status from the British government whereby it remained an independent state with absolute rights of self-government but would conduct foreign relations only through the British government. Charles was succeeded by his son Vyner Brooke in 1917. Vyner continued his father's policies until 1941 when Sarawak surrendered to the Japanese. After the Pacific War, political and economic changes in the region resulted in the cession of Sarawak to Britain. It was ruled as a crown colony until 1963 when it became part of the Malaysian Federation. Although the conventional view is that James and his successors were averse to foreign investment and did not actively encourage commercial enterprise in Sarawak in order that Sarawak could flourish "on traditional native lines tempered by British idealism", this has not been borne out by recent research on Brooke policies.

BUMIPUTERA The term *bumiputera* (literally 'sons of the soil') is applied to the members of those 'indigenous' ethnic groups of Malaysia who receive preferential treatment under the New Economic Policy. There are three broad categories:

(1) the Malays
(2) the Aborigines (*Orang Asli*)
(3) the natives of Sabah and Sarawak.

In Sabah, the natives include the Kadazan, Dusun, Murut, Bajau, Kelabit and Kedayan. In Sarawak, among the indigenous groups are the Iban ('Sea Dayaks'), the Bidayuh ('Land Dayaks'), the Melanau, Kenyah, Kayan, Bisayah and Penan. See also: PRIBUMI

BUNGA MAS DAN PERAK (THE GOLD AND SILVER FLOWERS) The Thai Kingdom of Ayudhya in the mid-fourteenth century exercised suzerainty over many Malay areas and in subsequent centuries was able to protect its Malay vassals from outside attack and raise the status of small Malay kingdoms. However, this association had its price. The vassal states were expected to demonstrate their loyalty by willingly dispatching men, food and weapons to serve Ayudhya's large armies. Even in times of peace, they submitted a triannual tribute known collectively as the *bunga mas dan perak*, 'the gold and silver flowers'. It consisted of two small trees, fashioned from gold and silver, and standing about a meter high. An eye-witness account in the early twentieth century describes the creation of gold and silver trees, faithful replicas even to the birds in their branches and attests to the meticulous workmanship involved in these works of art. Accompanying the trees were other costly gifts, weapons, cloth and slaves for both the ruler of Ayudhya and the provincial governor at Ligor, who was in charge of escorting the tribute to the Thai capital. Although the value of the *bunga mas* in earlier times is uncertain, nineteenth-century evidence notes that its total worth was in the vicinity of a thousand Spanish dollars. The necessary funds for the *bunga mas* were raised by the imposition of a poll tax on the inhabitants.

BURHANUDDIN AL-HELMY, DR. (1911–1969) was a prominent Malay politician and former leader of PAS (q.v.). He was born in Kota Bharu and educated in Malay, Arabic and English. He worked as a teacher, merchant and journalist and became involved in Malay nationalism and Islam. He served on the board of Malay publications and was the first president of the ***Lembaga Melayu***. When the religious wing of UMNO (q.v.) left the party, it joined forces with two other Malay groups to set up a purely religious Islamic welfare movement called PAS. In 1956, Burhanuddin Al-Helmy became president of PAS. PAS was committed to the promotion of Malay rights and became involved in politics to restore and protect Malay rights. Dr. Burhanuddin was opposed to cooperation with UMNO, which he believed had sold out the rights of the Malays. Under his leadership, PAS made considerable inroads into UMNO's support by appealing to Malays on religious and communal issues.

C

CABINET The actual government of the country is in the hands of the Cabinet (except for the period 1969–71 when government was shared with the National Operations Council). The Cabinet is drawn from the majority party in Parliament, mostly from the House of Representatives, although one or two members may be from the Senate. Members of the Cabinet are appointed by the *Yang diPertuan Agung* (q.v.) on the advice of the Prime Minister, who has discretion in choosing the Cabinet, giving due attention to political status, political support, representations and ability. In appointing members of the constituent parties of the ***Barisan Nasional*** (q.v.) he is guided by the wishes of the leaders of its component parties. The ministers are in charge of specific ministries although some ministers are designated as ministers without portfolio. The Cabinet usually meets once a week. The Prime Minister (or in his absence, the Deputy Prime Minister), presides. Secrecy is strictly observed at Cabinet meetings and consequently, knowledge of what Cabinet meetings are like is very limited. The Cabinet is collectively responsible to Parliament, which in practice means the House of Representatives. The Constitution (q.v.) requires that the Prime Minister be a citizen by operation of law, not by registration or naturalization. He cannot be a Senator, but must be in the House of Representatives. The Constitution is silent on any requirements about ethnic origin, but especially since 1969, the possibility of a non-Malay Prime Minister is scarcely conceivable in the foreseeable future.

CHAUVINISM In general, chauvinism refers to an aggressive patriotism. In the Malaysian context, it is usually used to describe the attitudes of individuals who are perceived to believe in the cultural superiority of their own ethnic group and who aggressively promote the interests of their own group, regardless of the sensitivities and needs of the other ethnic groups.

CHIN PENG (ONG BOON HUA/HWA) (1922–) the leader of the Communist Party of Malaya (q.v.), was born in Sitiawan, Perak (q.v.). Little is known of his career. He joined the CPM, which after Japan's invasion of Malaya in late 1941 swiftly seized and rode the wave of anti-Japanese sentiment in the country. The CPM organized a resistance force called the Malayan People's Anti-Japanese Army (MPAJA) (q.v.) with the ancilliary Malayan People's Anti-Japanese Union (MPAJU). The MPAJA became part of Force 136 and came under Allied Command for which it was supplied with liaison officers, radios and arms. There was a central committee comprising three members of whom Chin Peng was the real operative. After the war was over, and the MPAJA officially disbanded in December 1945, Chin Peng was awarded the Order of the British Empire for his cooperation with allied commandos during the war. Disappointed that the British were not granting independence to Malaya, Chin Peng slipped away into the jungle in 1948 to launch an insurgency against the British Colonial Government, which then declared Emergency Rule (q.v.) to deal with the insurgents. British strategies left the CPM increasingly isolated in the jungle and in 1945, the CPM agreed to discuss peace terms with the government. Face-to-face talks between Tunku Abdul Rahman (q.v.) and Chin Peng were arranged at the small town of Baling (q.v.) in late 1955. The talks were a failure as far as the CPM were concerned largely because Malayan security officials convincingly argued that any deal which allowed the Communists to re-enter the country's polity would simply rekindle their original immediate post-war campaign of subversion and propaganda. The CPM members, threatened and under renewed pressure, made their long march to find refuge in Southern Thailand. Chin Peng and several central leaders eventually ended up in Beijing. In December 1989, initiatives made by Thai leaders led to the signing of two peace agreements, one between Chin Peng and the Thai authorities and the other between Chin Peng and the Malaysian authorities whereby the CPM agreed to terminate its armed struggle against these countries.

CLARKE, ANDREW, SIR (1824–1902) was Governor of the Straits Settlements (q.v.) who paved the way for the expansion of British rule in Malaya with the introduction of the Residential System (q.v.) in 1874. He was born in Hampshire in the United Kingdom and was the eldest son of a lieutenant governor of Western Australia. He was educated in Canterbury and subsequently served in New Zealand. He arrived in Singapore in 1873 as Governor of the Straits Settlements. He was asked to report on anarchy in the Malay States and on the problem of Chinese secret societies. He was an able administrator who was willing to take the advice of local officials and businessmen who had long experience in Malayan affairs. On their advice and on his own judgement he intervened in the Perak succession dispute and signed the Treaty of Pangkor (q.v.) in 1874 with one of the claimants to the throne. The Pangkor Treaty paved the way for the appointment of a British Resident (q.v.) to administer the state. Subsequently, the Residential System was extended to Selangor, Negeri Sembilan and Pahang. The Residential System was a turning point in Malay history because it resulted in the extension of British colonial administration in the Malay Peninsula. Clarke was regarded as a hero for safeguarding British interests. His brief governorship ended in May 1875 when he accepted a seat on the Viceroy's Council in India and served as Minister of Public Works there.

COBBOLD COMMISSION The Cobbold Commission was a five-man Commission of Inquiry appointed to ascertain the views of the people of North Borneo and Sarawak regarding the proposed Malaysian federation. It was headed by Lord Cobbold, a former governor of the Bank of England. Other members of the Commission were Sir Anthony Abell, a former Governor of Sarawak, Sir David Watherston, a former Chief Secretary in Malaya (both nominated by the British government), and two Malayan representatives, Dato Wong Pow

Nee, Chief Minister of Penang and Mohamed Ghazali Shafie, Permanent Secretary to the Department of External Affairs. Its period of tenure was from 19 February until 18 April 1962. The Commission interviewed 4,000 people in both territories and considered some 2,200 written submissions from town boards, unions, religious, political and native leaders and individual members of the community. It held 50 hearings in 35 centers, often going deep into the interior by light aircraft or outboard motor-boat to meet isolated communities. Briefly, the Commission's main findings were that seventy per cent of the 1.3 million people of the Borneo Territories were in favor of Malaysia. However, the two states wanted to retain control over specific departments to safeguard certain rights. On 1 August 1962, the British and Malayan governments accepted almost all the unanimous recommendations of the Commission and decided in principle that the proposed Federation of Malaysia (q.v.) should be brought into being on 31 August 1963. This would entail the transfer of sovereignty over Singapore, Sarawak and North Borneo, and detailed constitutional arrangements for North Borneo and Sarawak, including safeguards for their special interests, would be drawn up after consultation with the legislatures of the two territories. These latter tasks were entrusted to an Inter-Governmental Committee comprising representatives from Britain, Malaya, North Borneo and Sarawak under the chairmanship of the British Minister of Colonial Affairs, Lord Lansdowne. On 27 February 1963, the Inter-Governmental Committee published its report. It made detailed recommendations on the form of constitutional arrangements Sarawak and North Borneo should take. Subsequently, in August 1963, a joint Ministerial Committee was set up to review the rights given to Sabah and Sarawak within the framework of Malaysia. Malaysia was inaugurated on 16 September 1963.

COCOA A report published in 1948 on the potential of cocoa as a cash crop for Malaya marked the beginning of serious attention being paid to the crop. As a result of the research and investment which followed, cocoa planting on a commercial scale finally took off in the 1970s. This was largely due to the policy of commodity crop diversification and within the space of two decades, Malaysia has grown from an insignificant producer of the commodity to the world's third largest in 1990, after the Ivory Coast and Brazil, contributing an estimated 10.4 per cent to the world market.

COMMONWEALTH Malaysia has been a member of the Commonwealth since Independence and Commonwealth forces played a vital role during both the Emergency and 'Confrontation' with Indonesia. The Tunku (q.v.) was one of the toughest opponents of *apartheid*, at the Commonwealth Prime Ministers' Conference in 1960, which ended with South Africa leaving the Commonwealth. In recent years there has been a weakening of ties with the Commonwealth, under Dato' Seri Dr. Mahathir Mohamad's (q.v.) administration. Now however, ties appear to have been strengthened and in October 1989, Malaysia hosted the Commonwealth Heads of Government Meeting in Kuala Lumpur.

COMMUNAL BARGAIN Prior to Independence, the leaders of UMNO (q.v.) and the MCA (q.v.) negotiated an unwritten agreement or 'bargain' which eventually found expression in the provisions of the Federal Constitution (q.v.). The agreement or pact conceded actual and symbolic Malay political predominance and a commitment to special policies (affirmative action to improve the socio-economic position of the Malays). In return the other races were given citizenship, a degree of protection for their cultural rights and freedom to pursue their economic activities. For the MCA, it meant the institutionalization of Malay political dominance in exchange for continuing relative Chinese economic predominance. The MCA leaders now feel that their economic predominance has been eroded with the implementation of the New Economic Policy (q.v.).

COMMUNAL POWER SHARING The concept of communal power sharing is based upon a rejection of the 'winner take all' principle commonly found in competitive political systems and a belief that the effective government of Malaysia's ethnically plural society is dependent upon the participation of all major ethnic groups. Thus, although UMNO (q.v.) did not need to

enter into coalitions with other political parties in order to form a government since it already had a sizeable parliamentary majority, its leaders nevertheless believed in and practised the limited sharing of political power within the ***Barisan Nasional*** (q.v.) structure. Critics however, believe that the formation of the National Front where all component parties are required to vote on the side of the government has in fact strengthened UMNO's dominant position.
See also: BARISAN NASIONAL

COMMUNALISM The term communalism is used in the Malaysian context to refer to the phenomenon of political or social action based upon competitive group solidarities, which derive their cohesion from relatively immutable factors such as language, religion, race and ethnic identity. Such competition invariably involves a degree of conflict. Communalism can be also used to describe a positive belief in the efficacy or desirability of or a predilection for, the organization of social and political action along communal lines. Communalism is frequently described as one of the greatest threats to Malaysia's security.

COMMUNIST PARTY OF MALAYA (CPM) The Communist Party of Malaya is an illegal organization that was committed to overthrowing the Malaysian Government by violence. It was established in 1930 and was active among labor unions which resulted in labor unrest in the 1930s. It was soon outlawed by the colonial authorities. During the Japanese Occupation of Malaya, the CPM spearheaded resistance activities against the Japanese. The CPM Secretary-General Chin Peng (q.v.) was awarded the Order of the British Empire Medal by the British Government after World War II for his co-operation with allied commandos fighting against Japanese occupation forces. When British rule was restored, the CPM (still an illegal organization) sought to extend its influence, mainly through infiltrating the labor movement. Conflict with the authorities escalated and in early 1948, the CPM central committee made preparations to go underground and launch an armed struggle against the colonial authorities. The government reacted by declaring a State of Emergency (q.v.) which lasted from 1948 to 1960. The Communist revolution was faced with serious difficulties: acute food shortages; heavy casualties stemming from the growing sophistication of the government's counter-insurgency campaign; squatter resettlement; implementation of registration systems and the control of food, medical and other essential supplies. In late 1955, face-to-face talks were arranged between the then Chief Minister, Tunku Abdul Rahman (q.v.) and Chin Peng at Baling (q.v.). The talks, as far as the CPM were concerned, were a failure. A successful military campaign against the communist guerilla insurgency and the CPM's inability to attract a mass following among the Malays led to the CPM's defeat. Subsequently, some military units of the CPM retreated across the Thai border to continue their activities. These included sporadic forays into Peninsular Malaysia from clandestine base camps. In 1970, the CPM was reported to have suffered severe factionalism resulting in the formation of two breakaway organizations, the CPM Revolutionary Front and the CPM Marxist-Leninist. Despite this factionalism, the CPM is usually treated as a single entity in media reports. The detention of some political figures and implementation of controls on political activities (e.g. the prohibition of public rallies) have been justified in terms of the threat posed by the subversive activities of the CPM. In recent years the CPM's activities have declined. Chin Peng has become synonymous with the so-called revolution. For most of the time since 1962, he has lived in Beijing. In 1987, the Thai military talked 700 CPM guerillas from "Revolutionary Front" and "Marxist-Leninist" breakaway factions into accepting amnesty. Those who surrendered were given land to farm and vague promises of Thai citizenship in future. The Thais continued with negotiations with the leaders of the remaining 900–1200 CPM forces and in late October, 1989 Chin Peng arrived in Thailand to participate in the final round of the 3-way peace negotiations among Malaysia, Thailand and the CPM. On 2 December, 1989, separate agreements were signed between Chin Peng and the Malaysian Government and the Thai Military at the Thai resort island of Phuket. The CPM abandoned its 41-year armed struggle to overthrow the Malaysian Government. This marks the most significant milestone in

Southeast Asian Communism for years. Whether the CPM will now wither and die as a political force remains to be seen. See also: EMERGENCY

CONFERENCE OF RULERS The Conference of Rulers acts as a safeguard for the position of the Rulers, their privileges, dignity and honor as provided for by the Constitution. One of its main functions is to elect the *Yang diPertuan Agung* (q.v.) and the *Timbalan* (Deputy) *Yang diPertuan Agung* every five years or when those posts fall vacant. The rulers are heads of Islam in their respective states and through the Conference they make decisions affecting Islam in the nation as a whole, including determining the dates for the start and end of the fasting month. The Conference also serves to resolve disputes between member states of the Malaysian federation. The Conference has a special responsibility to protect the special rights of the *bumiputera* (q.v.) and the legitimate rights of all Malaysians as provided under Article 153 of the Constitution. The assent of the Conference is essential for any change to Article 10 of the Constitution (which deals with sensitive issues). In general the Conference may discuss any issue related to the interests and security of the nation. Its proceedings are secret. The Conference is also attended by the chief ministers and *Menteri Besar* (q.v.) of the Federation. However, non-royal members (including state governors) cannot participate in matters connected with royal elections or privileges. The Conference may be convened by the Keeper of the Rulers' Seal at the command of the *Yang diPertuan Agung*, or by a minimum of three members of the Conference.
See also: PARAMOUNT RULER; GOVERNOR

CONFRONTATION From early 1963, Indonesia pursued a policy of 'Confrontation' towards Malaysia. 'Confrontation' stopped short of full-scale war, but included aggressive patrolling by Indonesian vessels between Sumatra and Malaya. Indonesia also used members of the North Borneo National Army to provoke a long series of incidents on the borders of the North Borneo states and Indonesia, bomb outrages in Singapore and dropping or landing troops on the coasts of

Malaya. Indonesian intervention also encouraged the already existing threat of communist subversion in Sarawak. In an effort to defuse the situation, tripartite meetings of representatives from Malaya, the Philippines and Indonesia were held and Malaya agreed to the visit by a United Nations team to ascertain the wishes of the Borneo territories' inhabitants on joining Malaysia. Although the UN Report found that the large majority of people favored Malaysia, Indonesia did not accept the Report. Relations deteriorated between the two countries, and Malaysia broke off diplomatic relations with Indonesia. Indonesia cut off trade with Malaysia and stepped up 'Confrontation'. Although economically 'Confrontation' did not hit Malaysia as had generally been expected, it caused resources to be diverted from development to military purposes. Informal discussions on ending 'Confrontation' led to an accord between the two countries in August 1966 whereby hostilities were to cease and diplomatic relations restored. Talks on the resumption of relations also included the formation of an association wider than ASA (q.v.) or Maphilindo (q.v.) and eventually in 1967, this took the formation of ASEAN (q.v.).

CONSTITUTION The Malaysian Constitution is derived from the Constitution of the Federation of (q.v.) Malaya which was promulgated on Independence Day, 31 August 1957. The Constitution of the Federation was the product of a constitutional commission consisting of constitutional experts from Australia, India and Pakistan. It was presided over by Lord Reid, a Lord of Appeal from the United Kingdom. The Reid Commission's Report was published in February 1957. It was then examined by a Working Committee set up by the British Government, the Conference of Rulers and Malayan political representatives. After detailed discussion in which the three major political parties, UMNO, the MCA and the MIC, played a major role and contributions by the general public, the Reid proposals were amended and finalized. It was then accepted by the Federal Legislative Council and passed as the country's new Constitution. On the formation of Malaysia on 16 September 1963, the existing Federation of Malaya Constitution was retained but amended and adjusted to allow for the admission of Sabah, Sarawak and Singapore and make provision for their particular requirements. The main features of the Constitution are:

(1) A constitutional monarch—the *Yang diPertuan Agung* (q.v.) who is elected for a term of five years by his brother rulers and who has to act in accordance with Government advice.
(2) A bicameral parliament consisting of
 (a) a Senate (*Dewan Negara*) (q.v.) comprising 70 members and
 (b) a House of Representatives (q.v.) (*Dewan Rakyat*).
 Elections to the House of Representatives are held every five years on the basis of universal adult suffrage, each constituency returning one member.
(3) The Cabinet headed by the Prime Minister consists only of members of the legislature and is collectively responsible to Parliament.
(4) In the Malay states, the Rulers retain their pre-independent positions except that generally they can no longer act contrary to the advice of the State Executive Council.
(5) The non-royal states are each headed by a *Yang diPertua Negeri* federally appointed for four years who also acts upon the advice of the respective state Governments.
(6) Each state has a unicameral legislature, elections to which are held every five years.
(7) The judiciary (except for Muslim courts and the native courts in Sabah and Sarawak) is wholly federal and judges for the upper and federal courts are independent and may not be removed from office before the compulsary retiring age of 65, except on the recommendation of a special tribunal convened for that purpose.
(8) Federal judges have the power to interpret the constitution and they also have the power to declare laws invalid and executive acts unlawful.

See also: REID COMMISSION

CONSTITUTIONAL CRISIS 1983 From August to December 1983, Malaysia underwent a major constitutional crisis, in which the national leadership of UMNO came to have serious disagreements with the country's hereditary rulers. The crisis originated in the refusal of the *Yang diPertuan Agung* (q.v.) to grant the royal assent to a series of constitutional amendments proposed by the elected Federal Government and duly passed by Parliament. Several of the amendments had the effect of significantly curbing the constitutional powers of the *Yang diPertuan Agung* and the state Rulers. Article 66(5) of the Federal Constitution was amended so that if, for any reason, a bill was not assented to by the *Yang diPertuan Agung* within 15 days of it being presented to him, he would be deemed to have assented to it. The eighth schedule of the Constitution was also amended, to oblige all states in the federation to change their respective state Constitutions incorporating the '15 day assent' provisions. Thus any bill passed by a state assembly would become law within 15 days, even if the Ruler of the State withheld his assent. Another amendment stripped the *Yang diPertuan Agung* of his powers to declare a state of emergency and vested them solely in the prime minister. Initial opposition by the Rulers to the amendments to the eighth schedule, developed into a confrontation with the prime minister. Royal assent to the bill was withheld. There was also concern that if other amendments, also included in the Constitution (Amendment) Bill 1983, were not given the royal assent, the administration of government would be disrupted. For example, if the Bill was not gazetted by 15 December 1983, the Election Commission would have been obliged to wait another ten years before being able to carry out a redelineation of Federal and State Constituencies. The Prime Minister, Dato' Seri Dr. Mahathir bin Mohamad (q.v.) and a delegation from the UMNO (q.v.) Supreme Council made attempts, albeit unsuccessful, to overcome the constitutional impasse. There was dissension among UMNO ranks and the Rulers also felt that they were being pressured by Mahathir. The crisis unexpectedly ended on 15 December 1983 when the Deputy *Yang diPertuan Agung* gave the royal assent to the Bill. The royal assent was granted after the Prime Minister, acting on behalf of the government, had given a written undertaking that the Bill would be further amended to modify the provisions which had led to the constitutional controversy. The amendments to the eighth schedule, which would have extended the federal royal assent provisions to the State Constitutions, were withdrawn, and the original 15 day period of review by the *Yang diPertuan Agung* was extended to 30 days. Finally, the provisions bestowing emergency powers on the Prime Minister were withdrawn. In effect, the State Rulers had agreed to accept restrictions on the ability of the *Yang diPertuan Agung* to refuse the royal assent, in return for the withdrawal of the rest of the amendments affecting their constitutional positions. Further amendments promised by the government as part of the settlement of the crisis, were carried out at a special one-day sitting of parliament on 9 January 1984.

D

DADAH A term officially adopted to describe narcotics. The Malaysian government regards the *dadah* menace as a major threat to national security. Under the Dangerous Drugs Act, there is a mandatory death penalty for drug trafficking offences and amendments to the Act, passed in 1985, empower the Minister for Home Affairs to order the detention without trial of suspected drug traffickers.

DAKWAH In Malaysia, the term is commonly used to describe organizations devoted to raising the level of Islamic consciousness in the Muslim community, and to carry out conversions. The government is concerned about deviant organizations and has attempted to control *dakwah* activities by establishing the ***Yayasan Dakwah Islamiah*** (***Islamic Dakwah Foundation***) which is responsible for the coordination of all dakwah groups in the country.

DAVID, V., Ph.D. (1932–) a popular politician and leading trade unionist, is widely acknowledged as 'BAPA PEKERJA' or father of the workers. He was born in Kuala Lumpur and educated in Kuala Lumpur and the U.S.A. where he obtained a doctorate in international relations in 1982. V. David was a founder member of the Selangor Mill Workers Union which later became known as the Selangor Mill and Factory Workers Union and subsequently the National Union of Factory and

General Workers. He served as General Secretary until the Union was banned in 1958. He is currently General Secretary of the Transport Workers Union and the Secretary General of the Malaysian Trades Congress (q.v.). He is also the founder and chairman of the Workers Institute of Technology, a training center for workers. In addition to his trade union activities, V. David is a prominent opposition politician. He was a founder member of the Selangor Labor Party which later merged with other state labor parties to form the Labor Party of Malaya (q.v.). He was also instrumental in the formation of the Gerakan (q.v.) and PEKEMAS (q.v.). He is currently the Chairman of the DAP (q.v.) Damansara Branch. V. David served as elected representative to the Selangor State Legislative Assembly and is a member of parliament. Because of his commitment to economic equality, social justice and political freedom, V. David was detained under the Emergency Regulations (1958) and Internal Security Act (q.v.) in 1965, 1969 and 1987–88.

DECENTRALIZATION The formation of the Federated Malay States (q.v.) in 1896, and the establishment of the Federal Council (q.v.) in 1909 resulted in the Malay Sultans and their State Councils increasingly being relegated to 'traditional' Malay affairs, which had been interpreted by the British as matters dealing with Islam and the Malay ceremonial. The loss of effective power wielded by the Malay Sultans caused concern among some officials and became a subject of debate in the Federal Council in 1922 when the post World War I economic recession led to a re-examination of 'policy'. There was also a desire for greater administrative economy. The British also wished to bring the Unfederated Malay States into the Federation; they did not attempt to do so by force but rather by trying to make conditions inside the Federation more attractive to the States outside. The 'decentralization' policy was pursued in the 1920s and 1930s by Governors Sir Lawrence Guillemard and Sir Cecil Clementi. The policy had limited results. Some administrative departments were handed over to the states from the Federation, state budgets rose and state administrations were strengthened. In 1935, the Chief Secretary was replaced by a Federal Secretary who was lower in status. The Unfederated States were not tempted by decentralization and remained outside the Federation.

DEMOCRATIC ACTION PARTY (DAP) The Democratic Action Party was formed following Singapore's separation from Malaysia in 1965. Some of its leaders had earlier belonged to the Singapore based People's Action Party. The DAP's aims are to strive for a 'democratic socialist pattern of society'. It professes an uncompromisingly 'non-communal' stance, committed to championing the rights of all Malaysians. The DAP is Malaysia's largest opposition party in terms of legislative representation and holds parliamentary seats as well as seats in various state assemblies. It may be described as having two principal roles: firstly, despite its commitment to non-communal politics, it has systematically championed the cause of non-Malay communities against perceived encroachments upon their constitutional rights. At the same time, the DAP is a communally disinterested, effective opposition, raising questions of general public concern and voicing its criticism of government actions that it perceives as eroding human and democratic rights. The DAP has, for many years provided the official leader of the opposition in the Malaysian Parliament and is represented on a number of parliamentary committees. In terms of its leadership, membership and sources of electoral support, the DAP is essentially a non-Malay party in which the Chinese members are predominant. It has also won significant support among middle-class non-Malays, with hopes of social mobility for themselves and their children and who are frustrated by the official policy of legal discrimination in favor of the Malays. For the most part, the DAP is an urban party. Despite its claims to be orientated towards all classes and communities, it has failed to establish effective links with rural Chinese and the Malay peasantry. In October 1987, almost the entire leadership of the DAP was detained under the Internal Security Act when the government swooped down on opposition parties, social interest groups, educationalists and church community leaders when communal tensions were heightened in a racially-charged atmosphere. Although most of them were released the following year, the DAP's secretary-general, Lim Kit Siang (q.v.) and his son were only released in 1989. Early in 1989, the government invited the DAP to participate in the National Economic Consultative Council (NECC) but the DAP refused to do so until Lim Kit Siang and his son were released. They were released several months later and the DAP then participated in the discussions of the NECC. The DAP continues to play a significant role in Malaysian politics despite limitations on political activities and actions of opposition parties. In the 1990 eighth general elections, the DAP, together with other non-Malay opposition parties, and ***Semangat*** '46 (q.v.) formed the ***Gagasan Rakyat*** (q.v.) an opposition front. The ***Gagasan Rakyat*** and APU (q.v.) had an electoral arrangement not to split opposition votes. Nonetheless the DAP and PAS (q.v.) carried out their internecine fight even after nomination day, thus eroding confidence in the opposition. The DAP swept the board in constituencies with more than 70 per cent Chinese, such as Penang (q.v.) and Kuala Lumpur, and Lim Kit Siang (q.v.) defeated Lim Chong Eu (q.v.) in Penang.

DEMOCRATIC MALAYSIAN INDIAN PARTY (DMIP) The Democratic Malaysian Indian Party is a minor political party, formed by a number of MIC (q.v.) dissidents in 1985. Membership is confined to Malaysians of Indian and Sri Lankan origin, and the party supports the ***Barisan Nasional*** (q.v.).

DEPARTMENT OF NATIONAL UNITY This Department's main objective is to foster harmonious inter-communal relations alongside national unity and integration in order to build a united Malaysian society. In order to achieve these objectives the Department is aided by an Advisory National Unity Panel chaired by the Minister in the Prime Minister's department responsible for the Department. The members of the Panel consist of outstanding and experienced leaders in the various fields of community work, social welfare, education, communal relations, the economy and women's interests. Its functions are:

(1) to develop programs which will create opportunities for the various ethnic groups in the country to get to know and understand each other better.

(2) to coordinate progress in bringing about integration and unity between states and districts so that national interests prevail over local ones.
(3) nurture a sense of patriotism and solidarity based on the principles of the National Ideology (*Rukunegara*).

See also: RUKUNEGARA; MAY 13 INCIDENT

DETENTION Detention without trial is provided for under Section 8(1) of the Internal Security Act (q.v.) 1960 (Revised 1972) which states that: "If the Minister is satisfied that the detention of any person is necessary with a view to preventing him from acting in a manner prejudicial to the security of Malaysia or any part thereof or to the maintenance of essential services therein or to the economic life thereof, he may make an order . . . directing that the person be detained." These powers have been the Government's principal instrument of political coercion and have been frequently used. Among those that have been detained under the Internal Security Act are alleged communist subversives, members of opposition parties, Islamic dissidents, trade unionists, environmentalists, members of social interest groups and church and community leaders.

DEWAN NEGARA/THE SENATE The Dewan Negara consists of 70 members of which 40 are appointed by the *Yang diPertuan Agung* on the basis that they

- possess experience and wisdom
- represent professional, commercial, functional and other groups
- represent minorities.

The remaining 30 are elected by the State Legislatures, each State returning two Senators; these may be members of the State Legislative Assembly or otherwise. The minimum qualifying age is 30 years. A president and deputy president are elected at the beginning of Parliament (or in the event of a vacancy in the post) by the members from one of their number. The clerk to the Senate is appointed by the *Yang diPertuan*

Agung; holds office until the age of 60 and can only be removed from office on the recommendation of a special tribunal convened for that purpose. All money bills must be introduced in the first instance in the House of Representatives. The Senate has restricted powers of veto; it may delay the passing of a bill only for a limited time. The Senate functions primarily as an 'auditor' which examines the legislative activities of the House of Representatives. The term of a Senator is 3 years and is not affected by the dissolution of Parliament. Parliament can by statute increase the member of Senators elected to three, provided that they be elected by direct vote, and decrease or abolish altogether the nominated senators.
See also: PARLIAMENT; DEWAN RAKYAT

DEWAN RAKYAT/THE HOUSE OF REPRESENTATIVES
The Dewan Rakyat (House of Representatives) consists of 177 members, each member representing one constituency. To present himself/herself for election,

(i) he/she must be a citizen resident in the Federation (he/she is automatically disqualified if declared insane or becomes bankrupt, if he/she holds a post the salary of which is paid from public funds or if he/she has been convicted of a criminal offence and has been punished with more than a year's imprisonment or a fine exceeding M$2000).
(ii) must be at least 21 years of age.
(iii) must not be a member of the Senate.

The 'life' of the House of Representatives is limited to five years, after which a fresh general election must be held; but the *Yang diPertuan Agung* has the discretion to dissolve Parliament before then if the Prime Minister so advises. The House of Representatives is presided over by the Speaker (*Yang diPertuan Dewan Rakyat*) and is elected at the beginning of Parliament (or in the event of a vacancy in the post) by members from one of their number. Two Deputy Speakers are elected in a similar process, and take the chair in the absence of the Speaker. If all are absent, the House appoints one of its

members *ad hoc*. The permanent machinery of the House is supervised by the Clerk to the House who is appointed by the *Yang diPertuan Agung*. He/she holds office until the age of 60 and can only be removed from office on the recommendation of a special tribunal convened for that purpose.
See also: PARLIAMENT; DEWAN NEGARA

DURBAR OF RULERS Following the formation of the Federated Malay States (q.v.), *Durbars* or official Conferences of Rulers were convened in 1897 and again in 1903 to bring the four rulers together, but despite the panoply surrounding them, the *Durbars* had only vague advisory powers. In 1927, the Rulers/Sultans ceased to be members of the Federal Council and instead a *Durbar* of Rulers was set up, consisting of the four Sultans, the High Commissioner, and the Federal Secretary. This body was the forerunner of the Conference of Rulers in the present constitution.

E

EAST INDIA COMPANY See English East India Company.

ECONOMIC PLANNING UNIT (EPU) The Economic Planning Unit is the central staff agency of the government for planning national economic development. It acts as the secretariat to the National Planning Council (NPC), the National Development Planning Committee (NDPC), the Foreign Investment Committee (FIC), the Economic Panel and the Special Privatization Unit. The EPU is divided into two main divisions, the Macro Planning Division under the direction of a Deputy Director-General and the Sectoral Planning Division under the direction of another Deputy Director-General. The broad functions of the EPU are:

(1) to formulate Government's broad objectives in development planning and to prepare the five-year development plans.

(2) to prepare the annual development budget for submission to the NDPC and thereafter the Cabinet.
(3) to coordinate the execution of various development projects.
(4) to evaluate the progress and results of the implementation of the five-year development plans and recommend changes when and where necessary.
(5) to maintain intelligence on the current state of the economy.
(6) to advise the Government on general economic problems.
(7) to plan and coordinate technical assistance and capital financing for the implementation of the five-year development plans and to serve as the secretariat for the Malaysian Technical Assistance Program for foreign countries, as determined by government.

EDUCATION Under colonial administration, there were several distinct tiers of education. The most prestigious consisted of the English language primary and secondary schools, attended by the children of the Malay aristocracy and wealthy urban Chinese and Indians. The University of Malaya was established in 1949 to provide tertiary education. A second tier was the secular Malay-medium primary school system, which the British established and supported. They also reorganized and assisted the Malay Arabic Quranic schools. Malay education was rudimentary, mainly for males and designed to avoid alienating rural Malay youth from peasant life. There were no secondary schools in the Malay medium. The third tier of education was the vernacular Chinese and Indian (Tamil) schools. The Chinese were encouraged to establish, oversee and finance their own primary and secondary schools. From 1924, for political reasons, the British introduced supervision over the curriculum and teacher recruitment and also gave grants to aid Chinese language schools. Tamil primary education was started on the rubber estates which were required to provide facilities. Tamil schools were also set up in the predominantly Tamil labor lines. There were no Tamil secondary schools. After Independence a national Malay-medium education system with a common syllabus was established. Government aided English-medium schools were replaced by

Malay-medium schools. Almost all subjects at the university level are also taught in Malay. Although Chinese-medium schools and Tamil medium schools have not all been converted to the Malay medium, there are anxieties among Chinese and Tamils about the long-term future of their schools. Generally, the education system today is a Malay national education system which is government controlled with a strong Islamic input.

ELECTION COMMISSION Article 113(1) of the Federal Constitution (q.v.) provides for an Election Commission whose members are appointed by the *Yang diPertuan Agung*. The Election Commission is charged with the responsibility of delimiting constituencies, preparing and revising electoral rolls and conducting elections to the Dewan Rakyat and Dewan Negara. The commission must review state and federal constituencies at intervals of not less than 10 years and not more than eight years and recommend changes. The Constitution had originally given the Election Commission the sole authority to delimit electoral boundaries but in 1962 the Alliance (q.v.) Government amended the Constitution to withdraw this power from the Election Commission and vest it in the Federal Parliament. Although the Election Commission is supposed to be a neutral and independent body to ensure fair elections, *The Election Watch Report* on the 1990 General Elections claims that the "conduct of the Election Commission . . . left much to be desired and brings into question the Commission's credibility. Having regard to the many irregularities in the electoral rolls reported to it or which in itself openly acknowledged, the Commission . . . failed to properly discharge its duties when, in spite of the irregularities it still used those electoral rolls in the General Elections."

ELECTION WATCH The Election Watch Committee was formed in February 1990 to monitor the Eighth General Elections and to ensure that the elections were properly and fairly conducted because of widespread allegations of electoral malpractice made by opposition parties and the general public. The committee comprised Tun Mohamed Suffian (Chairperson) (q.v.), Tan Sri Ahmad Noordin Zakaria, Raja Aziz

Addruse, Dr. Chandra Muzaffar (q.v.), Datuk Param Cumaraswamy, and Chooi Mun Sou, all prominent Malaysians, social activists and human rights campaigners. Despite criticism and allegations against it by the Prime Minister and the ***Barisan Nasional*** (q.v.), the Committee carried out its task and released its Report on the 1990 General Elections in November 1990. Briefly, the Committee concluded that although "the 1990 General Elections were by and large ***free*** . . . Election Watch does not consider the General Elections to have been ***fair*** . . . " and recommended various reforms to improve the electoral process and ensure fairer elections in the future.

ELECTORAL PACT An electoral pact is an agreement between political parties not to field rival candidates in a particular constituency and to allocate constituencies for contestation with the aim of maximizing the vote against their common opponent. In Malaysian political history such an electoral pact between the ***Gerakan Rakyat Malaysia*** (q.v.), DAP (q.v.) and PPP (q.v.) significantly increased the impact of opposition parties upon the Alliance (q.v.) at the 1969 General Elections. In the 1982 General Elections, the PSRM (q.v.) and DAP agreed to an electoral pact in Penang (q.v.), Johor (q.v.) and Pahang (q.v.), but the PSRM failed to win a seat in these areas. In the 1990 General Elections, the two main opposition coalitions—APU (q.v.) and the ***Gagasan Rakyat*** (q.v.) entered into an electoral pact not to split opposition roles. Despite an intensive fight between some of the component parties, the opposition swept the board in Kelantan (q.v.) and Sabah (q.v.) and won 46 per cent of the popular votes.

THE EMERGENCY During the Japanese Occupation of Malaya, the Communist Party of Malaya (q.v.) had been active in the resistance movement against the Japanese, known as the Malayan People's Anti-Japanese Army (MPAJA). Although the MPAJA was disbanded at the end of 1945, the communists decided to resort to armed violence, thus forcing the colonial authorities to proclaim a State of Emergency throughout Malaya on 18 June 1948. Among the reasons which induced the communists to resort to violence was the failure to penetrate and control trade unions by peaceful means. The tactics employed by the guerillas enabled them to kill and perpetrate acts of sabotage during raids and then to disappear into the jungle. The British-led police and military units were plagued by problems of morale and organization and a fresh initiative was needed to meet the situation. In 1950, the British implemented the Briggs Plan to eliminate the ***Min Yuen*** (mass organizations) and the communist main forces known as the Malayan Races Liberation Army (MRLA). Malaya was placed on a war footing and conscription for the military and police force introduced. Special powers were created to regulate security and destroy any communist guerilla support. The most striking operation was the establishment of 'New Villages' comprising Chinese squatters. The rebels had been obtaining food from these squatters, many of whom had settled on the land during the period of the Great Depression and the Second World War. The government resettled about half a million people in over 550 'New Villages'. Settlement in the villages was concentrated, which made it easier to defend them. There was also enforcement of strict food controls. Sir Gerald Templer (q.v.), who was appointed High Commissioner in 1952 also introduced local elections, village councils and granted citizenship to over half the Chinese population. He also provided security of tenure for the New Villagers. The main impact of the Emergency was over by about 1955 although it was not formally declared to have ended until 1960.

ENGLISH EAST INDIA COMPANY The English East India Company (EIC) was formed in 1600. It obtained the royal charter for the monopoly of trade in the countries between the American and African continents. It was not backed by state capital but was a private joint-stock company. Initially the EIC attempted to obtain a share of the trade in the Spice Islands. Dutch hostility however led to the withdrawal of the English from the Spice Islands and to their establishing themselves in Bencoolen in West Sumatra. In 1786, the EIC obtained Penang (q.v.) from the Sultan of Kedah (q.v.) in return for military assistance. In 1795, the EIC took over Melaka and in 1819, obtained Singapore. These three settlements, which were governed from India, the EIC's base in Asia, played an

important role in Britain's trade with China and India. In 1824, Britain and the Netherlands signed the Anglo-Dutch Treaty (q.v.) which divided the Malay Archipelago and the East Indies into the British and Dutch spheres of influence respectively. This set the stage for future British imperialism in the Malay peninsula.
See also: STRAITS SETTLEMENTS, ANGLO-DUTCH TREATY

F

FADZIL MOHAMED NOOR, USTAZ HAJI (1937–) is a prominent Malay politician and current leader of PAS (q.v.). He was born in Kedah (q.v.) and educated in Kedah and the Al-Azhar University of Cairo, Egypt. Upon his return, he served as lecturer with the Technology University of Malaya and joined ABIM (q.v.). He became active in PAS and assumed the presidency of the party. He is committed to the establishment of an Islamic State in Malaysia. In 1989, he entered into a cooperative pact with the ***Semangat*** '46 and other Malay parties to form an opposition to UMNO (q.v.). In the 1990 General Elections, PAS and ***Semangat*** '46 won all the parliamentary and state seats in Kelantan (q.v.).

FEDERAL COUNCIL After the formation of the Federated Malay States (q.v.), a further move towards centralization and uniformity was made with the creation of a Federal Council in 1909. The Federal Council was headed by the High Commissioner/Governor based in Singapore, assisted by the Resident-General in Kuala Lumpur. Other members comprised the Sultans (who had no power of veto), the four British Residents, and four 'unofficial' members, appointed by the High Commissioner/Governor. These unofficial members were European and Chinese representatives of planting and mining interests. In 1911, the position of Resident-General was abolished and his duties given to a 'Chief Secretary'. In practical terms the legislative powers of the Federated Malay States were diminished and the Federal Council became a vehicle for an extension of the authority of the High Commissioner/ Governor of Singapore.

FEDERAL TERRITORY This consists of Kuala Lumpur, the federal capital, which was surrendered by negotiation by the State of Selangor on 1 February 1974 and of the island of Labuan, surrendered by the State of Sabah in 1984.

FEDERATED MALAY STATES When the Residential System (q.v.) had been established in the four states of Perak (q.v.), Selangor (q.v.), Negeri Sembilan (q.v.) and Pahang (q.v.), there was a tendency for each Resident (q.v.) to go his own way in administration and some coordination became necessary. Consequently, a Federation Agreement was concluded between Britain and the four states in July 1895 and came into effect on 1 July 1896. The states were formed into a 'Federation' (q.v.) which was not a 'federation' in the accepted sense of a system of government in which powers are divided between a federal government and state governments. The Rulers of the four states agreed to accept a British Resident-General and to follow his advice; the only sphere in which they were not obliged to follow it was on questions touching Malay religion and custom. The four Residents were made responsible to the Resident-General, who was in turn responsible to the Governor of the Straits Settlements, who would in the future also be High Commissioner for the Federated Malay States. Every important government department in the four states was put under a single administrative head, responsible to the Resident-General for securing uniformity in the states. In 1909, a Federal Council (q.v.) was created, consisting of the Rulers, the Resident-General, the four British Residents, and four 'unofficial' members nominated by the Governor, who presided over the Council in his capacity as High Commissioner of the Federated Malay States. In 1911, the position of Resident-General was abolished and his duties given to a 'Chief Secretary'.

See: RESIDENT; RESIDENTIAL SYSTEM

THE FEDERATION AGREEMENT 1948 With the revocation of the Malayan Union (q.v.) in February 1948, the new

'Federation of Malaya' came into existence. By the Federation of Malaya Agreement 1948, the Central Government consisted of a British High Commissioner, an Executive Council, and a Legislative Council. The sovereignty of the Sultans (q.v.), the individuality of the states and Malay special privileges were upheld. The High Commissioner was entrusted with safeguarding both 'the special position of the Malays' and the 'legitimate interests of other communities'. The Legislative Council had official members and a large number of unofficial members, to be nominated by the High Commissioner. It was intended that, in time, some of the latter would be elected. At state level, there was a corresponding structure consisting of the Ruler/Sultan, an Executive Council and a legislative body, the Council of State with both official and unofficial members. Some important functions, such as land and education, were allocated to the state. But in the tradition of indirect rule, the Rulers undertook to accept the advice of the High Commissioner except in matters relating to the Muslim religion or the custom of the Malays. The Federal Legislative Council could also pass laws on subjects within the field of state functions, for the purpose of ensuring uniformity between states. Other features of the Federation Agreement included the provision for a Conference of Rulers (q.v.) and citizenship provisions. Citizenship was made more restrictive for non-Malays than in the earlier Malayan Union scheme, requiring residence of at least fifteen during the previous twenty-five years, a declaration of permanent settlement and a certain competence in Malay or English.

See also: MALAYAN UNION

FELDA After independence in 1957, the economic policies of the Malayan government were no longer principally determined by the concern of overseas investors or foreign governments. The government's main objective is to eliminate economic disparity among the ethnic groups. One disadvantaged group were the farmers. In 1954, in an effort to give farmers access to more land and reduce rural poverty, the government set up the Federal Land Development Authority (FELDA). Between 1956 and 1966, this body opened up large areas of land, each consisting of 1,600–2,000 hectares. Rubber or oil palm was planted and housing and other facilities provided for about 400 families. Some of the largest FELDA schemes are the Jengka Triangle Project covering some 132,000 hectares in Pahang, the Johor Tenggara Project, with 148,500 hectares in Johor and the Pahang Tenggara Project, involving one million hectares. Between 1956 and 1973, about 174,000 people of a total rural population of about 7,065,000 were resettled on FELDA lands.

FOREIGN POLICY The thrust of Malaysia's foreign policy is to project the image of Malaysia as an independent, sovereign democratic state, dedicated internally to forging national unity among its multi-racial population, and pursuing economic development, social justice and cultural progress; and externally, to promoting peace in the world, goodwill, friendship and understanding with all peace loving nations irrespective of political systems, adherence to ideals and purpose of the United Nations Charter, regional cooperation and opposing all forms of racism and colonialism.

FUNDAMENTAL LIBERTIES Part II of the Constitution entrenches a number of basic 'freedoms' some of these are absolute; others can be qualified by Parliament in certain circumstances. The following liberties are absolute:

- Right of Life
- Freedom from arbitrary arrest
- Prohibition of slavery
- Prohibition of retroactive penal legislation
- Prohibition of repeated trials
- Equality of all persons
- Prohibition of banishment of a citizen
- Freedom of movement (subject to laws relating to security, public order, public health and the punishment of offenders)
- Freedom of speech, assembly and association
- Freedom of religion
- Freedom of education
- Right to own property.

G

GAGASAN RAKYAT The ***Gagasan Rakyat*** was an opposition multi-ethnic coalition which joined forces with APU (q.v.) in an attempt to defeat the BN (q.v.) in the 1990 General Elections. The component parties in the coalition were the ***Semangat*** '46 (q.v.) headed by Tengku Razaleigh Hamzah (q.v.), the DAP (q.v.) under Lim Kit Siang (q.v.), the PRM (q.v.) under Dr. Syed Husin Ali, the AMIPF (q.v.) under M.G. Pandithan and the MSP (q.v.) under Yeoh Poh San. The two coalitions were held together by the sheer force of Tengku Razaleigh Hamzah's personality. In October 1990, the PBS (q.v.) joined the ***Gagasan Rakyat*** coalition. Unfortunately, the BN under Mahathir (q.v.) launched a big campaign, aided by its control of the media, to denigrate and demean the opposition and its leaders and successfully managed to retain its two-thirds majority.

GERAKAN RAKYAT MALAYSIA The ***Gerakan Rakyat Malaysia*** (commonly known as the Gerakan) was founded in Penang (q.v.) in 1968 as a moderate professedly multi-ethnic party committed to the just and equitable distribution of wealth. Despite its multi-ethnic platform and the presence of several prominent Malays in its ranks, the Gerakan's following was essentially non-Malay and confined largely to Penang and Selangor. At the 1969 General Elections the Gerakan assumed political power in Penang and Dr. Lim Chong Eu (q.v.), its President, became Chief Minister. Shortly afterwards, the party split, leaving Gerakan with only a narrow majority in the Penang Assembly. Most of its Malay leaders quit and Dr. Tan Chee Khoon (q.v.), along with his supporters in Selangor, went on to establish a rival party, PEKEMAS (q.v.). The Gerakan cooperated closely with the Federal Government and in 1972, after extended negotiations between Dr. Lim Chong Eu and Tun Abdul Razak (q.v.), agreed to a coalition with the Alliance (q.v.). Despite the MCA's opposition to the coalition, Tun Razak was anxious to shore up non-Malay support for, and participation in, the ruling coalition. The Gerakan has remained a component of the ***Barisan Nasional*** (q.v.). The coalition ultimately meant that the Gerakan lost its outright control of Penang, although Dr. Lim Chong Eu remained as Chief Minister. The Party also was responsible for several federal cabinet portfolios. By 1982, the MCA and Gerakan were actually allocated an equal number of seats in Penang. While remaining as Chief Minister, Dr. Lim Chong Eu resigned as President of the party in 1982 and was replaced by Dr. Lim Keng Yaik. A major problem of the Gerakan continues to be the tension between its professed multi-ethnic aims and its popular identification as a party comprised essentially of Chinese. Additionally, internal political bickering has resulted in a spate of resignations by party leaders and members and the loss of hundreds of members to its rival, the MCA (q.v.). The Gerakan lost heavily to the DAP (q.v.) in the 1990 General Elections, especially in Penang.

GOVERNOR Governors of Penang, Melaka, Sabah and Sarawak. When Malaya achieved independence in 1957, the nation comprised nine Sultanates and two settlements, namely Penang and Melaka. As the new Malayan nation was to continue to be a Federation, and since Penang and Melaka had been administratively autonomous, it was decided to maintain the status quo. Since neither Penang nor Melaka had a ruler at the time of independence, the head of each settlement was designated Governor (*Yang diPertua*). A similiar arrangement was extended to Sarawak, Sabah and Singapore when the three territories merged with Malaya to form the Federation of Malaysia in September 1963. In Sabah, however, the office is known as the *Yang diPertuan Negara*. In 1965, Singapore left Malaysia. The *Yang diPertua* are appointed by the Paramount Ruler (*Yang diPertuan Agung*) and are members of the Conference of Rulers. They are not, however, eligible to participate in the election of the Paramount Ruler. In the case of Penang and Melaka, candidates selected as *Yang diPertua* need not be persons born in either of the states concerned. Where Sabah and Sarawak are concerned, they have to be locals.
See also: CONFERENCE OF RULERS

H

HAMIM ***Parti Hisbul Muslimin Malaysia*** (the Malaysian Muslim Warriors Party or ***HAMIM***) was founded in 1983 by Datuk Haji Mohamad Asri Muda, who resigned as president of PAS in 1982, after a challenge to his leadership. ***Hamim*** was admitted to the ***Barisan Nasional*** (q.v.) coalition in 1985. It has failed to make much of an impact upon PAS. In early 1989, the party leadership made attempts to dissolve the party and induce all the members to join UMNO (q.v.). However, it failed to get the required number of votes for the dissolution of the party. Later in the year, the party withdrew from the ***Barisan Nasional*** coalition and joined the opposition ***Angkatan Perpaduan Ummah*** (APU) (q.v.).

HARRIS BIN MOHAMAD SALLEH, DATO (1930–), a leading politician in the East Malaysian state of Sabah (q.v.), was born in Labuan and educated in Kota Kinabalu. He worked as a teacher, then as a clerk and rose to the position of assistant district officer in Sipitang. In 1963, Harris left government service to enter politics and became the Secretary General of USNO (q.v.). He served in various ministerial posts. In 1975, Harris and Tun Muhammed Fuad Stephens, together with some veteran Sabah politicians, founded the ***Bersatu Rakyat Jelata Sabah*** (Sabah People's Union, commonly known as ***Berjaya*** (q.v.)). ***Berjaya*** wrested control from USNO in 1976 and with the untimely death of Stephens the same year, Harris became Chief Minister of Sabah. In 1985, ***Berjaya*** was defeated by the PBS (q.v.) and Harris contrived with his former opponent, Tun Mustapha (q.v.) to retain power. When he was thwarted, Harris resigned as president of ***Berjaya***. It is alleged that he is behind the formation of a new political party in Sabah.

HUSSEIN ONN, TUN (1922–1990) was a leading Malay politician and the third prime minister of Malaysia. He was born in Johor (q.v.) and had his early education there. He joined the Johor military forces as a cadet and later underwent training at the Military Academy in India. He joined the Indian Army and during the Second World War saw action in Egypt, Syria,

Palestine and Iraq. Subsequently, he served with the Intelligence Branch of the Military Headquarters in India. After the war, he joined his father Onn Jaafar (q.v.) in his political activities. He then joined the Johor civil service and served as an assistant district officer. Later he went to England to study law and qualified as a Barrister. On his return, he joined a legal firm in Kuala Lumpur. He rejoined UMNO in 1964. He was persuaded to stand for elections in 1969 and he won a seat in Johor. He served as the first secretary-general of UMNO and also headed the youth wing. In 1970, he was appointed Minister of Education and held that post until 1973. Subsequently, he was appointed Deputy Prime Minister and Minister for Trade and Industry from 1973–76. In 1976, on the death of the Prime Minister, Tun Abdul Razak (q.v.) Hussein Onn became Prime Minister. He retired in 1981. During his tenure as Prime Minister, he scrupulously maintained his family and himself free from business entanglements. He pressed charges of corruption and forgery against the powerful *Menteri Besar* (Chief Minister) (q.v.) of Selangor, who was convicted and sentenced to imprisonment. He also applied pressure on Tun Mustapha (q.v.) who ran Sabah as a personal fiefdom. Between 1977–78, he was also successful in asserting political domination over the powerful state governments of Perak, Melaka and Kelantan, thereby enhancing his image and that of his National Front (q.v.) Government. However, there was also an erosion of fundamental liberties in the country with the passage of the Societies (Amendment) Act 1981 which disallowed dissension in the country. In recent years, he spoke out against the violation of human rights in the country and was also active in human rights activities.

I

IMPLEMENTATION COORDINATION UNIT (ICU) This unit, which comes under the Prime Minister's Department, was established in 1971. Its principal objectives are to:

(1) ensure the implementation of government policies in particular the New Economic Policy, the Look East Policy,

the Privatization Policy and the Malaysia Incorporated Policy and to see that their goals are achieved
(2) ensure the implementation of all development projects/ programmes
(3) ensure the effective integration of federal and state development policies and programmes
(4) implement special programmes and projects specified by the government.

INDEPENDENCE OF MALAYA PARTY (IMP) Soon after Onn Jaafar (q.v.) resigned from UMNO (q.v.), he decided to form a multi-racial party which would seek independence and stress political and economic equality. This was the IMP, inaugurated in September 1951. The new party was initially supported by sections of the MCA (q.v.) and the MIC (q.v.) and Dato Onn hoped that UMNO would eventually cooperate with it. The Tungku (q.v.) would not allow members of the UMNO to join or assist the party, under penalty of expulsion. The IMP, despite an inadequate party machinery and organizational base, entered the Kuala Lumpur municipal elections in February 1952 and was decisively beaten. It also lost the support of the Chinese. It languished on for nearly two more years before being disbanded.
See also: PARTY NEGARA

INDUSTRIAL CO-ORDINATION ACT The Industrial Coordination Act (ICA) is a legislative initiative to accelerate the implementation of the New Economic Policy (q.v.) in the industrial sphere. Firms with a minimum paid-up capital of Malaysian Ringgit 250,000 or with more than 25 employees, are required to conform with NEP guidelines on *bumiputera* (q.v.) participation and ensure that an appropriate percentage of their employees are *bumiputeras* before an operating licence is granted. The Minister for Trade and Industry is empowered to refuse a company the licence to operate in, what he considers to be, the national interest. The ICA was a politically sensitive issue among the Chinese business community, as they perceived it as discriminating against the non-Malays. The ICA was blamed for Chinese reticence to invest in Malaysia and for actually impairing economic growth. In the face of such opposition the government has made several modifications to the Act and in 1985 it announced that the 'exemption threshold' under the Act would be raised to allow more freedom from government controls to smaller companies.

INTERNAL SECURITY ACT The Internal Security Act (ISA) was enacted in 1960 when the State of Emergency (q.v.) which had been declared in 1948 by the British Colonial Government for the purpose of combating the Communist Party of Malaya (q.v.) was formally terminated. An important feature of Emergency legislation was the power of preventive detention. With the passage of the ISA, this extraordinary power became a permanent feature of the ordinary (i.e. civil) law of the land. The power of preventive detention which (like all powers under the Emergency) had been regarded as a temporary aberration, now became permanently entrenched in the statute books as a power which could be exercised by the executive as part of the ordinary law of the land.

The Power to Detain Section 8(1) of the ISA empowers the Minister of Home Affairs to detain any person without trial if he is "satisfied that the detention of the person is necessary to prevent him from acting in a manner prejudicial to the security of Malaysia (or any part of it) thereof; or to the maintenance of essential services thereof or to the economic life thereof . . . "

The Duration Although Section 8(1) of the Act empowers a detention of an individual for a period of two years, it is not the usual practice to make such an order forthwith. Instead, the authorities prefer to exercise their powers of arrest under Section 73(1) of this Act. This provision empowers the authorities to hold and detain for a period of 60 days before making an order under Section 8(1). The 60 day period gives them the opportunity to investigate into the matter and determine whether a 2-year order should be made. Consequently, if no order is made after the lapse of 60 days, the detainee is set free. A detainee held under Section 73(1) of the Act does not have any right to make representations against his/her detention. It is only after a 2-year detention order under Section 8(1) is made against the detainee that he/she is entitled to this right. The 2-year period can be renewed upon its expiration by the Home Affairs Minister, with the consequence that a detainee can be incarcerated almost indefinitely.

The Rights of the the Detainee Under the ISA, a detainee must, after his/her detention under Section 8(1) of the Act, be served with a copy of the Order of the Minister empowering his/her detention as well as a statement in writing of the grounds on which the order is made and of the allegations of fact on which the order is based. This provision's aim is to furnish the detainee with sufficient particulars to enable him/her to make representations to an advisory board. In practice, this provision has been of little assistance to the detainee since quite often the allegations of fact are vague and uninformative and fail to establish that the allegations of fact amount to a threat to national security.

Conditions and Place of Detention A person detained under Section 73(1) for a period of 60 days is invariably held in solitary confinement at the main police station in the state concerned. The cells are small, badly lit, with poor ventilation and are completely cut-off from the outside world. The detainees are not allowed access to their lawyers during this period, although a limited number of visits by the immediate family are permitted under the most stringent conditions. The detainees are subjected to interrogation by teams of interrogators as well as other forms of psychological pressure designed to elicit confessions. Once a 2-year detention order is made under Section 8(1) the detainee is transported to a detention camp proper. Although the avowed object of the ISA is preventive, there is no doubt whatsoever that it has often been used as a punitive weapon to silence dissidents and political opponents of the government. In 1978, there were more than 1000 detainees held under the ISA. This figure began to decline, especially after 1982, when the process of release of detainees gathered momentum. By September 1987, the number had declined to 27. In October 1987, there was a fresh wave of arrests and 119 people were detained. By March 1988 (after some releases), the number of people detained was 86.

ISLAMIC FUNDAMENTALISM While the term is frequently used in the West to refer to extremist attitudes, the Malaysian Government makes a clear distinction between 'Islamic fundamentalism' and 'Islamic extremism'. In the broadcast on the BBC world service, Dato' Seri Dr. Mahathir bin Mohamad (q.v.), the Prime Minister of Malaysia explained thus: " . . . the word 'fundamentalists' carries different meaning for different people. As far as we are concerned, we are fundamentalists because we believe in the true teachings of Islam. And the true teachings of Islam means that we should be tolerant of other religions and other people and we should keep up with the times . . . therefore there should be no reason why others should worry about the so-called fundamentalist policies of the Malaysian Government."

ISLAMIC REVIVAL The term 'Islamic Revival' is generally used to describe the upsurge of Islamic religious awareness, confidence and identity which occurred in many Islamic countries, including Malaysia, in the 1970s. In Malaysia this revival coincided with both an assertion of Malay political primacy and official policies designed to accelerate Malay economic and educational opportunities in a very short period. The revival was originally most evident among urban Malay youths and its influence gradually spread to the rest of the Malay community. There was a greater awareness of the role of Islam in everyday life, a desire for greater knowledge of Islamic matters and a marked increase in attention to ritual and religious observance. It also resulted in some Malays adopting Middle Eastern forms of dress. This awareness has also led to a movement for observance of Islamic principles in affairs of state, ranging from demands that the *syariah* replace British law to demands that the structure of education be changed to conform with Islamic teaching. A number of *dakwah* (q.v.) (missionary) groups/organizations have also sprung up whose main objectives are to raise Islamic awareness among Muslims and to carry out conversions. The government responded to the Islamic revival by gradually accommodating demands for an increased Islamic orientation in official policies. This has led to the policy of Islamization. Some observers see the revival as a reassertion of Malay ethnic identity in view of the fact that the majority of the Muslims in the country are Malays.
See also: ISLAMIZATION

ISLAMIZATION Islamization is defined by the national leadership as the gradual and orderly absorption or injection of Islamic values into the administration of the country, while at the same time safeguarding the constitutional rights of non-Muslims. The policy, a response to the Islamic revival, has found expression in a number of projects including the Islamic university, Islamic bank and an Islamic insurance company. It has also been manifested in symbolic gestures, in the alteration of parliamentary prayers to an Islamic form, and the choice of Islamic architecture in many new government buildings. Despite official reassurance, Islamization has sometimes led to fears among non-Muslims, that their constitutional rights might be impinged. See also: ISLAMIC REVIVAL

J

JOHOR Johor emerged as a political entity as the successor state to the Malay empire of Melaka (q.v.), the first ruler of Johor being the son of the last Sultan of Melaka. As such all the states in the Peninsula and Sumatra which had acknowledged the overlordship of Melaka continued to acknowledge that of Johor. During the sixteenth and first half of the seventeenth centuries, from its capitals on the Johor River and in the Riau Archipelago, Johor became an important centre for trade, attracting vessels from China, India and the West as well as from within the region. In this period Johor was engaged in a triangular struggle with Aceh and the Portuguese in Melaka for the control of the trade of the Straits of Melaka. However, the Dutch conquest of Melaka in 1641 brought this struggle to an end and crippled Johor's trade. By the end of the century the state was weak and divided, circumstances which led to the substitution of the direct Melaka line of rulers by the *Bendahara* branch. In the eighteenth century Johor's politics were overshadowed by the Minangkabau of Sumatra and the Bugis from the Celebes. Bugis underkings succeeded in making themselves the real rulers of Johor until their power was broken by the Dutch in 1684. The existence of Malay and Bugis factions at the Johor court in 1819 provided the British empire-builder, Stamford Raffles (q.v.), with the opportunity to play one group off against the other and acquire the island of Singapore as a British base and center of trade. This event precipitated the dismemberment of the Johor-Riau Empire. Bugis-dominated Riau emerged as the Sultanate of Riau-Lingga under Dutch protection, while mainland Johor was controlled by the Malay faction headed by the *Temenggung*. By the 1880s Pahang, Trengganu and Negeri Sembilan, whose rulers had still owed a shadowy allegiance to the Sultan of Johor at the beginning of the century, now ruled as independent monarchs, and the *Temenggung* line had successfully ousted the *Bendahara* line from the position of Sultan. The *Temenggungs* provided a series of capable rulers, amongst whom the most notable was Temenggung Abu Bakar who elevated himself to Maharaja and then in 1885 to Sultan. Known as 'the father of modern Johor' Sultan Abu Bakar skilfully exploited his close relationship with the British in Singapore to develop and modernize the state. He was also successful in resisting British pressure to bring Johor under their closer control. His son and successor, Sultan Ibrahim, tried to pursue the same policies but he reigned at the high noon of British imperialism and in 1914 with great reluctance was forced to accept a British 'General Adviser', thereby bringing Johor more or less in line with the position of the other states of the Peninsula under British protection.

K

KARPAL SINGH (1940–) a leading opposition politician and human rights campaigner, was born in Penang (q.v.). He was educated in Penang and Singapore where he obtained his law degree. He currently has legal offices in Penang and Kuala Lumpur. Karpal Singh joined the DAP (q.v.) in 1970 and is Chairman of the DAP—Penang state branch, National Deputy Chairman of the DAP and legal advisor to the DAP. He is currently member of parliament for Bukit Glugor constituency in Penang. Karpal Singh was detained under the Internal Security Act (q.v.) in 1987 and finally released in 1989. He is a popular lawyer who is willing to defend the underdog.

KEDAH Kedah is reckoned to be the most ancient state in the Malaysian federation. Situated on one of the main transit routes across the Peninsula on the great East-West trade routes, the country was destined to become a prosperous centre for settlement and trade. Some of the earliest known Stone Age sites are located in the state, and it is the only state in the Peninsula which has remains from the Hindu-Buddhist inspired kingdoms in Malaysian history—in the numerous temple sites in the Bujang Valley. However, Kedah's exposed position made it vulnerable to outside forces. In the seventh and eighth centuries AD, Kedah was a vassal of the great Sumatran empire of Sri Vijaya. With the decline of Sumatran power, the state fell under the influence of the advancing Thais from the north. The rise of Melaka in the fifteenth century gave Kedah a respite from the Thais and led to the Islamization of the state. After Melaka's fall to the Portuguese, however, the old threats returned. During the seventeenth century Kedah was attacked by the Portuguese and ravished by the Acehnese, out to destroy it as a rival producer of pepper. The imminence of a Thai attack in the last quarter of the eighteenth century led Kedah to hand over the island of Penang to the British. But this did not save the state from Thai conquest in 1821, and for the next 25 years Kedah was under direct Thai rule. The Sultan of Kedah was restored as a Thai vassal in 1843, but Setul, Kubang Pasu and Perlis were taken from the state to form separate vassal principalities of their own. In 1909, by a treaty in which Kedah played no part, the Thais transferred their suzerainty over Kedah to the British. This led to the appointment of a British Adviser, but the Kedah Government was successful in retaining more control over its own affairs than was the case in the other Malay states which fell under British control. In 1941 Kedah (with Kelantan) was the first state to be invaded by the Japanese. During the Japanese Occupation the state was once more handed back to Thai authority. After the war, Kedah was returned to British authority and joined the Federation of Malaya in 1948.

KEKUATAN RA'AYAT ISTIMEWA (KRIS)/PEOPLE'S ASSOCIATION OF PENINSULAR INDONESIA During the Japanese Occupation of Malaya, the Japanese encouraged Malay nationalist movements which they thought they could control. One such organization was KRIS which advocated independence for Malaya and union with Indonesia.

KELANTAN Kelantan has been a center of human activity and settlement since prehistoric times, and has existed as a political entity for over a thousand years. Important prehistoric remains of Stone Age men have been found at Gua Cha, Gua Musang and at other sites in the interior of the state. Kelantan was probably a vassal of Sri Vijaya. The state was converted to Islam during the period of fifteenth century Melaka, and the modern Sultanate can trace its origins back to this period. Kelantan enjoyed a long period of autonomy after the fall of Melaka, but was inevitably affected by the relentless pressure of Thailand into Kedah and neighboring Patani. By the beginning of the nineteenth century the state was the most populous in the peninsula, but its politics were dominated by the Thais and the Malays of Trengganu. Despite a resurgence of autonomy in the middle of the century, by 1900 Kelantan was recognized as a tributary state of Thailand. In 1909, as a result of a treaty signed between Thailand and Britain, the British assumed overlordship of Kelantan and a British Adviser was appointed to Kota Bharu. Kota Bharu was the site for the first landing of Japanese troops in the peninsula in 1941. During the Japanese Occupation period, Kelantan was placed under Thailand. After the war, it reverted to the British. Kelantan became part of the Federation of Malaya in 1948. In the recent 1990 General Elections, the BN (q.v.) lost Kelantan to the opposition.

THE KELANTAN UPRISING/TO' JANGGUT REBELLION Soon after the imposition of British rule in Kelantan (q.v.), a peasant rebellion broke out at Pasir Putih in 1915, led by one Haji Mat Hassan, popularly known as To' Janggut. The Kelantan uprising was a localized reaction to the newly introduced land regulations in the state. The district office, a colonial institution, was sacked and the bungalows and property of the European planters burned and looted. The colonial authorities quickly suppressed the uprising and To' Janggut was killed in action. His body was hung upside down at the Kota Bharu town padang (square) for several days as a lesson to the rebels.

KESATUAN INSAF TANAH AIR (KITA) The ***Kesatuan Insaf Tanah Air*** (National Awareness Party or KITA) was formed in 1974 to provide a political platform for a diverse group of independent MPs and assemblymen who had either resigned or been expelled from their parties. Following its failure to win a single seat at the 1974 General Elections, the party virtually disintegrated and existed in name only, under the leadership of Samsuri bin Misu. KITA participated in negotiations among minor parties to establish a ***Barisan Rakyat*** (q.v.). In 1985, KITA was dissolved.

KESATUAN MELAYU MUDA (KMM)/ UNION OF MALAY YOUTH During the Japanese Occupation of Malaya, the Japanese pursued racial policies based on expediency, which attempted to mobilize some sections of the local population in their favor. They also encouraged Malay nationalist movements which they thought they could control. Among those was the KMM, a left wing group under the leadership of Ibrahim bin Yaacob, founded in 1937 to advocate independence of Malaya and union with Indonesia.

KITINGAN, JOSEPH PAIRIN, DATO (1940–) a leading politician and Kadazan leader and currently Chief Minister of Sabah (q.v.), was born in Papar, Sabah. He was educated in Sabah and Australia where he qualified as an advocate and solicitor. He joined the Sabah State Legal Service where he served as legal officer, deputy public prosecutor and State Council. In 1974 he joined the private sector and soon entered politics. He was a founder member and vice-president of ***Berjaya*** (q.v.). When ***Berjaya*** ousted USNO (q.v.) in 1975, and became the ruling party in Sabah, Kitingan served in various ministries. As President of the Kadazan community, he soon became disenchanted with Harris' (q.v.) pro-Muslim policy and in 1985, left ***Berjaya*** and formed the ***Parti Bersatu Sabah*** (the Sabah United Party)—PBS (q.v.). The PBS won a resounding victory in the 1985 state elections and although the leaders of ***Berjaya*** and USNO attempted to take power, Kitingan formed the new state government in April, 1985. In fresh elections held in May 1986, the PBS won a convincing two-thirds majority in Sabah. Kitingan has also managed to retain his leadership of the Kadazan community in Sabah. In the 1990 General Elections, Kitingan withdrew the PBS from the BN (q.v.) coalition and joined the opposition headed by Tengku Razaleigh (q.v.). He consequently lost favor with Mahathir and was arrested on charges of corruption in early 1991. He was released on bail of $M1.5 million and his case has yet to be heard.

KONGRES INDIA MUSLIM MALAYSIA (KIMMA) The ***Kongres India Muslim Malaysia*** (KIMMA) was formed in 1977 by a small group of Indian Muslims disgruntled with the treatment they had received within the Malaysian Indian Congress (MIC) (q.v.) which they perceived as being Hindu-dominated. The founders of KIMMA had hoped that the new party would become the representative of Malaysia Indian Muslims within the ***Barisan Nasional*** (q.v.). However, they were unable to muster either sufficient support among Indian Muslims or the agreement of component parties of the ***Barisan Nasional*** to play this role. KIMMA has failed to win representation in any legislature. It is concerned mainly with protecting the rights of Indian Muslims in the country. In the 1990 General Elections, KIMMA, in a surprise move, joined the APU (q.v.) coalition.

L

LABUAN Up till 1846 Labuan was part of the dominions of the Sultan of Brunei. In that year Brunei, bowing to direct British naval pressure, was obliged to cede the island to the British. But the British hope that their new colony would quickly develop into a new Singapore serving the trade of northern Borneo was soon shattered, while the island's coal resources proved to be of such low quality as to be commercially useless. Thus in 1890 the British Colonial Office was happy to hand over the administration of the island to the newly-created government of the British North Borneo Company (Sabah) (q.v.), while in 1905 the Company was equally happy to hand the island back to the Colonial Office which added it two years later to the colony of the

Straits Settlements (q.v.), administered from Singapore. Labuan remained an unprogressive part of the Straits Settlements until 1941, and after the Pacific War was made part of the new British colony of North Borneo. Labuan got its independence as part of Sabah with the creation of Malaysia in 1963, and was transferred to the jurisdiction of the Federal Government in 1984.

LEE HAU SHIK, HENRY, COLONEL, TUN, SIR (1900–1988) was a prominent Chinese community leader and statesman. He was born in Hong Kong and educated there and in the United Kingdom where he graduated with a B.A. degree. On his return to Malaya, he became the chairman of a local bank. He was also a tin miner and owned the China Press, a publishing company. During the Second World War, he served as a colonel in the Allied Forces. With the encouragement of the British, he and other Chinese community leaders founded the MCA (q.v.) in 1949 mainly as a welfare organization. Lee was also instrumental in the formation of an alliance with UMNO (q.v.) which was seen as the only hope for a viable independent Malaya. Between 1953 and 1959, he served as a government Minister for Transport (1953–56) and Finance (1957–59). He was also a member of the Merdeka (q.v.) Mission to London. He then decided to retire from politics and devoted his energies to his business interests. As a leading tin miner, he was a member of the Malayan Tin Delegation to all International Tin Meetings between 1946 and 1960 and was also a member of the Tin Advisory Committee from 1946–1955.

LEE LAM THYE (1946–), a prominent statesman and leading opposition politician, was born in Ipoh, Perak (q.v.). He was educated in Perak and became a school teacher and trade unionist. He served as secretary of the National Union of Commercial Workers. He was a founder member of the young socialist movement in Perak and also helped establish the Ipoh branch of the DAP (q.v.). He was deputy secretary general of the DAP, chairman of the DAP Federal Territory Branch, honorary advisor to numerous clubs, associations and welfare committees, and member of parliament for the Bukit Bintang constituency in Kuala Lumpur. In a surprise move, he resigned from all his party posts and decided not to stand in the October

1990 General Elections, citing differences with the party leadership as his main reason.

LEONG YEW KOH, TUN (1888–1963) was a leading Chinese community leader and statesman. He was born in Salak North, Perak, a little town founded by his miner father. He was educated in China and returned to Malaya when he was thirteen and resumed his schooling in Perak and Penang. At the age of twenty he was awarded a scholarship to study law, politics, economics and sociology at London University. On his return to Malaya, he practised as a lawyer in Ipoh. He returned to China in 1932 and worked as an administrator there. During the Second World War, he was appointed district officer in Yunan Province and also served as the manager of a provincial bank. Subsequently, he joined the army where he held the rank of Major-General. After the war, he returned to Malaya and resumed his practice. The British viewed him as a Chinese Community leader and appointed him as a member of the Consultative Committee on Constitutional Proposals for Malaya. He also served on the Federal Council. During the Emergency (q.v.) period, he and other prominent Chinese founded the Malayan Chinese Association (MCA) (q.v.) in 1949 partly in response to the formation of UMNO (q.v.) and as a welfare organization to lure the Chinese away from communism. The MCA and UMNO then formed a new political alliance which was viewed as the only hope for a viable independent Malayan government. Leong Yew Koh stood for elections in Perak and won and was subsequently appointed Minister for Health in the first Cabinet. In 1957, when an independent Malaya was proclaimed, he was appointed first Governor of Melaka (q.v.) a post he retained until 1959.

LIGHT, FRANCIS, SIR (1740–1794) was a merchant adventurer in the English East India Company (EIC) (q.v.) who is regarded as the founder of Penang. He was born in Suffolk, England and joined the Royal Navy. Subsequently, he left the navy to take a command under the EIC in India. As an agent and country trader he sought a British possession in Malayan waters and was impressed with Penang's location. He convinced the EIC of Penang's suitability as a British outpost in Malayan waters and was entrusted with the negotiations with the Sultan of Kedah (q.v.) (whose possession Penang was). In August 1786, he took formal possession of Penang in the name of King George III of England. The Sultan ceded Penang in return for certain guarantees, including protection against possible attacks from Siam or Burma and from any future uprisings by his own relatives. The establishment of Penang by Light transformed the EIC into a territorial power with an obvious stake in the security of the area. Only a year after its founding, all Malay rulers of standing had written to Light in an effort to gauge English willingness to lend material aid. The expected material aid did not materialize and Kedah forces attacked Penang but were beaten by the British and in 1791, the British occupation of Penang was subsequently confirmed in a treaty with Kedah. Light was appointed the first Superintendent of Penang and under his administration, Penang flourished as a colony. Penang also became the foundation stone of British expansion in Malaya.

LIM CHONG EU, DR. (1919–), a leading politician, was born in Penang (q.v.). He was educated in Penang and Britain where he obtained a medical degree. On his return to Malaya, he went into private practice. He soon entered politics and was appointed chairman of the political sub-committee of the MCA (q.v.). Along with a few others, Lim felt that the MCA did not fight strongly enough for Chinese interests and in 1958 challenged the incumbent Tan Cheng Lock (q.v.) for the presidency of the party. He defeated Tan by 89 votes to 67 and was elected MCA president. Lim's emphasis on an equal relationship with the UMNO (q.v.) brought him into an open conflict with the UMNO leadership and a crisis within the MCA. In 1959, Lim resigned from the presidency of the MCA and in 1961 left the party. In 1962, together with his supporters, Lim founded the United Democratic Party (UDP) (q.v.). The UDP was a non-communal party although it was dominated by MCA dissidents. It emphasized the equal rights of all Malaysians. The UDP cooperated with the Socialist Front (q.v.) where Lim came into contact with Dr. Tan Chee Khoon (q.v.). When the UDP was disbanded in 1967, Lim, Tan Chee Khoon and a few others founded the ***Gerakan Rakyat***

Malaysia (q.v.) in 1968. Soon after the 1969 Riots (q.v.), Lim fell out with Tan Chee Khoon and a few other leaders over the issue of cooperation with the Alliance (q.v.). Lim's decision to join the Alliance Coalition was followed by his appointment as Chief Minister of Penang in 1969, a post he held until 1990. He served as President of the Gerakan from 1971–1980. In the 1990 General Elections, Lim Chong Eu lost to Lim Kit Siang (q.v.) of the DAP (q.v.) in Penang and had to give up the Chief Ministership of the state.

LIM KIT SIANG (1941–), a prominent politician and Parliamentary Opposition Leader, was born in Batu Pahat (q.v.) in Johor (q.v.). He was educated in Batu Pahat and took an external law degree from London while he was in detention. Lim worked as a teacher in a Chinese school in Johor before becoming a journalist in Singapore from 1961–65. He also served as secretary-general of the Singapore National Union of Journalists. When Singapore left Malaysia in 1965 and the DAP was formed in 1966, Lim joined the DAP and became the editor of the *Rocket*, the organ of the DAP. Although he unseated the Chief Minister of Penang in the 1990 General Elections, the DAP was unable to obtain a majority to govern the state. Lim is a strong supporter of Malaysian Malaysia and has campaigned for equal rights. It is widely believed that the main reason for his detention under the ISA (q.v.) from May 1969 to October 1972 and from October 1987 to early 1989 was due to his activities in exposing corruption among government ministers and for championing the cause of the Chinese community. See also: DAP

LING LIONG SIK, DATO' SERI, DR. (1943–), leading politician and currently president of the MCA (q.v.) was born in Kuala Kangsar in Perak (q.v.). He studied in Taiping and at the Federation Military College. He obtained a medical degree from the University of Singapore in 1966 and went into private practice. He then joined the MCA and was elected a member of parliament for Mata Kucing in Penang in 1974. He served as Deputy Minister in the Ministries of Information, Finance and Education and in 1986 was appointed Minister of Transport, a post he has held since that time.

LONDON AGREEMENT After the tasks of the Cobbold Commission (q.v.), the Inter-Governmental Committee and the joint Ministerial Committee were completed regarding the formation of Malaysia, an agreement was signed on 9 July 1963, known as the London Agreement. This represented the final step towards the formation of Malaysia.

LOOK EAST POLICY In late 1981, Prime Minister Dato' Seri Dr. Mahathir Mohamad (q.v.) announced Malaysia's Look East Policy to lift Malaysia's economy on the road to rapid industrial growth and to prod Malaysians to be more productive by adopting work ethics from Japan and Korea. In a memorandum to senior government officers, the Prime Minister stated that to Look East

> "means emulating the rapidly developing countries of the East in the effort to develop Malaysia. Matters deserving attention are diligence and discipline in work, loyalty to the nation and to the enterprise or business where the worker is employed, priority of groups over individual interests, emphasis on productivity and high quality, upgrading efficiency, narrowing differentials and gaps between executives and workers, management systems which concentrate on long term achievement and not solely on increases in dividends or staff incomes in the short term, and other factors which can contribute to progress for our country. Looking East does not mean begging from the East or shifting the responsibility for developing Malaysia to them. Responsibility towards our country is our own and not that of others. Looking East also does not mean buying all goods or granting all contracts to companies of the East, unless their offer is best."

The Look East policy naturally paved the way for greater economic involvement of Japanese interests in Malaysia. Japanese commitments for investments rose from $M69.1 million in 1981 to $M139.8 million in 1982, with Japan topping the list of investors in both years. The Look East Policy became a spent force after a brief spurt of life. The essential problem was that Malaysia consistently bought more from Japan than the latter was buying from Malaysia. Another related issue included the large invisible bill involving freight and insurance. There were often irritants in the relationship such as Japanese protectionist barriers against imported manufactures from Malaysia, the slow rate or lack of technology transfer and the practice of transfer pricing by Japanese multinationals to avoid taxation in Malaysia. Japan's blocking of the Malaysian Airline System's bid to operate a flight to the United States with Northwest Orient Airlines via Tokyo (which was only settled after a meeting between the Malaysian Prime Minister and his Japanese counterpart) dealt a moral blow to the Look East Policy. The chief lessons that Malaysia learnt were that Japan's path to success is not replicable for such countries as Malaysia and that each country's development is rooted in historically distinct and contextually different experiences.

LOW, HUGH, SIR (1824–1905) was a British Resident (q.v.) in Perak (q.v.), who is regarded as the founder of British administration in the Malay States. He was born in 1824 in England. From youth, he had an interest in botany and journeyed to the tropics to study orchids. He soon came to the notice of James Brooke (q.v.) who appointed him as one of his officials. At the age of 24, he became Inspector to Labuan. He was an able administrator who introduced sound taxation, promoted agriculture and mining and kept the peace among the different communities. He lived in Sarawak (q.v.) for over 30 years. In 1877, he was appointed Resident of Perak. He spent 12 years in Perak and it was due to his able administration that Perak became the most prosperous of the Malay States. Among his achievements were the creation of a state council in which there was participation by the Sultan and Malay Chiefs, the appointment of Malay police, the abolition of debt-slavery, the establishment of a revenue system, the reorganization of mines and the promotion of commercial crops such as rubber, tea and coffee. During his tenure, the first railway line was built in the state and country. He thus laid the basis for a sound administrative system which was used as a model for the other states. He retired in 1889 at the age of 65.

M

MAHATHIR BIN MOHAMAD, DATO' SERI, DR. (1925–) is the current Prime Minister of Malaysia. He was born in Alor Setar, Kedah and was educated there. He qualified as a doctor from the University of Malaya in Singapore in 1953. He served in government medical service for four years and then resigned to go into private practice and became a very successful general practitioner in Alor Setar. He had become active in politics since 1945 when he joined various Malay organizations, including the Kedah Malay Union and the Kedah Malay Youth Movement. In 1946, he joined UMNO (q.v.). In 1964 he stood for election in Kedah and won a seat. Even then, he was known as a rising star among the young Turks of UMNO. In 1969, he lost his seat to a PAS (q.v.) candidate. He believed that Tunku Abdul Rahman (q.v.) was not redressing the imbalance among the races and because of his anti-Tunku activities, was expelled from UMNO in 1969. Later he wrote the highly controversial *The Malay Dilemma* outlining the problems of the Malays. When Tun Abdul Razak (q.v.) became the Prime Minister, Mahathir was re-admitted to UMNO and re-elected to the Supreme Council. In 1975, he became one of the three Vice-Presidents of the Party. He was returned unopposed in the 1974 General Elections (PAS was now a member of the National Front (q.v.)). He was appointed Minister of Education in 1974 and during his tenure (1974–78) there was a wave of student unrest in the country. He was responsible for introducing amendments to the Universities and University Colleges Act which wiped out university autonomy. Universities and other institutions of higher education were now administered by the Ministry of Education. In 1976, he was appointed Deputy Prime Minister and two years later became Minister of Trade and Industry as well. In this latter position, he embarked on several promotional trade missions to encourage international investment in the country. He intervened in the Malaysian Airlines System dispute and in the Malaysian Trades Union Congress (q.v.) dispute over the amendments of the trade union laws. He used the Internal Security Act (q.v.) to settle the two issues. In 1981 when

Hussein Onn stepped down as Prime Minister, Mahathir became the Prime Minister and Minister for Home Affairs. Since then there have been further curbs on fundamental liberties and in 1983, he was deemed responsible for the constitutional crisis (q.v.) in the country. In 1987, he detained 119 people under the Internal Security Act in the "Operation Lallang" (q.v.) to diffuse a volatile political situation in the country. During his tenure as Prime Minister, he has strengthened his own position and UMNO has emerged more dominant than ever. In the 1990 General Elections, he used all weapons at his disposal to retain the BN's two-thirds majority.

MALAY A Malay is a person of the Malay race. In the Twelfth Schedule of the Federal Constitution, a Malay is defined as a person who:

(i) habitually speaks the Malay language
(ii) professes the Muslim religion and
(iii) conforms to Malay customs.

MALAYA Before the formation of Malaysia in 1963, West Malaysia was known as Malaya. It included the nine Malay states of Johor, Kedah, Kelantan, Negeri Sembilan, Pahang, Perak, Perlis, Selangor and Trengganu and the Straits Settlements of Melaka and Penang. Malaya as a political entity came into being with the inauguration of the Federation of Malaya in 1948. The usage of the term Malaya is now largely geographical and refers to the Malay Peninsula.

MALAYAN A Malayan was a person who was a citizen of the Federation of Malaya, irrespective of racial origin.
See: MALAYA

MALAYAN CONSULTATIVE COUNCIL FOR BUDDHISM, CHRISTIANITY, HINDUISM AND SIKHISM This council was established on 6 August 1983 on the recommendation of the National Unity Board. Its main function is to provide a means by which the four religions it represents can convey their views on issues which affect them to the government. It has three main aims: to promote understanding, mutual respect and co-operation between people of different faiths; to study and resolve problems affecting all inter-religious relationships and to make representations regarding religious matters when necessary. The membership includes the Malaysian Buddhist Association, the Council of Churches of Malaysia, the National Evangelical Christian Fellowship, the Malaysian Hindu Sangam, the Khalsa Dewan Malaysia, the Sikh Naujawan Sabha, and the Kebajikan Sikh, Selangor dan Wilayah Persekutuan.

MALAYAN UNION Soon after the British took over again in Malaya after the Second World War, they proposed and set up in 1946 a new type of government, the Malayan Union, which was to include the whole of the Malay Peninsula and to exclude Singapore. To the British, the Malayan Union was a necessary step toward the granting of independence to a united nation in which each group would have equal rights. The Malayan Union Scheme embodied the creation of a unitary state comprising the Federated Malay States (q.v.), the Unfederated Malay States (q.v.), Penang (q.v.) and Melaka (q.v.) with a central government, a governor, and legislative and executive councils. The Malay Sultans were to retain their positions but sovereignty was to be transferred to the British Crown which would be represented in Malaya by a British Governor. All citizens of the Malayan Union would have equal rights, including admission to the administrative civil service. Finally, Malayan citizenship was to be extended to all without discrimination as to race or creed. The Malayan Union Scheme was effectively opposed by the Malay rulers and a new political force which arose to channel Malay opposition to the Union. This was the United Malays National Organisation (UMNO) (q.v.). The scheme was revoked in the entirety after 1 February 1948 when the Federation of Malaya was created by the Federation Agreement of 1948 (q.v.).

MALAYSIA The Federation of Malaysia consists of the Peninsular States of Johor, Kedah, Kelantan, Melaka, Negeri Sembilan, Pahang, Penang, Perak, Perlis, Selangor and Trengganu, together with the North Borneo States of Sabah and Sarawak. Malaysia came into being as a political entity in 1963. Singapore was originally part of the Federation but ceased to be a member in 1965. In 1974, the Federal Territory covering Kuala Lumpur and its environs came into being. In 1984, the island of Labuan, off the coast of Sabah, was also proclaimed a federal territory.

MALAYSIAN A Malaysian is a person irrespective of racial origin, who is a citizen of Malaysia. Before the formation of Malaysia in 1963, the term "Malaysian" was used to include persons racially akin to the Malays, who were Muslims and spoke a similar language, but who originated from a territory other than Malaya, for instance from Indonesia.

MALAYSIAN ADMINISTRATIVE MODERNIZATION AND MANPOWER PLANNING UNIT (MAMPU) This unit, located within the Prime Minister's Department, was established in 1971 and is responsible for effecting changes in the management and administration of the public sector in order to improve its effectiveness, efficiency and productivity in accordance with national requirements. It undertakes its responsibilities by being the prime mover in effecting change and acting as consultant and facilitator to other government agencies.

MALAYSIAN CHINESE ASSOCIATION (MCA) The MCA was founded during the Emergency (q.v.) in 1949, at the suggestion of the British colonial authorities, as a social welfare agency for the Chinese community in Malaya and to assist in the task of wooing the Chinese away from Communist influence. The MCA soon took on the role of representing Chinese interests to the colonial authorities and by 1952, had become a political party. In that year, its Selangor Branch entered into an electoral arrangement with UMNO (q.v.) to contest the Kuala Lumpur municipal elections, a partnership which laid the foundations for the Alliance (q.v.). Wealthy and influential elements of the Chinese elite, and in particular members from the various Chinese chambers of commerce have always sought to play a predominant role in the MCA, a fact which has inevitably led to the MCA being branded by its opponents as the party of ***towkays***. The MCA, representing Chinese communal interests, served as the 'second pillar' of the tripartite Alliance and was allotted several important portfolios, including that of the post of Finance Minister. In addition, it was allowed to provide the Chief Minister for the Alliance government in the predominantly Chinese state of Penang. However, at the 1969 General Election, the party fell victim to ethnic outbidding, suffered severe electoral reverses, including the loss of the seats of a number of cabinet ministers and was defeated in Penang at the hands of the ***Gerakan Rakyat Malaysia*** (q.v.). Thereafter the MCA played a markedly reduced role in the ruling coalition. Tun Abdul Razak (q.v.), against the MCA's wishes chose to strengthen Chinese participation in the government, by expanding the Alliance structure and absorbing several of the parties which had been responsible for the MCA's losses in 1969. Moreover, the MCA was no longer allocated key financial Cabinet portfolios. Despite a sizeable formal membership and the fact that it is the second largest political party in Malaysia, the MCA has consistently failed to win a majority of the Chinese vote. Its principal rival is the Democratic Action Party (q.v.). To a large extent, the MCA's political impact has been lessened by the irreconcilable tensions inherent in its need to champion the Chinese position, whilst at the same time making efforts to appease UMNO by attempting to gain acceptance within the Chinese community of the New Economic Policy (q.v.). The MCA has also been obliged to accept the continuing and growing presence of its rival, the Gerakan, in both the ***Barisan Nasional*** (q.v.) and the government. In recent years, the MCA has suffered from severe factionalism resulting in the emergence of rival 'Acting' Presidents. Moreover, even after these disorders had been settled with the assistance of UMNO mediation, the image of the party was further eroded by the arrest in 1986, of its President, Mr. Tan Koon Swan, by the Singapore authorities on several charges of fraud involving his involvement in the collapse of the Pan-Electric Industries Limited Group. (He has since been released.) Additionally several Chinese leaders were arrested for their role in the mismanagement of deposit-taking cooperatives which resulted in thousands of poor Chinese losing their life savings invested with these cooperatives. Many analysts believe that the MCA has failed to grow in political sophistication, giving up constitutional safeguards and producing inept politicians when statesmen were needed. The present President is Dr. Ling Liong Sik who seems determined to reverse the fortunes of the MCA. To improve the MCA's chances he gathered a corps of Chinese intellectuals to advise him on strategies for the 1990 General Election. Some of these intellectuals represented the MCA in the discussions on the National Economic Consultative Committee (q.v.). In the 1990 General Elections, the MCA lost to the DAP in constituencies with more than 70 per cent Chinese, such as Penang and Kuala Lumpur.

MALAYSIAN INDIAN CONGRESS (MIC) The Malaysian Indian Congress was formed in 1946. It is one of the original members of the tripartite Alliance Party (q.v.) which it joined in 1955. It is a communal political party concerned with the interests of the Indian community in Malaysia. However, it represents mainly the interests of the South Indians, although this was not so in the initial years. As well as functioning as the representative of the Indian community within the ***Barisan Nasional*** (q.v.), the MIC also performs a number of welfare functions as well as being involved in business enterprises through its financial arm Maika Holdings. Due to the limited size of the Indian community in Malaysia relative to other ethnic groups and their scattered distribution, MIC candidates were unable to win Parliamentary representation on a purely communal basis. This difficulty has been overcome through participation in the ruling coalition, which ensured that the MIC received a quota of both Federal and State seats as well as representation in the Federal Cabinet. This has led to compromises on the part of the MIC. In the cabinet reshuffle (June 1988), the President of the MIC, Datuk Seri S. Samy Vellu (q.v.), the Minister for Works, was moved in a direct swop to Energy, Telecommunications and Posts, a post held by a Sarawakian, Datuk Leo Moggie (q.v.). Works is deemed slightly more senior than Posts. Given the political situation in Sarawak, and the expansion of the road networks there and the fact that the Minister for Works enjoys the power to win and maintain political support through the issuing of tenders, the

Prime Minister hoped to win support for his candidates in Sarawak. Additionally, the MIC has suffered from factionalism within its predominantly Tamil leadership as well as the resignation of some disgruntled Indian Muslim members who subsequently founded their own separate minor parties.

MALAYSIAN SOLIDARITY PARTY The Malaysian Solidarity Party (MSP) was formed in 1989. It is a non-communal based party comprising former SDP (q.v.) and MCA (q.v.) members. Its main concerns are national unity and the emergence of a two-party system in the country. Its pro-tem Chairman is C.S. Wong (formerly of the MCA) while the Secretary-General is Yeoh Poh San (formerly of the SDP). The Malaysian Solidarity Party is a component party of the ***Gagasan Rakyat*** coalition.

MAPHILINDO From early 1963, Indonesia pursued a policy of 'Confrontation' (q.v.) towards Malaysia. During a temporary lull in 'Confrontation', tripartite meetings of representatives of Malaya, the Philippines and Indonesia were held in July and August 1963 which culminated in the formation of a new organization of the three countries, Maphilindo. Maphilindo stressed the 'Malay origin' of the three countries. The organization was inoperative because Confrontation was renewed.

MARINA YUSOFF (1941–) is a leading Malay politician. She was born in Kelantan and educated in Kota Bharu and Kuala Lumpur. She obtained a law degree from the United Kingdom. She started work in the legal and judiciary service and later became a legal advisor and personnel manager in a leading bank. Subsequently, she set up her own legal firm and became a property developer. Marina Yusoff soon joined UMNO (q.v.) and was elected to the Supreme Council. After a falling out with Mahathir Mohamad (q.v.) she left the party in 1987 and is a founder member of ***Semangat*** '46 (q.v.). She is currently one of the Vice-Presidents of the Party.

MAT SALLEH REBELLION The Mat Salleh Rebellion represented a unified movement against the British North Borneo

Chartered Company (q.v.) in Sabah. It erupted in 1895 and was not fully quelled until 1905. Mat Salleh, a native chief, was of mixed Bajau and Sulu parentage and drew upon a combination of Muslim and indigenous symbols of authority. Muslims saw him as *Mahdi*, the Coming Saviour. His use of flags, Islamic standards and the umbrella of royalty gave him a prestige and mystique lacking in more localized uprisings. Mat Salleh's grievances against the Chartered Company were never totally clear but it may be surmised that the introduction of a new tax on imported rice and another to help finance a cross-country railroad exacerbated a general discontent. He was killed in 1900 but jungle warfare continued for another five years. Today he is regarded as one of Sabah's great heroes and is buried at Tambunan where a monument has been erected in his honor.

MAY 13 INCIDENT Malaysia was rocked by violent intercommunal riots in the wake of the 1969 General Elections, during which the Alliance (q.v.) government suffered severe reverses at the hands of predominantly non-Malay opposition parties. The term refers to the riot incidents of communal violence which began on May 13. The riots were confined almost entirely to Kuala Lumpur and the surrounding areas in Selangor and resulted in the killing of a large number of people and considerable destruction of property. Parliament was suspended and Malaysia was governed for almost two years under a National Operations Council (q.v.). The events of May 13, 1969 represented a watershed in Malaysian politics. The government undertook a refashioning of political life and economic structures to restore long-term national stability. This was done through the formulation of a national ideology, the removal from open public discussion of major contentious issues thought likely to incite communal discord and the implementation of new social and economic programs to protect and advance Malay rights. The 'spectre of another May 13' is occasionally raised by political leaders as a warning of the dangers of unrestrained or irresponsible political behavior.
See also: BARISAN NASIONAL; NEW ECONOMIC POLICY

MELAKA (State) The present State of Melaka owes its existence to the rise of the port of Melaka in the fifteenth century, to which it served as hinterland. The city-state-empire of Melaka was founded by Parameswara, a fugitive Sumatran prince, around 1400, and during the course of the next hundred years rose to become the greatest entrepôt of the region and the center of the Malay world. Its conversion to Islam within this period served to make Melaka the focal point for the spread of the religion throughout the Peninsula and other parts of the Malay-Indonesian archipelago. The traditions and style of Melaka were inherited by the various Malay principalities of the Peninsula after the port's capture by the Portuguese in 1511. The Portuguese occupied Melaka for over a hundred years until they were finally driven out by the Dutch in 1641. Melaka remained a Dutch possession till 1795 when it was occupied by the British, and although it was restored to Holland in 1814 it was transferred permanently to Britain by the Anglo-Dutch Treaty of 1824 (q.v.). Under Western colonial rule Melaka did not maintain its position as the leading port of the region. The Portuguese failed because they were under constant attack by the Malays of Johor and the Acehnese, and later on by the Dutch as well. The Dutch deliberately made Melaka subordinate to their capital in the Indies at Batavia (Jakarta), although they did make Melaka their base for controlling the trade of the Peninsula. Under the British, Melaka remained an economic backwater, overshadowed by Penang and Singapore. It formed part of the Crown Colony of the Straits Settlements (q.v.), but after the Second World War joined the Malayan Union (q.v.) and then the Federation of Malaya (q.v.).

MELAKA TOWN Melaka is the oldest and historically most interesting town in Malaysia. Founded around 1400, it emerged in the fifteenth century as a regional entrepôt with the right to command the patronage of foreign merchants. Its great success and honored place in Malaysian history was not only due to its prosperity and renown as a trading center. Building upon an illustrious past, it established a pattern of government and a lifestyle which was emulated by subsequent Malay kingdoms and became the basis of what was later termed

"traditional Malay culture and statecraft". It served as an inspiration and a source of strength to all those states which considered themselves its heirs. In 1511 it was captured by the Portuguese and subsequently the Dutch took over control in 1641. Present day Melaka contains some of the oldest colonial buildings (Portuguese and Dutch) in East Asia along with some of the oldest Malay, Chinese and Hindu religious structures in the country. In this century, Melaka was selected to be the site where Tunku Abdul Rahman (q.v.), the first Prime Minister, proclaimed Independence Day on 20 February 1956. It is the repository of the documents and memorabilia relating to the independence movement which are housed in the Proclamation of Independence Memorial.
See also: MERDEKA

MERDEKA *Merdeka* (Independence) was granted to the Federation of Malaya by Britain on 31 August 1957. *Merdeka* Day is celebrated as a national holiday and ceremonies and a grand parade are held. Of late, a theme for each year had been selected by the government. The most recent theme is *BERSATU* or Unity among the Malaysian peoples. In 1985, the Proclamation of Independence Memorial, housing documents and memorabilia on the independence movement and the actual transfer of power, was opened in Melaka, close to the site where Tunku Abdul Rahman (q.v.) had proclaimed Independence Day on 20 February 1956.

THE MILITARY The Malaysian armed forces do not play a significant role either in society or the economy. The armed forces are overwhelmingly Malay, non-political and geared principally to the provision of security against internal Communist guerillas. The navy and air force are relatively small and there is no national conscription. The armed forces have remained outside politics. Of late, the government has emphasized the threat of external aggression, and the armed forces are undergoing training in preparedness of this threat.

MOGGIE, LEO, ANAK IROK, DATUK (1941–) a popular Sarawak politician and Dayak leader, was born in Kanowit, Sarawak (q.v.) and educated in Sarawak, New Zealand and the

U.S.A. He served as assistant district officer and later as district officer for the Kapit region. He was appointed Director of the Borneo Literature Bureau and subsequently Deputy General Manager of the Borneo Development Corporation. He then left government service and joined the Sarawak National Party (SNAP) (q.v.). He contested the state seat of Machan and the parliamentary seat of Kanowit in 1974 and won both seats. Subsequently he served in the Sarawak State Government. In 1978, he was appointed to the Malaysian cabinet as Minister of Energy, Telecommunications and Posts. Moggie was dissatisfied with SNAP and following a crisis in the party in 1983, he left the the party to form the ***Parti Bansa Dayak Sarawak*** (PBDS) (q.v.). The PBDS joined the ***Barisan Nasional*** (q.v.) coalition in 1984. In 1989, Moggie became Minister for Works and Posts in the Malaysian Cabinet.

MOHAMAD NAJIB BIN TUN HAJI ABDUL RAZAK, (1953–) a rising politician and son of the second prime minister of Malaysia, was born in Pekan, Pahang (q.v.). He was educated in Pahang, Selangor and in the United Kingdom, where he obtained a B.A. degree in 1974. On his return to Malaysia, he entered politics. He was elected member of parliament for Pekan in 1976 and served as a government deputy minister between 1978 and 1982 in a number of ministries including Energy, Telecommunications and Posts, Education and Defence. In 1982, he was appointed the *Menteri Besar* (Chief Minister) (q.v.) of Pahang. He has also been a Deputy President of the UMNO (q.v.) Youth Wing and sits on the UMNO Supreme Council. He is currently Minister of Defence.

MOHAMAD SUFFIAN BIN HASHIM, TUN (1917–) is a former Lord President of the Malaysian Judiciary. He was born in Kuala Kangsar and educated in Perak (q.v.) and in the United Kingdom where he qualified as a Barrister-at-Law. He was appointed Malay broadcaster and later became the head of the Malay section of the British Broadcasting Corporation, Overseas Section (1945–46). In 1946, he returned to Malaya and joined the legal service and had a remarkably successful career. Starting as a magistrate, he became in turn, deputy public prosecutor, legal advisor, solicitor general, high court judge, federal judge, chief justice and served as Lord President of the judiciary from 1974 to 1982. He has translated the Constitution of the Federation of Malaya into the Malay language and has also written an introduction to the Constitution of Malaya. He is a member of the World Bank Administrative Tribunal, Washington D.C., Vice President of the International Labor Organization Administrative Tribunal, Geneva and holds important regional and national positions. He is also chairperson of the self-appointed Election Watch Committee which has been formed to monitor the forthcoming general election to ensure that it is properly and fairly conducted. He is an outspoken critic of the prime minister's assault on the judiciary and has deplored the erosion of human rights in the country. In 1990, he and five other prominent Malaysians formed the Election Watch (q.v.) to monitor the Eighth General Elections.

MOSQUITO PARTY A term of derision applied to minor parties lacking an extensive network of support. Such parties are considered by their detractors as sources of minor irritation rather than serious contenders for political power.

MTUC The Malaysian Trades Union Congress is a society (registered under the Societies Ordinance of 1949) whose members are registered trade unions which have voluntarily affiliated themselves to it. The Congress is in effect a forum in which the seventy-odd affiliated unions are able to work out common policy affecting labor generally. It is completely non-political and has always stressed its abstention from politics. It is however in a strong position to represent, particularly to the government, any matter which requires common action to be taken, particularly if legislation is required. In its corporate capacity, the MTUC is represented on the Employees Provident Fund Board, the National Joint Labor Advisory Council and the Central Apprenticeship Board. The Congress plays no part in solving individual trade or industrial disputes that being the individual responsibility of its affiliate members. On the other hand, it considers specific problems which may have a bearing on any matter affecting industrial relations as a whole. In this it performs a valuable service in promoting industrial democracy. The MTUC is affiliated to the International Confederation of Free Trade Unions.

MUSA HITAM, DATUK (1934–) is a leading Malay politician and until 1986, was Deputy Prime Minister. He was born in Johor (q.v.) and educated at the English College. He graduated from the University of Malaya (then located in Singapore) with a B.A. degree in 1959. A decade later, he obtained an M.A. in international relations from Sussex University in the United Kingdom. Soon after graduation in 1959, he joined the civil service as an assistant district officer. In 1964, he became the political secretary to the Minister of Transport. Subsequently he became the executive secretary of UMNO (q.v.) in charge of party administration. In 1968, he entered Parliament and in 1969, was appointed Assistant Minister to the Deputy Prime Minister. He was expelled from UMNO for his anti-Tunku Abdul Rahman (q.v.) activities and went to the U.K. to do a masters degree. Upon his return, he rejoined UMNO and in 1973 was appointed Deputy Minister of Trade and Industry. His rise in UMNO was rapid and he served in a number of positions as government minister, including Education, Trade and Industry and Home Affairs. In 1981, he and Tunku Razaleigh Hamzah contested the Deputy UMNO President's post and he defeated the latter. He thus assumed the Deputy President's post and also became the Deputy Prime Minister. By 1986 he had fallen out with Mahathir Mohamad (q.v.) and was defeated for the Deputy President's post by Mahathir's candidate. When UMNO was deregistered in 1988, he chose to remain an independent but in 1989 joined UMNO ***Baru*** (q.v.). He is currently a special envoy of the government.

MUSTAPHA BIN DATU HARUN, TUN DATU (1918–), a leading politician in the East Malaysian State of Sabah (q.v.) was born in Kudat. He was educated in Kudat and worked as a clerk there. During the Japanese Occupation of Sabah (then known as British North Borneo), Mustapha escaped to the Philippines to join a guerilla resistance group. Subsequently he became a sergeant in the regular army and was attached to the secret service. In 1945, he was posted to North Borneo with the rank of Captain. He was appointed a native chief and entered local politics. He served as a member of the Legislative Council (1954), Executive Council (1956) and in 1961, formed the United Sabah National Organization (USNO) (q.v.). With the exception of a brief period when he was not president of the party, Mustapha has dominated USNO. In 1963, he was appointed *Yang diPertuan Negara* (q.v.) of Sabah. In 1967, he became Chief Minister of Sabah with Kuala Lumpur's help because of his efforts to bring Sabah into line with national policies. Once in power, Mustapha ran Sabah as a personal fiefdom, a feat made possible by Sabah's immense resources from timber concessions. It has been alleged that he entertained notions of separation from Malaysia and of forming a new nation consisting of Sabah and the three Philippine areas of Sulu, Mindanao and Palawan. There were even claims that he channelled arms to Moslem rebels in the southern Philippines. To undermine his authority, Tun Abdul Razak (q.v.), the then Prime Minister, appointed a chief of police and a head of armed forces in Sabah who were loyal to Kuala Lumpur. When an opposition party, ***Berjaya*** (q.v.) arose in 1975, Tun Abdul Razak quickly accepted it as a member of the National Front. Tun Mustapha finally resigned in October 1975, but still dominated Sabah politics as leader of USNO. After Tun Abdul Razak's death, the new Prime Minister, Hussein Onn continued to apply pressure on Tun Mustapha and was finally rewarded by the latter's removal from power through Berjaya's victory in the Sabah elections of April 1976. Mustapha then became a member of the opposition. After a three-way contest between the ***Parti Bersatu Sabah*** (PBS) (q.v.), Berjaya and USNO at the 1985 state elections, the PBS emerged victorious and Mustapha failed to form a minority USNO-Berjaya government. Nonetheless, he contrived to take over control in Sabah (he was Chief Minister for a few hours) but was foiled in his attempts when the High Court ruled against him. He is currently an opposition politician in Sabah. In May 1991, he dissolved USNO to form the Sabah UMNO chapter.

MUZAFFAR, CHANDRA, Ph.D. (1947–) is a leading political scientist and human rights activist who was born in Sungei

Petani, Kedah. He holds a doctorate in sociology from the University of Singapore. Muzaffar has written many books and articles on themes ranging from religion to development and the state of democracy in Malaysia. In 1977, he and a few others founded ALIRAN (***Aliran Kesederan Negara***) (q.v.) a prominent social reform movement in Malaysia. In 1988, he resigned from his teaching position as a university lecturer to devote full attention to ALIRAN. Apart from his social and political commentaries on Malaysia, Muzaffar is an executive committee member of the Asian Human Rights Commission, a member of the Consultative Board of SOS Torture, and is the coordinator of the Informal Movement for Freedom and Justice in Malaysia. Muzaffar was detained under the Internal Security Act (ISA) (q.v.) on 27 October 1987 and released on 18 December 1987. In 1990, he and five other prominent Malaysians formed the Election Watch (q.v.) to monitor the 1990 General Elections.

N

NATIONAL ANTHEM The national anthem, adopted at independence in 1957, is reportedly based on a tune which was popular in the Seychelles in the 1880s. The tune was picked up by the sons of a former ruler of Perak (q.v.) who was exiled to the Seychelles for his complicity in the murder of the first British resident (q.v.) of Perak, soon after the signing of the Pangkor Treaty (q.v.). According to royal sources in Perak, the tune was selected as the *ad hoc* Perak state anthem when the Perak ruler was visiting London in 1881. By different routes the tune, known as *Terang Bulan*, became popular in local opera and later in the cabarets of pre-war Malaya. *Terang Bulan* has remained the state anthem of Perak. The words of the anthem are:

Negaraku tanah tumpahnya darahku
Rakyat Hidup Bersatu Dan Maju
Rahmat Bahgia Tuhan Kurniyakan
Raja Kita Selamat Bertakhta

Rahmat Bahgia Tuhan Kurniyakan
Raja Kita Selamat Bertakhta

NATIONAL FLAG The national flag consists of fourteen red and white stripes (along the fly) of equal width, a union or canton of dark blue, a crescent and a star. The red and white stripes stand for the equal status in the federation of the member states and the federal government. The union or canton of dark blue in the upper quarter of the flag next to the staff represents the unity of the people of Malaysia. The union contains the crescent, which is the symbol of Islam, and the star, the fourteen points of which symbolize the unity of the thirteen states of the federation with the federal government. The yellow of the crescent and the star is the royal color of the Rulers.

NATIONAL FLOWER The national flower is the *bunga raya* (*hibiscus rosa sinensis*). The flower was probably introduced to Malaysia by way of trade from its original homeland in China, Japan and the Pacific Islands, around the twelfth century. The *bunga raya* is found abundantly in Malaysia. It grows in several varieties of color: the red, five petalled type was selected as the national flower.

NATIONAL LANGUAGE The national language of *Bahasa Malaysia* is established as such under Article 152 of the Constitution, which also safeguards other languages by stipulating that no person may be prohibited or prevented from using (except for official purposes) or from teaching or learning any other language. As the national language, *Bahasa Malaysia* must be used for official purposes which includes its use by federal and state governments, and as defined by the contitutional amendment of 1971 by all authorities (including local authorities) and statutory bodies. By the same constitutional amendment, the status of *Bahasa Malaysia* may not be questioned, and any amendment to Article 152 can only be made with the consent of the Conference of Rulers. The provisions regarding the use of the national language for official purposes in Sabah and Sarawak are also special to these two states, in particular with regard to the law courts where a native language in current use may be used in such courts and for any code of native law and customs. By the 1963 Language Act, the official script of the national language is *Rumi* (Roman script) but the use of *Jawi* (Arabic script) is not prohibited.

NATIONAL OPERATIONS COUNCIL Following the May 1969 riots (q.v.), the then Deputy Prime Minister, Tun Abdul Razak (q.v.), was appointed Director of Operations and given wide executive and legislative powers. He was also empowered to appoint the members of the National Operations Council (NOC) (q.v.) to assist him in the task of maintaining order and developing policies to restore national stability. At the same time, provision was made to set up State Operations Committees and District Operations Committees; the Director of Operations appointed their members and directed their activities. Simultaneously, steps were taken to increase the size of the army. Civilian members of the NOC included the Minister for Home Affairs, Minister for Information and Broadcasting, the Presidents of the MCA (q.v.) and MIC (q.v.), the Director of Public Services and the Permanent Secretary of the Foreign Affairs Ministry. Among the military and police representatives were the Chief of Staff of the Armed Forces, the Inspector-General of Police and a senior army officer. The Cabinet (and the ministerial system) continued to exist; it was still headed by the Tunku (q.v.) as Prime Minister but it was no longer responsible to Parliament. The NOC had to deal with what was largely a security situation, which initially focused its attention on specific and immediate problems. The NOC was dissolved in mid-1971 when parliamentary rule was restored, but its security functions were vested in a new body, the National Security Council (q.v.).

See also: MAY 13 INCIDENT; NATIONAL SECURITY COUNCIL

NATIONAL SECURITY COUNCIL The security functions of the National Operations Council (NOC) (q.v.), which was dissolved in 1971, was transferred to the National Security Council (NSC) which is a body responsible for co-ordinating policies relating to national security. It is also responsible for the overall direction of security measures. The NSC is under

the jurisdiction of Parliament. Among others, its membership includes the Chief of the Armed Forces, the Inspector-General of Police and the Secretary-General of the Ministers of Defence, Home Affairs and Information.
See also: NATIONAL OPERATIONS COUNCIL

NEGERI SEMBILAN Negeri Sembilan is unique in comprising a federation within the Malaysian federation. The basic population of the state consists of Minangkabau settlers from Sumatra who started to settle in the hinterland of Melaka (q.v.) during the period of the Melaka Sultanate in the fifteenth century. For generations these Minangkabau settlers were content to live according to their custom and social system (a matriarchial system) under the protection of the Malay Sultans of Melaka, and after the fall of Melaka to the Portuguese, under the protection of the Sultans of Johor. However, by the beginning of the eighteenth century Johor's rulers were no longer in a position to protect the Minangkabau of Negeri Sembilan from the pressure and incursions of the Bugis who had established themselves in neighboring Selangor and at the mouth of the Linggi River. So they turned to the traditional royal house at Pagar Ruyong in their Sumatran homeland for a prince who could unite and defend them. This finally resulted in the proclamation of Raja Melewar as the first *Yang diPertuan Besar* of Negeri Sembilan in 1773 near Rembau. It is not clear which were the original nine states of this new confederation, but today there are only six, namely Sri Menanti—incorporating the territories of Ulu Muar, Jempol, Gunung Pasir, Inas and Terachi—Sungei Ujung, Johor, Jelebu, Rembau and Tampin. The history of Negeri Sembilan after 1773 was turbulent, particularly when the largest member of the confederacy, Sungei Ujung, became the scene of a tin rush in the middle of the nineteenth century and the Linggi River a much disputed channel of trade. This general political instability marked by succession disputes and civil war in Sungei Ujung itself disrupted the tin trade with the Straits Settlements (q.v.) and threatened to injure their prosperity; this led to British intervention in 1874 and the establishment of a British Resident in Sungei Ujung. Opposition to this development from the rest of Negeri Sembilan led to a brief but bloody clash with British forces the following year. But during the 1880s Yam Tuan Besar (*Yang diPertuan Besar*) Antah gradually accepted the British presence and placed his Sri Menanti confederation under British protection in 1887. Rembau and Tampin joined Sri Menanti two years later. Finally in 1895 Negeri Sembilan was reconstituted as a federation of six states (as listed above) under the *Yang diPertuan Besar* Muhammad as a result of a treaty between the *Yang diPertuan Besar*, the four major chiefs (Undang) and the British, with a British Resident for the whole. The son and successor of the Yam Tuan Besar Muhammad, Yam Tuan Besar Abdul Rahman (q.v.), was appointed the first *Yang diPertuan Agung* (q.v.) of an independent Malaya.

NEW ECONOMIC POLICY (NEP) Soon after Parliament was suspended and a state of emergency declared in Malaysia in the wake of the May 13 Incident (q.v.), a National Operations Council (NOC) (q.v.) under Tun Abdul Razak (q.v.) was appointed to govern the country. The NOC set up a National Consultative Council (NCC) (q.v.). The NCC formulated new economic guidelines which were inaugurated in the New Economic Policy (NEP) (q.v.) in 1971 to be implemented over the period to 1990. The two principal objectives of the NEP were the reduction and eventual eradication of poverty irrespective of race and the reduction and elimination of the identification of race with economic function. The second objective primarily implied reducing the concentration of the Malays in subsistence agriculture and increasing their employment in the modern rural and urban sectors of the economy. It also included increasing the proportion of Malay ownership of industrial and commercial share capital. This restructuring was to be secured through the proceeds of sustained economic growth, and not through a redistribution of existing resources away from the non-Malay communities. In essence, the NEP was a programme of affirmative action in favor of the Malays. The NEP led to the creation of a number of public enterprises which provided assistance to Malay entrepreneurs, established business concerns which in time were transferred to private Malay interests, and purchased shares in established companies on behalf of the Malay community. The Malay language was introduced as the medium of instruction at all levels of education and there was a formalization of privileged access for Malays in areas such as the allocation of public sector housing, university entrance, civil service employment and in the allocation of commercial licences.

NEW VILLAGES As part of counter-insurgency measures adopted during the Emergency (q.v.), the colonial authorities relocated Chinese squatters in controlled settlements or hamlets, known as New Villages. These settlements subsequently became permanent townships and were important areas for political contestation among Chinese-based political parties. In 1985, the Federal government announced an overall development plan to improve living conditions in the New Villages. See also: EMERGENCY

NORTH KALIMANTAN COMMUNIST PARTY (NKCP) Like its Peninsular Malaysian counterpart, the NKCP is an illegal organization pledged to overthrow the government by violent means. The NKCP was formed in 1970, from remnants of Communist guerilla units in Sarawak. Following the surrender of a number of guerillas in Sarawak in 1974, under an official amnesty, NKCP is now believed to have relatively limited capabilities in achieving its goal.

O

ONN BIN JAAFAR, DATO SIR (1895–1962) was a leading Malay nationalist and the first President of UMNO (q.v.) who led Malay opposition to the Malayan Union (q.v.) in 1946. Onn was born in Johor, the son of the *Menteri Besar* (Chief Minister) (q.v.) of Johor. He had his initial education in Johor and in the United Kingdom and later returned to Malaya to resume his studies at the Malay College, Kuala Kangsar. He started his career as a clerk in the General Advisor's office in Johor and rose to become the *Menteri Besar* of the state. He was a soldier and a journalist and published a Malay newspaper in Singapore. He started the Peninsular Malay National Movement

(PMNM) (***Pergerakan Melayu Semananjung***) which had a membership of over 110,000 in Johor. When the British inaugurated the Malayan Union (q.v.) in 1946, Malay associations, including the PMNM agreed to form the ***Pertubuhan Kebangsaan Melayu Bersatu*** or United Malays National Organization (UMNO). UMNO was inaugurated in May 1946 in Johor and Onn was chosen as its first President. As President, Onn led the campaign against the Malayan Union and mobilized Malay support against the British. The British revoked the Malayan Union in 1948 and Onn negotiated with them in the talks that led to the Federation Agreement in 1948. Onn then proposed that UMNO be open to all the other races and urged the Malays to follow the path of non-communalism. His idea was rejected and he resigned from UMNO in 1951. He also resigned as *Menteri Besar* the same year. Subsequently, he was appointed chairperson of the Rural and Industrial Development Authority and when the Cabinet system was introduced, was given the portfolio of Member of Home Affairs. In 1951, he sponsored the move to form the Independence of Malaya Party (q.v.), a non-communal organization. The party did not attract a large Malay following and subsequently was replaced by the ***Parti Negara*** (PN) (q.v.) in 1954. The PN soon became a Malay communal party and sought to become the champion of Malay rights. The PN lost badly in the 1954 Johor state elections and the 1959 general elections when Onn was its only successful candidate. Onn died in 1962 and after his death the PN was disbanded in 1964.

OPERATION *LALLANG* In October 1987, open bickering between the UMNO (q.v.) and the MCA (q.v.) resulted in a racially charged atmosphere in Malaysia. The tension was only broken by the use of detention powers by the government. 119 people were detained without trial in October and November 1987 under the Internal Security Act (q.v.) in what the authorities termed "Operation *Lallang*". Those detained included prominent politicians, trade unionists, Chinese educationalists, environmentalists and members of social interest groups. They have since been released.

ORDINANCES Laws enacted by the Federal Legislative Council before Independence. They remain in force until repealed. See also: ACTS OF PARLIAMENT

P

PADI (RICE) Rice cultivation represents the oldest agricultural activity in the country. In the nineteenth century, the greater part of Malaysian rice production came from dry or hill padi, associated with low yields, shifting cultivation and soil exhaustion. Wet padi cultivation was also practised in states like Kedah, Kelantan and Negeri Sembilan. With the economic changes which took place in the nineteenth century and the influx of large numbers of immigrants, the country became largely dependent on foreign imports to meet its food requirements. By the end of the century, this dependence had become so marked that the colonial authorities had to embark on the first major rice cultivation scheme in the Peninsula, with the opening up of the Kerian (Krian) District of North Perak to padi cultivation. The impact of the First World War (1914–18) and the serious rice shortages which immediately followed, prompted further measures to reduce the country's dependence on rice imports, while the effects of the Great Depression led to the implementation of a serious rice development policy. A Drainage and Irrigation Department was established in 1932 primarily for that purpose and by 1941 two new development schemes (Sungei Manik in lower Perak and Tanjung Karang in Selangor) had been launched in addition to the one in Kerian. While padi cultivation comes second to rubber in terms of land area taken up and the number of people involved, it continued to be a depressed area of low incomes, and indebtedness. The industry is identified primarily with the *bumiputra* (q.v.) community. After the Second World War, great strides were taken in the direction of reducing Malaysia's dependence on rice imports and in raising the productivity (through better seed selection, irrigation and double-cropping) and living standards of padi planters. The

Green Revolution in the 1970s has allowed Malaysia to achieve near self-sufficiency in rice production.

PAHANG Pahang has been an area of human settlement since the earliest times. Important neolithic finds have been found on the banks of the Tembeling River, a tributary of the Pahang River. There are also many references to Pahang by Chinese writers, who state that in the thirteenth century the state was a vassal of Sri Vijaya. Pahang emerged as a distinct political entity in the fifteenth century during the period of the Melaka Sultanate, when a son of the Melaka ruler was made its Sultan. From the fifteenth to the nineteenth century Pahang remained a vassal state, first of Melaka, then Johor-Riau. By the beginning of the nineteenth century Pahang had become established as the fief of the *Bendaharas* of Johor-Riau. The dismemberment of that empire after the British occupation of Singapore and the Anglo-Dutch Treaty of 1824 enabled the *Bendahara* line to become virtually independent. After a prolonged civil war in the middle of the century *Bendahara* Wan Ahmad proclaimed himself Sultan and sovereign ruler in 1882. But Pahang's statehood was shortlived. British interest in Pahang's mineral resources and the general British forward movement in the Malay Peninsula resulted in Sultan Ahmad being forced to accept a British Resident at his court in 1888. A bitter revolt against British influence led by the Orang Kaya Semantan, Tok Bahaman, broke out in 1891 and took the British five years to quell. In 1896 Pahang became one of the four Federated Malay States (q.v.), and followed the rest of the country into the Malayan Union (q.v.) and the Federation of Malaya (q.v.) after the Second World War.

PAHANG REBELLION The extension of British control into Pahang (q.v.) was followed by a period of conflict known as the Pahang Rebellion. This Rebellion or War has come to symbolize the struggle to safeguard Malay tradition, Malay values, and the sense of Malay independence against outside intrusion. The Rebellion was spearheaded by the Orang Kaya (district chief) of the *ulu* district of Semantan, Abdul Rahman, commonly known as Dato Bahaman. Bahaman's income dropped substantially with the introduction of British rule and he mounted a campaign of civil disobedience in which the people of Pahang defied state regulations. The Rebellion lasted four years and for the most part involved guerilla warfare. One legendary fighter who emerged was Mat Kilau who fled the state and was given sanctuary by the people of Kelantan (q.v.) and Trengganu (q.v.). During the dying days of the campaign remnants of the rebels became associated with a holy man from Trengganu whose presence imbued their cause with the spirit of *jihad*, a holy war against infidels. The rebels were pursued to Trengganu and Kelantan by a British force in 1895 and subsequently most of the leaders were arrested in Kelantan by the Siamese authorities and taken to Bangkok. The Pahang Rebellion represented only a small setback to the British expansionist movement.

PALM OIL In the period when rubber dominated the agricultural export scene, a few estates with an eye to overseas markets began growing a new crop, oil palm (*Elaeis guineenis*). It had been introduced into the peninsula in the 1850s but was mainly cultivated as an ornamental plant. Only in 1917 was it cultivated on a commercial basis. However, no large-scale development occurred until 1924 when other companies began to plant oil palm. The industry was confined to large plantations usually located near some rubber estate in order to take advantage of the existing infrastructure. Most of the oil palm estates were consequently along Malaya's west coast. The number of hectares under oil palm increased and from a production of 3,350 tonnes in 1930 or 1 per cent of world output, it had risen in 1939 to 58,300 tonnes or 11 per cent of world output. By 1940, Malaya ranked fourth among world producers of palm oil (after Nigeria, the Belgian Congo and the Netherlands East Indies). Up until the outbreak of the Second World War, oil palm cultivation in the Peninsula was exclusively in European hands, largely because of the heavy capital outlay and sophisticated technical processes involved in the processing of the crop. After the Second World War, Malaya became the world's foremost producer of palm oil. This was a consequence of troubled political conditions in rival producing countries and the encouragement given to its development in Malaya. During the 1960s, Malaysia became established as the world's largest producer and exporter of palm oil, a position it has held ever since. Not only has much research and investment gone into the industry but the government has enabled smallholders to participate in oil palm cultivation, primarily through bodies like FELDA (q.v.).

PANGKOR TREATY/ENGAGEMENT Until the 1870s, the full impact of the British presence was confined to the Straits Settlements (q.v.) and despite the continual petitions from the Straits Settlement merchants, London did not want any further British involvement at official level. The increasing importance of tin and unsettled political conditions in the western Malay states resulting from rivalries among Malay chiefs over the possession of important tin fields, together with the related disputes between antagonistic Chinese secret societies and the growing significance of the Malay peninsula, led to British intervention in Perak in 1874. By the Pangkor Treaty/Engagement the British recognized Abdullah (one of the claimants to the Perak throne) as Sultan (q.v.) in return for his agreement to accept a British Resident whose advice "must be asked and acted upon on all questions other than those touching the Malay religion and custom". The British signed similar treaties with Selangor(q.v.), Negri Sembilan (q.v.) and Pahang (q.v.). The Pangkor Treaty therefore accelerated the process of British intervention in the affairs of the peninsular states and is commonly accepted as a convenient means of demarcating the beginning of Malaya's colonial period. Its significance lies in the fact that it represented a turning point in the formal relationship between Britain and the Malay States. Subsequently British authority was formalized in several separate administrative units which became known by the term 'British Malaya'.
See also: RESIDENT; RESIDENTIAL SYSTEM

PARAMOUNT RULER (YANG DIPERTUAN AGUNG) When the Malayan nation was formed in 1957, there were nine rulers whose sovereignty, except for a brief period during World War II and between April 1946– January 1948, when the Malayan Union (q.v.) was in force, had remained intact. Although by the Federation of Malaya agreement (q.v.) in

1948, a central administration had been established over the peninsula (excluding Singapore), the position of each ruler in his own state continued to be legally and socially very strong. The rulers are also the head of Islam in their respective states. With the birth of Malaya, it was decided that there should be a Paramount Ruler who was to be elected from among the nine monarchs. The Paramount Ruler would serve for a period of five years. He was to be elected by the Conference of Rulers. Those who are eligible to participate in the election are the rulers themselves. There are certain rules governing the election of the Paramount Ruler. Seniority is an important consideration and over the years, any state whose ruler has not served in the office, has priority over the others. A ruler who is nominated has the option of withdrawing. No ruler is automatically deemed to succeed another. Since 1957, nine rulers have served as the Paramount Ruler. The present Ruler is Sultan Azlan Shah (q.v.) who is from Perak. At this juncture, all the states have had a ruler who has served/is serving in that office.

See also: CONFERENCE OF RULERS; GOVERNOR AND APPENDIX 1

PARLIAMENT Parliament consists of the *Yang diPertuan Agung* (q.v.) 'in Parliament'—i.e. the *Yang diPertuan Agung* in the House of Representatives (q.v.) and the Senate (q.v.). The *Yang diPertuan Agung* does not however, preside; he addresses the two houses as and when necessary, but by convention this is only done at the beginning of each parliamentary session, which commences each year. The proceedings of parliament are 'privileged', viz, they cannot be questioned in any court; nor can a member be sued for anything he says or does in Parliament itself. Parliament consists of two houses, the House of Representatives (*Dewan Rakyat*) and the Senate (*Dewan Negara*). Parliament is the period from one general election to another covering a period of five years from the date of the first meeting of parliament held after a general election. The existing Parliament is the Seventh Parliament. The previous one was the Sixth Parliament from 1982–1986. The First Parliament was from 1959 to 1964. At the end of its term, the Parliament will be dissolved. Within sixty days (in the case of

Peninsular Malaysia, and ninety days in the case of Sabah and Sarawak) of the dissolution of Parliament, a general election must be held and within a hundred and twenty days of that date Parliament must be summoned to meet.
See also: DEWAN RAKYAT; DEWAN NEGARA

PARTI BANSA DAYAK SARAWAK (PBDS) The ***Parti Bansa Dayak Sarawak*** (Sarawak Dayak Party) or PBDS was formed in 1983 under the leadership of Datuk Leo Moggie (q.v.) after he, and a number of his supporters left the Sarawak National Party (q.v.) following an internal factional dispute. It is a communal party orientated towards the Dayak community. At the 1983 Sarawak state elections the new party won 6 of the 14 seats it contested and in 1984, it formally joined the ***Barisan Nasional*** (q.v.) coalition. In the 1987 Sarawak elections, the PBDS won 15 of the 48 state seats.
See also: PARTI PESAKA BUMIPUTERA BERSATU; SARAWAK NATIONAL PARTY

PARTI BERSATU RAKYAT BUMIPUTERA SABAH The United *Bumiputera* People's Party (commonly known as Bersepadu) was registered in 1984 by expelled Berjaya (q.v.) Vice-President Datuk Pangiran Othman Rauf. The party, supported mainly by Malays of Brunei origin, was committed to preserving *bumiputera* (q.v.) interests and had no Chinese members. It was also pledged to preventing Berjaya from retaining power. At the 1985 Sabah state elections, all 37 Bersepadu candidates lost their deposits. During the subsequent crisis over the legitimacy of the PBS government, Bersepadu publicly expressed support for the right of Datuk Pairin Kitingan's (q.v.) PBS (q.v.) to replace Berjaya as the ruling party.

PARTI BERSATU SABAH (PBS) The ***Parti Bersatu Sabah*** (Sabah United Party) or PBS was founded by Datuk Joseph Pairin Kitingan (q.v.), a Catholic Kadazan lawyer who had resigned from the then ruling party Berjaya (q.v.) after a disagreement with its leader Datuk Harris Salleh (q.v.). The new party was registered only 50 days before the state elections of April 1985. Pairin succeeded in mobilizing opposi-

tion to Berjaya, mainly among Chinese and Kadazans disgruntled about what they perceived as the pro-Muslim policies of the Harris Government. The PBS won a resounding victory in the 1985 State Elections and after an attempt by the leaders of Berjaya and USNO to foil it, formed the new state government on 22 April with Pairin as Chief Minister. After facing considerable harassment from its opponents, the party won a convincing two-thirds majority in fresh state elections in Sabah held in May 1986 and was admitted as a member of the ***Barisan Nasional*** (q.v.) coalition in June 1986. In a surprise move, the PBS withdrew from the BN coalition, after nomination day, in the 1990 General Elections and joined forces with Tengku Razaleigh Hamzah (q.v.). Kitingan and the PBS survived a smear and dirty tactics campaign launched by the BN and the PBS swept the board in the state elections.
See also: BERJAYA; UNITED SABAH NATIONAL ORGANIZATION

PARTI BERTINDAK RAKYAT SABAH (UNITED SABAH PEOPLE'S ACTION PARTY) BERSIH The United Sabah People's Action Party (commonly known by the acronym ***Bersih*** which means "clean" in Bahasa Malaysia) is a minor Sabah-based party formed in 1983 by former USNO leader Pandikar Amin Haji Mulia. At the 1985 Sabah state elections, all 16 ***Bersih*** candidates lost their deposits.

PARTI BURUH SARAWAK (SARAWAK UNITED LABOR PARTY) PLUS The Sarawak United Labor Party is a minor Sarawakian party, based in Sibu. It was founded in 1985. Its present President is Tang Lung Chiew.

PARTI CINA BERSATU SABAH/SABAH CHINESE CONSOLIDATED PARTY (PCBS) The Sabah Chinese Consolidated Party or ***Parti Cina Bersatu Sabah*** is a minor party which was formed in 1980. It claimed to represent the Chinese community in Sabah. At the 1981 state elections, it joined with USNO (q.v.) and ***Pasok*** (q.v.) in an electoral pact to oppose the ruling ***Berjaya*** (q.v.) and won one seat. However, following the resignation of the PCBS's sole assemblyman, this seat was subsequently recaptured by ***Berjaya***. The PCBS decided not to contest the 1985 state elections and instead supported Datuk Pairin Kitingan's (q.v.) PBS (q.v.) in this election.

PARTI CINA SABAH/SABAH CHINESE PARTY (PCS) The Sabah Chinese Party was formed in 1986, as a minor party claiming to represent the Chinese community of Sabah.

PARTI ISLAM SE MALAYSIA / ISLAMIC PARTY OF MALAYSIA (PAS) The Islamic Party of Malaysia (also known as ***Parti Islam*** or by its acronym PAS) originated as an Islamic-orientated affiliate of UMNO (q.v.). After breaking away from UMNO, the organization was eventually registered as a political party in 1955. Since then, with the exception of a brief period when the party was part of the ***Barisan Nasional*** (q.v.) coalition, PAS has been the principal source of Malay opposition to UMNO. PAS is committed to Islam as a complete system of faith and political ideology and rejects secularism. The party was therefore opposed to what it regarded as the essentially secular nature of the Malaysian constitution. The nature of the party's commitment to Islam as an ideology, although criticised for being vague, has allowed PAS considerable flexibility in its political activities. Since Islam is an integral part of the Malay identity and outlook, such an ideological approach has provided PAS with both a degree of symbolic legitimacy and a persuasive idiom for communicating its message. Three broad areas are identifiable in the political appeal of PAS. The first of these is a direct appeal to Islamic values and Malay sensibilities about the role and status of Islam in Malaysia. Secondly, PAS has also championed Malay communal interests. Finally, PAS has also sought to attract the support of the Malay peasantry and rural folk. While these areas of appeal have provided sources of strength for PAS, they have also served to limit the party's political impact at the national level. PAS has been strongest in the predominantly Malay and strongly Islamic states of Kelantan (q.v.), Trengganu (q.v.) and Kedah (q.v.). The electoral fortunes of PAS have fluctuated. The party controlled Trengganu from 1959 to 1961 and governed Kelantan from 1959 to 1977. From 1973 to 1977, PAS was a component of the ruling coalition. However, in 1977, after a dispute over the right of the party to nominate the *Menteri Besar* (q.v.) (Chief Minister) of Kelantan, PAS left the ***Barisan Nasional***. A state of emergency was imposed on Kelantan by the Federal Government and was subsequently lifted to allow state elections, at which PAS was defeated by an electoral pact between UMNO and Berjasa. In the 1980s, PAS increasingly sought to change its previously strident pro-Malay stance, arguing that a truly Islamic system would guarantee security and justice for all, regardless of ethnic origin. Following the ousting of Datuk Mohamad Asri Muda from the Party's leadership in 1982, and his replacement by Haji Yusof Rawa, PAS has accelerated its efforts to persuade Malaysia's non-Muslims that it does not pose a threat to their position. PAS has condemned UMNO's commitment to nationalism as being incompatible with the universalism of Islam. Under the new President, Fadzil Mohamed Noor (q.v.), and Deputy President, Abdul Hadi Awang, PAS has obtained a good command of the northern and east coast Malay states. PAS has also formed a pact of 'cooperation and understanding' with one-time foe, Tengku Razaleigh Hamzah (q.v.), who heads the ***Semangat*** '46 (q.v.). In so doing, they have forged an alliance between the center and right of Malay politics for the first time in 11 years. The joint movement born out of this pact is called the ***Angkatan Perpaduan Ummah*** (APU) (q.v.)—Movement for the Unity of Muslim People/Muslim Unity Movement. The APU Coalition which was joined by Berjasa (q.v.), Hamim (q.v.) and KIMMA, aimed to unseat the ***Barisan Nasional*** at the 1990 General Elections. PAS and ***Semangat*** '46 won all 39 state seats and all 13 parliamentary seats in Kelantan in the 1990 General Elections despite attempts by the BN to frighten or coerce voters in the state. The current chief minister of the state is from PAS. PAS has been unable to come to an understanding with the DAP and the internecine fight between them eroded confidence in the opposition during the elections. See also: SEMANGAT '46; ANGKATAN PERPADUAN UMMAH

PARTI NASIONALIS MALAYSIA (NAS MA) The ***Parti Nasionalis Malaysia*** (Nationalist Party of Malaysia) was formed in 1985 as a multi-ethnic party open to all Malaysian citizens. Among its founding members were a number of prominent politicians and trade union leaders including Hajjah Zainab Yang (President of the Lorry (truck) owners association), Raja Datuk Nasron Ishak, a veteran UMNO member and Ahmad Nor and Fadzil Abdullah (trade unionists) respectively. However, the party was crippled at the outset by disagreement between its leaders, many of whom have since resigned. The party's present Secretary-General is Khairuddin Sulaiman, a former President of the Johor Sessions Court.

PARTI NEGARA (NATIONAL PARTY) Following the demise of the Independence of Malaya Party (IMP) (q.v.), Onn Jaafar (q.v.) founded the Party Negara (PN) in 1954. The PN became a Malay communal party and sought to become the champion of Malay rights. The PN's support consisted almost entirely of old IMP members although it did not carry all of them. It lost badly in the 1954 Johor state elections and the 1959 General Elections when Dato Onn was its only successful candidate. Dato Onn died in 1962, and although the party contested the 1964 elections, all its candidates lost and the party faded away.
See also: INDEPENDENCE OF MALAYA PARTY

PARTI PERSAUDARAAN ISLAM (PAPERI)/Islamic Solidarity Party The Islamic Solidarity Party was a clandestine political organization used as a 'front' by the Communist Party of Malaya. It was established to generate support for the Communists through its involvement in Islamic issues.
See also: COMMUNIST PARTY OF MALAYA

PARTI PESAKA BUMIPUTERA BERSATU (PBB) The ***Parti Pesaka Bumiputera Bersatu*** (PBB) was formed in 1973 following the merger of the Iban-based ***Parti Pesaka*** and the Muslim-supported ***Parti Bumiputera***. The Party is dominated by its Muslim wing which has resulted in a significant loss of Iban support for the PBB. It is the dominant party in Sarawak and its leader, Datuk Patinggi Haji Abdul Taib Mahmud (q.v.), is the Chief Minister of the state. It is also a member of the ***Barisan Nasional*** (q.v.) coalition. In the 1983 state elections, the PBB won 19 of the 48 seats in the ***Council***

Negeri (State Assembly). It is the senior component in the state ruling coalition which also includes the Sarawak United People's Party (SUPP) (q.v.) and the Sarawak National Party (SNAP) (q.v.). The Parti Bansa Dayak Sarawak (PBDS) (q.v.) was also a member of the ruling coalition but was expelled from it in 1987. In the face of rising ethnic Iban political awareness, the federal government has asked that the state's ruling coalition include the PBDS as the fourth component of the coalition.

See also: PARTI BANSA DAYAK SARAWAK; SARAWAK NATIONAL PARTY; SARAWAK UNITED PEOPLE'S PARTY

PARTI PUNJABI MALAYSIA The Malaysian Punjabi Party (***Parti Punjabi Malaysia***) was registered in 1986, with the declared aim of working for the effective political representation of Malaysia's 60,000 Punjabis, regardless of their religious affiliations. The party is, in effect, an interest group, since its leaders have declared that they will not participate in electoral politics.

PARTI RAKYAT SABAH/SABAH PEOPLE'S PARTY (PRS) The ***Parti Rakyat Sabah***, formed in early 1989, is open to all Malaysian citizens and its founders intend to attract the Kadazans, the Malay-Muslims and Chinese residents of Sabah. It is multi-racial by constitution and the party organization provides for representative deputy leaders from all the communities. It is headed by Datuk Dr. James Ongkili, who was Deputy Chief Minister of Sabah when ***Berjaya*** (q.v.) was in power. When ***Berjaya*** lost the 1985 state elections, it became almost defunct. Most of the new party leaders were formerly ***Berjaya*** members or supporters. The party did not win a single seat in the 1990 elections.

PARTI SOSIALIS RAKYAT MALAYSIA (PSRM)/The Malaysian People's Socialist Party The Malaysian People's Socialist Party, commonly known as the PSRM, was originally founded as the ***Parti Rakyat*** (People's Party) (q.v.) under the leadership of the late Ahmad Boestamam (q.v.), a prominent former radical Malay nationalist. The party's proclaimed ideology was *Marhaenism*, an adaptation of President Sukarno's doctrine. In 1969, a group of younger members, led by Kassim Ahmad, displaced Boestamam, changed the party's name to ***Parti Sosialis Rakyat Malaya*** (PSRM) and proclaimed its ideology to be ***Sosialisme Saintifik*** (Scientific Socialism). The PSRM continued ***Parti Rakyat***'s policy of disapproval of the expanded Federation of Malaysia. Under its new leadership, the PSRM concentrated upon seeking the support of peasants and urban workers and committed itself to such policies as the redistribution of land to the landless, the eradication of middlemen in the rural economy and the provision of easy credit to farmers and fishermen. Since 1969, PSRM has failed to win a single seat at either the state or federal level. In addition, a number of its leaders were detained without trial under the Internal Security Act. In 1980, the National Congress rejected moves to adopt Islam as the official ideology of the party but amended its constitution to commit the PSRM to achieve justice and truth based on Islamic principles. The party also discarded ***Sosialisme Saintifik*** but re-affirmed its commitment to socialist principles. In addition, the party's name was changed to ***Parti Sosialis Rakyat Malaysia***, thereby signalling the party's acceptance of the legitimacy of the Malaysian state. Kassim Ahmed resigned from his post (and party) in 1984. Although the PSRM is professedly multi-ethnic and has some non-Malays in its ranks, the party's support comes mainly from Malays. Since the PSRM lacks representation in any legislature, its activities consist largely of issuing press statements on political issues, championing the cause of disadvantaged groups, and, when a permit is available, publishing and circulating its party newspaper, *Mimbar Sosialis*. In 1990, the party changed its name to ***Parti Rakyat Malaysia*** under the leadership of Dr. Syed Husin Ali, a social activist and former academic. The party joined the ***Gagasan Rakyat*** (q.v.) opposition coalition.

PASOK MOMOGUN (PARTI KADAZAN ASLI SABAH)
Pasok Momogun is a revival of the United National Pasok Momogun Party first formed in 1962 which merged with United National Kadazan Organization (UNKO) in 1964 to form United Pasok-Momogun Kadazan Organization (UPKO)

and dissolved with it in 1967. It is essentially a Kadazan party with strong Murut backing.

PATANI LIBERATION FRONT The Patani Liberation Front is an insurgent group of Thai Muslims predominantly seeking the independence of the largely Malay populated southern provinces of Thailand. The Patani Liberation Front has links with Malaysian Malays living along the Thai-Malaysian border, as well as with the Communist Party of Malaya. The group is not supported by the Malaysian government.

PEACE PACT The formation of Malaysia in 1963 led to hostility from Indonesia and the breaking of diplomatic relations with both the Philippines and Indonesia. On 1 June 1966, a peace pact designed to end Indonesia's three-year confrontation (q.v.) against Malaysia was agreed upon in Bangkok by Malaysia's Deputy Prime Minister, Tun Abdul Razak (q.v.) and Indonesia's Foreign Minister, Mr. Adam Malik. Following the peace agreement between Indonesia and Malaysia, the Philippines took concrete steps to recognize Malaysia and on 3 June, Malaysia and the Philippines resumed full diplomatic relations after a lapse of three years. On 11 August 1966, the Peace Agreement between Malaysia and Indonesia was signed in Jakarta between Tun Abdul Razak and Adam Malik, signalling the end of the three-year confrontation. By 31 August 1967, Malaysia and Indonesia resumed full diplomatic relations.

PEKEMAS ***Parti Keadilan Masyarakat Malaysia*** (the Social Justice Party of Malaysia) was founded in 1970 by Dr. Tan Chee Khoon (q.v.) following factional splits within the ***Gerakan Rakyat Malaysia*** (q.v.). Promoting itself as a moderately socialist, multi-ethnic party, ***Pekemas*** sought to attract the support of trade unionists. However, a number of its members defected to the DAP (q.v.). The party won only two seats in the 1974 General Election. The party's main strength and financial support came from Dr. Tan Chee Khoon. In 1976, Dr. Tan suffered a stroke, and Ahmad Boestamam, veteran Malay nationalist, became president. He also subsequently resigned due to ill health. Early in 1978, most of the leading members of ***Pekemas*** defected to the DAP and the party failed to win a single seat in the 1978 General Elections. *Pekemas* was dissolved in 1981.

PENANG Formerly part of Kedah (q.v.), Penang was acquired in 1786 on behalf of the English East India Company (q.v.) as a naval and trading base by a private trader named Francis Light (q.v.) from the Sultan of Kedah. The island was acquired on what turned out to be a false undertaking to protect the Sultan from his enemies, but once surrendered, Kedah was unable to regain control of Penang. In 1800, after all attempts to do so had failed, Kedah surrendered the land between the Kerian and Muda rivers on the mainland opposite to the British. The British named the island after the heir to the British throne, the Prince of Wales, as its acquisition fell on his birthday, and the island's new capital, Georgetown, after the reigning British monarch, George III. The territory on the mainland was named Province Wellesley after the Marquis of Wellesley, the British Governor-General of India at the time. Penang Island which had been barely inhabited in 1786, swiftly rose up to become an important entrepôt for the trade of the vicinity and acquired a polyglot population. Sugar became an important industry in Province Wellesley in the nineteenth century. Penang and Province Wellesley formed part of the Straits Settlements (q.v.) until the Japanese conquest in 1941. In 1946 Penang joined the Malayan Union (q.v.) and in 1948 became a member state of the new Federation (q.v.).

PEOPLE'S PROGRESSIVE PARTY (PPP) The PPP was founded in 1955 by two lawyers of Ceylon-Tamil origin, the late D.R. (q.v.) and Datuk S.P. Seenivasagam. The PPP is essentially a non-Malay, Perak-based opposition party. The PPP's appeal was based largely upon its championing of non-Malay grievances and the personal following of the Seenivasagam brothers. Its control of the Ipoh municipality gave it a local political base with limited opportunities for patronage. At the 1969 General Elections, the PPP won four parliamentary and 12 Perak assembly seats. In 1972, a state-level Alliance-PPP coalition was negotiated between Tun Abdul Razak (q.v.) and Datuk S.P. Seenivasagam and the PPP subsequently joined the *Barisan Nasional* (q.v.). The PPP lost very badly in the 1974 General Elections and Datuk S.P. Seenivasagam was appointed as a Senator after losing his parliamentary seat. Following his death in 1975, (his brother died in 1969) the party suffered a factional split and a rival party, the United People's Party was set up by R.C.M. Rayan. The PPP also lost control of Ipoh when the State Government appointed a MCA nominee as the new Municipal President. Today the PPP plays little more than a token role in the affairs of the ***Barisan Nasional***. The present leader is Senator Paramjit Singh. The PPP performed poorly in the 1982 General Elections when it won only the Chemor state seat in Perak.

PEPPER Pepper, one of the traditional exports of Southeast Asia, has been cultivated on a regular basis on the Malay Peninsula since 1790—first in Penang, and then in Singapore and Johor. However, in the nineteenth century, the focus of pepper cultivation shifted to Sarawak. Records indicate that it had been cultivated there prior to the 1870s. Charles Brooke's liberal land and labor policies provided the impetus for its revival in the 1880s and 1890s. At first centered on the Bau region, it soon spread to the Rejang Basin, Binatang and Sarikei. By the early twentieth century, pepper had become an important export crop in Sarawak. It was subjected to price fluctuations, particularly in the 1920s but recovered in the 1930s when Sarawak became the world's second largest producer. Today, Malaysia is the world's fourth largest pepper producer, after Indonesia, India and Brazil.

PERAK The Perak River Valley is one of the oldest homes of man, as attested by finds near Lenggong in Upper Perak. The present Sultanate traces its origins to Sultan Muzaffar, the eldest son of the last Sultan of Melaka, who established the dynasty in or around 1528. Because of its rich tin deposits Perak constantly faced outside threats to its sovereignty. The state was ravaged by the Acehnese in the sixteenth century. After 1641 the Dutch attempted to establish a monopoly over Perak's tin trade by building forts on Pangkor Island and at the mouth of the Perak River, but without great success. In the eighteenth century Perak was threatened by Bugis, Selangor in the south and by the

Thais in Kedah in the north. The state was only saved from Thai domination in the 1820s with British assistance. As the nineteenth century progressed, the growing importance of tin on the world market led to an influx of Chinese miners into the state. In the second half of the nineteenth century, political conditions became unsettled to the point of chaos as a result of rivalry among Malay chiefs over the possession of important tin fields. Related disputes between antagonistic Chinese secret societies, together with the growing importance of the western flank of Malaya, subsequent to the opening of the Suez Canal, led to British intervention in Perak. In order to protect their interests the British imposed the Pangkor Engagement (q.v.) on the Perak Chiefs. Opposition from the Perak Chiefs resulted in the assassination of the first British Resident (q.v.) and a brief war, after which the state became a model for the development of the British 'Residential System' (q.v.). In 1896 the state became one of the four Malay states forming the Federated Malay States (q.v.), and after the Japanese Occupation became part of the Malayan Union (q.v.) and then of the Federation of Malaya (q.v.). The Dindings which had been annexed by Britain and made part of the Straits Settlements (q.v.) after 1874 were returned to Perak in 1935.

PERLIS Perlis originally formed part of Kedah (q.v.). On restoring the Sultan of Kedah to his throne in 1842 after their conquest of the state in 1821, the Thais separated Perlis and established it as a vassal principality in its own right. Syed Hussain, the son and successor of Syed Harun who had been made territorial chief by a previous ruler of Kedah, was recognized by the Thais as the Raja of the new principality. Perlis was never rejoined to Kedah. In 1909 by the Treaty of Bangkok between Britain and Thailand, Perlis was transferred from Thai to British suzerainty and a British Adviser appointed to the State. A formal treaty between Britain and Perlis was not signed till 1930. During the Japanese Occupation Perlis was 'handed back' to Thailand. On the return of the British, Perlis became part of the Malayan Union (q.v.) and then of the Federation of Malaya (q.v.).

PERMODALAN NASIONAL BERHAD (PNB) *Permodalan Nasional Berhad* (PNB) was incorporated in 1978, as a wholly-owned subsidiary of the state-owned ***Yayasan Pelaburan Bumiputera*** (Bumiputera Investment Foundation) with the aim of encouraging *bumiputera* (q.v.) economic participation. PNB's role is to acquire a portfolio of shares in Malaysian companies with a sound growth potential. In 1981 PNB launched the ***Amanah Saham Nasional Berhad*** (National Unit Trust Scheme or ASN) which allowed *bumiputeras* to acquire shares in a portfolio of investments. By 1984, some 1.7 million *bumiputera* investors (35.6 per cent of eligible investors) had purchased shares in the trust, although many of them were relatively small shareholders. The ASN was the subject of political contention and the government accused PAS (q.v.) of trying to undermine the scheme, by the latter branding it as un-Islamic.

PERNAS PERNAS or ***Perbadangan Nasional Berhad*** was incorporated by government in 1969, with the aim of promoting *bumiputera* (q.v.) employment, *bumiputera* management experience and increasing *bumiputera* ownership in the commercial and industrial sectors. Through nine wholly-owned subsidiaries and over fifty other subsidiaries and associated companies, PERNAS is involved in a wide variety of economic activities. As a state trading corporation PERNAS is an affirmative action organization and in 1981, nine profitable PERNAS companies including Sime Darby and Goodyear Malaysia, were transferred to the ***Amanah Saham Nasional*** scheme under the direction of ***Permodalan Nasional Berhad***.

PERTUBUHAN KEBANGSAAN PASOK NUNUKRAGANG BERSATU (PASOK) The National United Pasok Nunukragang Party, or ***Pasok*** as it is usually known, was formed in 1978, and tried to establish a Kadazan identity in Sabah politics and the preservation of Kadazan culture. At the 1981 state elections, ***Pasok*** entered into an electoral pact with USNO (q.v.) and the Sabah Chinese Consolidated Party (q.v.), but lost in all 26 constituencies, which it contested. At the 1985 state elections ***Pasok*** managed to win one seat, but the party's assemblyman subsequently defected to the PBS.

PETROLEUM Petroleum and natural gas are now Malaysia's most valuable exports. The petroleum industry had its beginnings in

Sarawak where the first oil well was opened at Miri in 1910. Petroleum quickly rose to become the mainstay of Sarawak's economy for the next three decades prior to the Second World War, although it was clear by 1940 that Miri's resources were becoming depleted. After 1945 the Miri wells were rehabilitated and production resumed although it continued to decline steadily. In the early 1970s, there was an almost simultaneous discovery of oil fields off-shore from Sarawak, Sabah and Trengganu. By the end of the decade, Malaysia emerged as a net producer of petroleum. Associated with the discovery of these large off-shore oil fields were large areas of natural gas. Malaysia's crude oil is of high quality; light, and low in sulphur content. Malaysia's estimated remaining discovered reserves of crude oil were 3.0 billion barrels (GB) at 1 January 1986. The size of reserve places Malaysia in the twenty-second position in the world and at nineteenth on a reserve per capita basis. Where gas is concerned, Malaysia, with remaining discovered non-associated gas reserves of 43 trillion cubic feed (TCF) at 1 January 1986, ranks thirteenth in the world on a reserve basis and sixteenth on a reserve per capita basis.

THE PHILIPPINES' CLAIM TO SABAH In 1962, when plans for the formation of Malaysia were underway the Philippines government informed the British government that it wished to discuss its claim to the territory of Sabah, then a British Crown Colony. This claim was based upon a legal dispute concerning treaty arrangements made in the nineteenth century between the Sultan of Sulu and European merchants. These arrangements subsequently led to the formation of the British North Borneo Company (q.v.) which administered North Borneo until it was ceded to the British Crown in 1946. The Philippines government disputed the interpretation of the treaty and claimed that the Philippines had a legal claim to the possession of Sabah. This claim was rejected by the British who proceeded with the inclusion of Sabah in the expanded Federation of Malaysia. The Philippines refused to recognize the new Federation and severed diplomatic relations with Malaysia in 1963. In 1966, full diplomatic relations were restored, following mediation by the government of Thailand. In 1967, ASEAN was formed. Despite this regional grouping, the

Philippines government has never formally renounced its claim to Sabah.

PLURAL SOCIETY The notion of a 'plural society' was developed by J.S. Furnivall, who studied economic and social relationships in Indonesia during the colonial period and compared British and Dutch colonial policy. Furnivall defined the plural society as "comprising two or more elements or social orders which live side by side, yet without mingling in one political unit". In such a society, economic activities and settlement coincide with ethnic divisions. British colonial policy in Malaya resulted in the large-scale immigration of Chinese and Indians who came to work in the tin mines and the plantations. In order to control their activities, the British created separate systems of government to administer the ethnic groups. Consequently, the cultural and economic gap between the different communities was maintained and resulted in the development of a plural society. In Malaya, the plural society meant that there was ethnic differentiation in terms of settlement, occupation, education, culture and religion and this obstructed assimilation among the different ethnic groups. One of the principal aims of the New Economic Policy is to eliminate the identification of race with economic function.

PRIBUMI In Sabah, the term *pribumi* rather than *bumiputera* (q.v.) was used to refer to those communities regarded as indigenous and therefore eligible for special privileges. When ***Parti Bersatu Sabah*** (q.v.) came to power in Sabah in 1985 the classification *pribumi* was replaced by that of *bumiputera*.

R

RAFFLES, THOMAS STAMFORD, SIR (1781–1826) was a merchant adventurer in the English East India Company (EIC) (q.v.) who is regarded as the founder of Singapore. He was born at sea off the island of Jamaica, his father being a captain of a West Indian merchant ship. He started his career as a clerk in the London office of the EIC and in 1805 was appointed assistant secretary, with the rank of Junior Merchant in Penang. Two years later, he became Registrar of the Courts and rose to become Licenser or Censor of the Press. During this period he became proficient in the Malay language and translated Malay literature and histories into English. After the Napoleonic Wars, when Melaka was to be abandoned by the British, Raffles campaigned for it to remain a British possession. In 1810, Raffles was appointed Agent of the Governor General to the Malay States. He was a member of the British expeditionary force in 1811 to take Java during the Napoleonic Wars to prevent its falling to the French. After a successful mission, he was appointed Lieutenant-Governor of Java. During his period of administration, he established the well-known land-rent system in Java. In 1816, Java was returned to the Dutch and Raffles was appointed Governor of Bencoolen in Sumatra. He was convinced that Britain should control the maritime route between India and China and had strongly opposed the return of Dutch possessions after the Napoleonic Wars. Consequently he was convinced of the need to establish a British entrepôt somewhere in the region which could become another staging post along the maritime route to China. When he was instructed to set up a post in the southern approaches to the Melaka Straits, Raffles first considered Riau but found the Dutch already entrenched there. Subsequently, in January 1819, he signed a treaty with the *Temenggung* of Riau-Johor, the territorial chief of Singapore, which gave the British the right to establish a factory on the island. To impart legality to the rights he acquired on Singapore, Raffles recognized Husain, elder son of Sultan Mahmud, as the legitimate successor in Riau-Johor. The founding of Singapore ushered in a new period in Malayan history because it confirmed the dominance of British commercial interests in the region. Singapore's free trade policies drew commerce away from other areas and it became the greatest entrepôt in the region. As the nineteenth century progressed, the economies of the Malay states gradually became more linked with those of the British settlements. Raffles was appointed Governor of Fort Malborough, Singapore, a post he held until 1823. He established the Raffles Institution in 1823 for the education of sons of upper class natives. Unfortunately he was accused of corruption and as a result of tragedies and public censure, returned to England. Raffles was a vocal exponent for the furtherance of British political control in order to generate trade and his writings continued to inspire other Englishmen with a vision of empire.

RAFIDAH AZIZ, DATIN PADUKA (1943–), a leading woman politician and currently head of the Women's Wing of UMNO (q.v.), was born in Selama in Perak. She was educated in Kelantan, Johor and Kuala Lumpur and obtained a Bachelor of Arts degree in Economics (1966) and Masters in Economics (1970) from the University of Malaya. After a short stint as an academic, she entered politics in 1974. She served as Deputy Finance Minister in 1976 and was appointed Minister of Public Enterprises in 1980. She is the first woman to be appointed to an important government ministry and has worked for the advancement of women in Malaysia.

RAZALEIGH HAMZAH, TAN SRI TENGKU (1937–) is a prominent Malay politician and leader of the ***Semangat*** '46 Party (q.v.). He was born in Kelantan and educated in Kota Bharu and Ipoh. He graduated with an economics degree from Queen's University, Belfast, in 1959. He then started law studies which were interrupted when his father died. He returned to Malaya in 1961 to take over the family business concern. Soon after his return, he joined UMNO (q.v.) and by 1967 had become deputy leader of the Kelantan State UMNO Liaison Committee. In 1971, he was elected to the Supreme Council of UMNO and was appointed head of UMNO in Kelantan. He was also appointed Treasurer of the Party. He also held a number of important posts such as Chairman and Managing Director of Bank Bumiputera, Chairman of PERNAS (q.v.) and Chairman and Chief Executive of PETRONAS (q.v.) with the rank of Cabinet Minister. He gained election as Vice-President of UMNO in 1975 and in 1976 was appointed Minister of Finance. He held that post until 1984 when he was appointed Minister for Trade and Industry. He is generally acknowledged as the main architect of the ***Barisan Nasional***'s (q.v.) sweeping victory over PAS (q.v.) in the state and general elections in Kelantan in 1978. Within two years of becoming Finance Minister, he was elected Chairman of the International Monetary Fund's Annual Meeting, Chairman of the Asian Development Bank and the Islamic Bank. In 1981, he challenged Musa Hitam (q.v.) for the number two post in UMNO and lost. Subsequently in 1988, he challenged the Prime Minister for the top post in UMNO and lost by a very narrow margin. When UMNO was deregistered, he set up the ***Semangat*** '46 Party as a rival party. In the 1990 General Elections, he made attempts to overcome ethnic polarization within the opposition and his outstanding contribution was the forging of the APU (q.v.) coalition and ***Gagasan Rakyat*** (q.v.) coalition. Essentially, these two coalitions were held together by the sheer force of his personality. He is an immensely popular leader in Kelantan.

REID COMMISSION The Reid Commission was formed in 1955 to prepare a constitution for an independent Malaya. The members of the Commission included Lord Reid, a Lord of Appeal in Ordinary, Sir Ivor Jennings, Master of Trinity Hall, Cambridge University, an authority on constitutional law, Sir William McKell, a former Governor-General of Australia, B. Malik, a former Chief Justice of the Allahabad High Court, and Mr. Justice Abdul Hamid of the West Pakistan High Court. There was to have been a Canadian representative who backed out on medical grounds. Although no Malayans were represented, the Commission consulted the UMNO (q.v.), the MCA (q.v.) and MIC (q.v.). The Commission's document was accepted as the *Merdeka* ('Independence') Constitution on 15 August 1957, the Legislative Council ratified the Constitution and on 31 August, the independence of the Federation of Malaya was proclaimed.
See also: CONSTITUTION

RESIDENT In the last quarter of the nineteenth century, the British intervened in the affairs of the Western Malay states with the signing of the Pangkor Engagement (q.v.) with Perak (q.v.) in 1874. Under the terms of the Agreement, the Perak Ruler, elevated to the throne by the British, agreed to accept a British officer, styled Resident in his state, whose advice the

ruler would follow in all matters except those touching Malay customs and the Islamic religion. British Residents were subsequently appointed to Selangor, Sungei Ujung and Pahang. Under the Residential System, the British Residents became the *de facto* rulers in the Western Malay states. In 1896, the four states were merged to form the Federated Malay States (FMS) (q.v.) and the office of the Resident-General was created to head the Federation. In the remaining peninsular states, the British appointed Advisers rather than Residents. The Advisers had less executive powers compared to the Residents. During the period of the Japanese Occupation, these two systems of administration were discontinued. After the Second World War, the formation of the Malayan Union (q.v.) in 1946 and the Federation of Malaya (q.v.) in 1948, led to a natural death of the two systems.
See also: MALAYAN UNION; FEDERATION OF MALAYA; RESIDENTIAL SYSTEM

RESIDENTIAL SYSTEM By the Pangkor Engagement (q.v.) of 1874 between Britain and Perak, provision was made for the appointment of a Resident (q.v.) (and Assistant Resident) to Perak "whose advice must be asked and acted upon [on] all questions other than those touching Malay Religion and Custom". This system was known as the Residential System and was afterwards applied to the States of Selangor, Pahang and Negeri Sembilan. Technically, the Resident was an adviser rather than a ruler; in practice he was expected to be more than this. The Residential System was therefore a system of indirect rule.
See also: RESIDENT

RUBBER Malaysia's involvement with rubber began with seeds of the rubber-producing plant, *Hevea brasilinsis* which had been collected in Brazil, sent to germinate in Kew, and then sent to Ceylon and Singapore. The seedlings from Singapore were planted in Perak and by the mid 1890s, rubber was planted commercially in Malaya. Rubber was an ideal crop for the Malay Peninsula and fulfilled the government's aim of diversifying the economy and not being too reliant on tin. In 1897, special land regulations were introduced in the FMS (q.v.) to encourage rubber cultivation. The first rubber boom occurred in 1905–08 with the expansion of the motor-car industry and a second boom period was from 1909 to 1912. By 1910, there were already 200,000 hectares under the new crop and by 1914, the area had doubled again, the planted area being progressively extended over the next fifteen years at an average of 40,000 hectares a year. By 1930, rubber covered two-thirds of the cultivated area of the peninsula and had established itself as the most important export crop. In the 1930s, expansion was much slower, although the area under cultivation continued to increase. Most of the rubber estates were in the west coast states. The industry virtually collapsed during the period of the Japanese Occupation but made a swift recovery after the war to resume its former position as one of the twin pillars of the Malayan economy (by 1948, production was 708,000 tonnes, some 150,000 tonnes more than the previous record in 1940). In the 1950s Malaya lost its position as the world's largest producer of natural rubber to Indonesia and faced the ever-increasing competition from synthetic rubber. The Korean War bolstered rubber's recovery. Rubber was not spared the fate of fluctuating price levels and there was a depression in rubber in 1920–21 which led to the introduction of the Stevenson Restriction Scheme (1922–28). The scheme which was designed to protect European capital in the rubber companies of Malaya, Borneo and the Netherlands East Indies, instead resulted in the U.S. diversifying its sources of rubber and enabled Malaya's competitors (especially the Netherlands East Indies) to make up the leeway lost by Malaya's headstart. The problems experienced by the industry remained unrelieved during the period of the Great Depression. In 1934, an International Rubber Regulation Agreement was signed among the rubber producers of Southeast Asia limiting production with a fixed quota per country for an initial period of four years. Although the Agreement did help to restore rubber prices, it served to disadvantage Malayan producers because of the pecularities of the quota system and in particular it was disadvantageous to the smallholders in the industry. By 1930, smallholders (largely Malay farmers), cultivated about one third of the total area under rubber in the Peninsula and contributed some two-fifths of the Peninsula's total rubber production. However, as it always had been from the very beginning because of the initial capital costs involved, the rubber industry was dominated by the estates (large plantations), four-fifths of which, prior to the Second World War, were in European hands. Consequently, the interests of smallholders were neglected and it was only after independence that these interests were effectively taken into account. Furthermore, since independence, great emphasis has been laid on restructuring the rubber industry so as to give Malaysians a greater stake in estate ownership and production and to give better opportunities to smallholders. In the 1980s, rubber continues to be Malaya's predominant export crop, covering the largest cultivated area and holding fourth position in terms of export value.

RUKUNEGARA The *Rukunegara* (literally 'pillars of the nation') is Malaysia's 'national ideology' and was formulated during the period of emergency rule following the Thirteen May Incident of 1969 (q.v.). The *Rukunegara* is a set of general principles consisting of:

- Belief in God (*Kepercayaan kepada Tuhan*)
- Loyalty to King and Country (*Kesetiaan kepada Raja dan Negara*)
- The Supremacy of the Constitution (*Keluhuran Perlembagaan*)
- The Rule of Law (*Kedaulatan Undang-undang*)
- Mutual Respect and Good Social Behaviour (*Kesopanan dan Kesusilaan*)

The *Rukunegara* represented an attempt to generate public consensus on the fundamentals of Malaysian statehood. For many years this national ideology was vigorously promoted but has gradually become less prominent in official pronouncements.

S

SABAH Sabah owes its existence as a separate state to the activities of Western adventurers in the region in the last quarter of the nineteenth century. Prior to that the territory had consisted of

scattered chieftaincies and autonomous communities owing a general allegiance to the Sultans of Brunei. But in 1704 the land east of Marudu Bay was ceded to the Sultan of Sulu in return for Sulu help in a succession dispute, a cession which 250 years later was to provide the basis for the Philippines' claim to the state. By the last quarter of the nineteenth century Brunei's control over Sabah was extremely tenuous, and with little difficulty an American trader obtained a lease over the greater part of the country from the Sultan. This lease passed into the hands of an Austrian baron and finally into those of an English businessman called Alfred Dent. Dent signed treaties with both Brunei and Sulu converting the lease into a cession, and in 1881 succeeded in establishing the Chartered Company of British North Borneo (q.v.) to manage the acquisition. From that date until the Japanese conquest of 1941 Sabah was ruled by the Company and was known as British North Borneo. It was placed under British protection in 1888. Odd pieces of territory not acquired by the original cession were gradually obtained and the Company's administration managed to survive a serious rebellion against its rule led by a Sulu prince, Mat Salleh, at the end of the century. After the Japanese Occupation the Chartered Company surrendered its rights to the British Government and Sabah became a British Crown Colony. Sabah was able to achieve its independence from Britain by agreeing to Tunku Abdul Rahman's (q.v.) Malaysian proposal and becoming part of Malaysia in 1963. This development was challenged by both Indonesia and the Philippines, but Indonesian opposition came to an end in 1966 and in the same year the Philippines gave its recognition to Malaysia.
See also: MAT SALLEH REBELLION

SAMBANTHAN, VEERASAMY THIRUGNAN, TUN (1919–1979) was a leading member of the Indian community in Malaysia. He was educated in Perak and south India. After graduation, he became a rubber planter in Perak. He worked among Indian workers, promoting the Tamil language and culture. Later he became active in Malayan politics. He served as President of the Malayan (later Malaysian) Indian Congress (MIC) (q.v.) from 1955–1971 and was largely responsible for the transformation of the Party from an active, political organisation to a conservative, traditional one, emphasising Indian culture, religion and language. As President of the MIC, a component of the ruling Alliance Party (q.v.), he was appointed Minister of Labor (1955–57), Minister of Health (1957–59), Minister of Works, Posts and Telecommunications (1959–71), Minister of National Unity (1972–74) and Chairperson, National Unity Board (1974–78). He also promoted education and thrift among Indian workers and established the National Land Finance Co-operative Society in 1960 to provide an opportunity for land ownership among Indian workers during the period of the fragmentation of rubber estates.

S. SAMY VELLU, DATO' SERI (1936–), politician and currently President of the MIC (q.v.) was born in Kluang, Johor. He was educated in Selangor and qualified as an architect. He joined the MIC in 1959 and was elected member of parliament for Sungei Siput, Perak in 1974. He was re-elected to this seat in 1978, 1982 and 1986. In 1978, he became Deputy President of the MIC and in 1980 assumed the presidency of the party. He held a government position as Deputy Minister in Housing and Local Government before being appointed Minister for Works and Utilities in 1979. He is presently Minister for Telecommunications and Posts.

SARAWAK The nucleus of modern Sarawak is the area around the Sarawak river which formed a province of the Brunei Sultanate. Sarawak's emergence as a separate political entity began when an English adventurer, James Brooke (q.v.), was granted territory between Tanjung Datu and the Samarahan river in 1841 in return for his services in helping Raja Muda Hassim of Brunei quell a rebellion in the province. In the years which followed, James Brooke, who assumed the title of 'Rajah', consolidated his position by establishing firm government and by destroying Malay-Iban seapower. He also added to his domains by further acquisitions of territory at the expense of Brunei. By 1868 when he died his territory of Sarawak stretched up to Tanjung Kidurong. His nephew and successor, Rajah Charles Brooke, built on these foundations and Sarawak continued to expand at the expense of Brunei until with the acquisition of Lawas in 1905 the state had acquired the

boundaries it holds today. The third Brooke ruler, Rajah Vyner, succeeded his father in 1917 and ruled Sarawak until 1941. Brooke rule is to be remembered more for what was left undone than for what was transformed. After the brief Japanese interregnum, Vyner ceded Sarawak to Britain and it became a Crown Colony in 1946. This provoked considerable opposition amongst the Malay community in the state and gave rise to a strong anti-cession movement which culminated in the assassination of the second British colonial governor in 1949. This led to the collapse of the movement but left a schism in Malay politics which has made itself felt for a long time. The colonial status of Sarawak came to an end through the medium of the Malaysia proposal put forward by Tunku Abdul Rahman (q.v.) in 1961. Sarawak joined the new federation in 1963, public opinion having clearly indicated its preference for Malaysia and despite the armed opposition of Indonesia.
See also: BROOKE, JAMES

SARAWAK NATIONAL PARTY (SNAP) The Sarawak National Party (SNAP) was formed in 1961 as a party open to membership from all ethnic groups, although its supporters have been largely Ibans with some Chinese participation. In its early years, SNAP sought to win electoral support as the protector of state rights against encroachments by the Federal Government. The Party provided the chief minister and deputy chief minister for the 1963–66 period. After its leader, Datuk Stephen Ningkan was toppled as Chief Minister in 1966, through the use of federal emergency powers, SNAP became an active opposition party at both the state and federal levels. At the 1974 General Elections, SNAP won 18 of the 48 State Assembly seats and 8 Federal seats, thereby demonstrating its significant electoral following. It joined the ***Barisan Nasional*** (q.v.) in 1976. In 1983, internal bickering and factionalism within SNAP resulted in the establishment of a new party, the ***Parti Bansa Dayak Sarawak*** led by Datuk Leo Moggie (q.v.), which won 6 seats from SNAP at the subsequent state elections. SNAP is a component of the Sarawak state ruling coalition together with ***Parti Pesaka Bumiputera Bersatu*** (q.v.) and ***Sarawak United Berjasa Party*** (q.v.).
See also: PARTI BANSA DAYAK SARAWAK

SARAWAK UNITED PEOPLE'S PARTY (SUPP) The Sarawak United People's Party was formed in 1959 on a non-communal, 'socialist' platform. It is a multi-racial party whose membership is largely Chinese-based. SUPP was one of the first opposition parties in Malaysia to negotiate an accommodation with the Alliance (q.v.) government in the period after the 1969 General Elections. Following a state-level coalition with the Sarawak Alliance in 1971, SUPP pledged the support of its MPs for the Federal Government. In return, its President, Ong Kee Hui, became the first non-Alliance member of the Federal Cabinet. When the ***Barisan Nasional*** (q.v.) was created, SUPP became a founder-member. It is currently a component party of the ruling coalition at both state and federal levels. At the 1982 Federal General Elections, SUPP won 5 seats. At the Sarawak State elections in the following year, SUPP won 11 of the 48 seats in the *Council Negeri* (State Assembly). Its present leader is Datuk Amar Stephen Yong Kuat Tze.
See also: PARTI PESAKA BUMIPUTERA BERSATU; SARAWAK NATIONAL PARTY; PARTI BANSA DAYAK SARAWAK

SEENIVASAGAM, DHARMA RAJA (1921–1969), a leading politician, was born in Ipoh. He was educated in Perak and the United Kingdom where he trained as an advocate and solicitor. On his return, he set up a family legal firm with his brother S.P. Seenivasagam. The Seenivasagam brothers were founder members of the Perak Progressive Party which later became the Peoples Progressive Party (PPP) (q.v.) in 1955. D.R. Seenivasagam served as Acting Vice-President (1953–54) and General Secretary of the PPP in 1955. The PPP's appeal was based largely upon its championing of non-Malay grievances and the personal following of the Seenivasagam brothers. D.R. Seenivasagam was a member of the Ipoh and Menglembu Municipal Councils between 1954 and 1957 and was elected to the Federal Legislative Council in 1956. He became a member of Parliament in 1959.

SEJARAH MELAYU The *Sejarah Melayu*, the so-called 'Malay Annals' has been handed down in a number of different versions, the earliest of which is now dated from the early seventeenth century. Many of the stories it contains had been a part of Malay culture for generations. The work is generally regarded as the foremost example of classical Malay prose style, a literacy masterpiece as well as a Malay perception of the past. The aim of the *Sejarah Melayu* was "to set forth the genealogy of the Malay rajas and the ceremonial of their courts for the information of [the King's] descendants . . . that they may be conversant with the history and derive profit therefrom . . . ". It contains information concerning the founding of Melaka. But the *Sejarah Melayu* does not purport to adhere to a strict chronology or provide a precise rendering of events in the past. It was not written according to the Western conception of a historical document. It should be regarded as a particular genre of Malay literature whose primary concern was the edification of future generations.

SELANGOR The heartland of Selangor has been the Klang River Valley rather than the Selangor River to the north, from which the state takes its name. In the Klang River Valley important neolithic remains have been found. In the days of the Melaka Sultanate, Klang was the appanage of Tun Perak, the *bendahara* of the Sultanate. The state's rich tin deposits ensured that it became a much contested ground after the fall of Melaka to the Portuguese. The original population of Minangkabau settlers had to make way for Bugis intruders, while the Dutch made largely ineffectual attempts to control the tin trade by building forts at Kuala Linggi and Kuala Selangor. By the middle of the eighteenth century the Bugis had succeeded in establishing the present Sultanate, its original base being at Kuala Selangor, and they were fairly successful in resisting Dutch attempts to control them. The increased demand for tin in the nineteenth century gave rise to an influx of Chinese tin miners and promoted the rise of powerful tin chiefs such as Raja Jumaat of Lukut (now in Negeri Sembilan) which upset the traditional balance of power within the state. As a result a prolonged civil war broke out in the 1860s involving Bugis and Malay noblemen and Chinese tin miners, and this in turn provided the British with a pretext for intervention in 1874 when the Sultan agreed to accept a British Resident (q.v.). The state prospered under the Residential System, and in 1896 formed one of the four Federated Malay States (q.v.) established that year. After the Japanese Occupation the state became part of the Federation of Malaya (q.v.). In 1974 the Sultan of Selangor ceded the territory of Kuala Lumpur so as to enable the nation's capital to be on federal land.

SEMANGAT '46 / SPIRIT OF 1946 The *Semangat* '46 was formed by dissident members of the UMNO after the deregistration of UMNO (q.v.) by court order in 1988. Originally, this splinter group tried to register the party under the name UMNO '46. However, the application was rejected because the mainstream UMNO had registered itself under the name UMNO ***Baru*** (new UMNO). The party subsequently changed its name to ***Semangat*** '46 (Spirit of 1946—after the year the original UMNO was formed) and was registered in May 1989. The party's constitution is the same as that of the old UMNO. The aim of the party is also the same as that of the old UMNO—namely to safeguard the legitimate communal interests of the Malays, as the indigenous population, against the challenges posed by immigrant communities of different ethnic origins. ***Semangat*** '46 is headed by Tengku Razaleigh Hamzah (q.v.), once one of the top five leaders of the original UMNO and now an implacable rival of Prime Minister Dato' Seri Mahathir Mohamad. ***Semangat*** '46 formed a pact of 'cooperation and understanding' with PAS (q.v.). The joint movement born out of the pact is called the ***Angkatan Perpaduan Ummah*** (q.v.) (Movement for the Unity of the Muslim people)—an appeal that glosses over the Islamic-Malay nationalist differences between the two, concentrating only on the common goal of unity of Malays and Muslims. Two other Malay parties (formerly component parties of the ***Barisan Nasional*** (q.v.)), ***Berjasa*** (q.v.) and ***Hamim*** (q.v.) also joined the coalition followed by KIMMA (q.v.) in 1990. Tengku Razaleigh also heads the ***Gagasan Rakyat*** (q.v.) coalition and forged an alliance between the two opposition coalitions in the 1990 General Elections. ***Semangat*** '46 therefore attempted to overcome ethnic polarization in order to unseat the BN. In the state of Kelantan, PAS and ***Semangat*** '46 won all of the 13 Parliamentary seats and all of the 39 State seats to defeat the BN.
See also: UMNO

SENSITIVE ISSUES By the Constitution (Amendment) Act of 1971, passed by Parliament in its first session after the 13 May Incident any matter, right, status, position, privilege, sovereignty or prerogative established or protected by the constitutional provisions relating to citizenship; the national language and the right of any person to use (except for official purposes), teach or learn any language; the special position of Malays and natives of Borneo and the protection of the legitimate interests of other communities; and the sovereignty and prerogatives of the Rulers—issues about which the different communities in the country are sensitive—are removed from the arena of public discussion, including the legislature. Under the same Act, an emergency amendment made to the Sedition Act by the Emergency (Essential Powers) Ordinance no. 45, 1970, was made virtually permanent. The amendment renders it seditious to question any of the issues listed above. See also: MAY 13 INCIDENT

SOCIALIST DEMOCRATIC PARTY (SDP) The Socialist Democratic Party (SDP) was formed in Penang in 1978 by dissident members of the DAP (q.v.), including Ismail Hashim (former DAP Vice-President), and Yeap Ghim Guan (former DAP Penang State Chairman). The SDP's differences with the DAP were largely due to personality clashes. Its constitution and policies were similiar to those of the DAP. After 1978, several former DAP activists, including Fan Yew Teng, joined the SDP and Fan Yew Teng later became Secretary-General. In 1986, Ahmad Nor, former President of CUEPACS and Yeoh Poh San, former MCA Secretary-General joined the party. The SDP's electoral participation was on a minor scale and it never won a single seat in a State Assembly or Parliament. The Party is now defunct.

SPECIAL BRANCH The Special Branch (SB) is an integral part of the Royal Malaysian Police responsible for the acquisition, collation and dissemination of security intelligence. The SB monitors the activities of political parties, organizations and individuals and reports alleged threats of national security to the Minister of Home Affairs, who is empowered to initiate

prosecutions or order the detention of suspects under the Internal Security Act.
See also: INTERNAL SECURITY ACT

STATE ECONOMIC DEVELOPMENT CORPORATIONS (SEDCs) SEDCs were established in each state between 1965 and 1973 as part of official policies to foster *bumiputera* (q.v.) economic participation and capital accumulation. They have been involved in establishing companies, joint ventures and investments in local companies. The National Unit Trust Scheme (***Permodalan Nasional Berhad***) is the controlling body of all the subsidiary companies of the respective SEDCs and plays a major role in directing the affairs of the SEDCs.
See also: PERMODALAN NASIONAL BERHAD; NEW ECONOMIC POLICY

STEPHENS, TUN FUAD/DONALD (1920–1976), a popular Sabahan politician and Kadazan leader, was born in Kudat, Sabah. He was educated in Sabah and became a teacher. When the Second World War broke out, Stephens left for Singapore. He returned in 1945 and became a contractor to the Public Works Department. In 1949, he joined the *North Borneo News* as the newspaper's west coast correspondent. In 1953, he started his own paper, *The Sabah Times*. Subsequently, he bought over *The North Borneo News* and merged it with his own paper. He was a member of the Legislative Council and the Executive Council and served on various committees. As Chairman of the Kadazan Society, he founded the United National Kadazan Organization (q.v.) in 1961 and was its first president. In 1962, in anticipation of the formation of Malaysia, he helped establish the Sabah Alliance Party and served as chairman of the executive committee. He also served as chairman on the Malaysian Solidarity Committee and was a joint leader of the North Borneo Team in the Intergovernmental Committee of Malaysia. He was a signatory to the Malaysia agreement in London. When Malaysia was formed in 1963, Stephens became the Chief Minister of the State of Sabah. Because of his independent stance, he was relegated to the Ministry of Sabah Affairs and Civil Defence. In 1965, he resigned from the Ministry and was appointed Malaysia's ambassador to Australia. After his return he entered Sabah politics and joined USNO (q.v.). In 1975, he and other veteran Sabah politicians formed ***Berjaya*** (q.v.) to oust control from Tun Mustapha (q.v.) and USNO. USNO was defeated in the 1976 state elections and Stephens became Chief Minister. His untimely death in a plane crash shortly afterwards dealt a blow to Sabah society and politics.

STRAITS SETTLEMENTS Early European interest in the Malay Archipelago lay in the spice trade. In the seventeenth century, the Dutch ousted the Portuguese and the British and controlled this trade. By the late eighteenth century, British interest was renewed in the Malay Archipelago because of the expansion of the China trade which had to pass through the Malay Archipelago. The British were looking for settlements to further their trade with China and bases from which to prevent French domination of the Indian Ocean. In 1786, Captain Francis Light (q.v.), acting for the English East India Company (q.v.), leased the island of Penang from the Sultan of Kedah who was anxious for assistance against the Siamese (Thais). The Company agreed to pay an annual sum for Penang and for the adjacent area of Province Wellesley which was leased in 1800. Melaka was added to the Company's possessions when the British took it over in 1795 as a result of the Dutch War against the French, who had occupied Holland the year before. It was later returned to the Dutch, but by the Anglo-Dutch Treaty of 1824 (q.v.) was exchanged for Bencoolen and the East India Company's possessions in Sumatra. In 1819, Sir Stamford Raffles (q.v.), an official of the East India Company, acquired the island of Singapore from the *Temenggung* of Riau-Johor, the territorial chief of Singapore. In 1826 these three settlements were formed into a single administrative unit called the Straits Settlements and were governed from India. Straits Settlements officials and merchants were unhappy with this arrangement and successfully petitioned for the transfer of the Straits Settlements to the colonial office which was accomplished in 1867. The merchants viewed the Malay states as potential fields of investment and the Straits Settlements became the springboard for British expansion into the Malay Peninsula.

SULTANS/RULERS The Ruler of each of the nine Malay States of the Peninsula is the Sultan. The Ruler of Perlis is known as the Raja of Perlis and the Ruler of Negeri Sembilan is styled *Yang diPertuan Besar* (Yam Tuan Besar) of Negeri Sembilan, who is the sovereign monarch despite the selection of one of them as Paramount Ruler. Each is, within his state, the fountain of honor, justice and mercy and every act of government is made on his behalf and or under his name or authority. The Rulers meet together at the Conference of Rulers at which the *Yang diPertuan Agung* presides. In exercising their sovereign functions, the Rulers have severally bound themselves under the State Constitutions to act on the advice of their Executive Councils but the prerogative of mercy is exercised on the advice of the State Pardons Board.
See also: CONFERENCE OF RULERS; GOVERNORS

SUMA ORIENTAL (Complete Treatise of the Orient) The *Suma Oriental* was written by Tome' Pires, a Portuguese apothecary, who was sent to Melaka in 1512 after its conquest by Portugal. The sixth book, based on Pires' own observations and 'what the majority affirm' deals with Melaka, its origins, administration and trade. Pires intended the *Suma Oriental* to be an authentic account of Melaka's history that could be used as a reference book by the Portuguese administration.

SWETTENHAM, FRANK ATHELSTANE, SIR (1850–1946), a British administrator, and widely acknowledged as 'the father and founder of modern Malaya', was born in Derbyshire in the United Kingdom. At the age of twenty, he joined the Straits Settlements Civil Service where he soon mastered the Malay language. His fluency in Malay and skill as a diplomatist led Governors Clarke (q.v.) and Jervois to employ him as an interpreter and special commissioner and he participated in the preparations for the Treaty of Pangkor (q.v.) for Perak (q.v.). In 1874, he was appointed as Assistant Resident to Selangor (q.v.). Thereafter, his career centred on the Peninsula. He was appointed Assistant Colonial Secretary for Native Affairs (1876–82) and then successively as Resident to Selangor (1882–89) and to Perak (1889–95). He earned considerable credit for the creation of the Federation (q.v.) and was its first Resident-General from 1896 to 1901. He is also credited for the extension of British control over the Northern Malay States. In 1901, he became Governor of the Straits Settlements and High Commissioner to the Malay States. He retired in 1904.

T

TAN CHEE KHOON, TAN SRI, DR. (1919–), a popular politician who became known as 'Mr. Opposition', was born in Kuala Lumpur. He trained as a doctor in Singapore, and opened a practice in Kuala Lumpur where he joined the Labor Party (q.v.), the main ideologically-oriented non-communal political party in Malaya. He was instrumental in forging a coalition of the opposition parties, known as the Socialist Front (q.v.), in 1957. In 1964, Tan was elected Labor Member of Parliament. When the Socialist Front broke up in 1966, and the Labor Party opted out of constitutional politics, Tan and a few others founded the ***Gerakan Rakyat Malaysia*** (q.v.) in 1968. The ***Gerakan*** was split by factionalism and Tan left to found the ***Pekemas*** (q.v.) or the Social Justice Party in 1970. He resigned as President in 1976 due to ill health. In addition to his political career he served on the National Unity Board, the Malaysian Medical Association, the Malaysian Medical Council, and is active in the Human Rights Movement in Malaysia.

TAN CHENG LOCK, DATO, SIR (1883–1960) was a prominent Chinese community leader and statesman. He was born in Melaka to a prominent *baba* (q.v.) family, who had interests in the planting industry and in shipping. He was educated in Melaka and Singapore and started out as a schoolmaster in Singapore. As an educationalist, he was a member of the committee to set up the Raffles College in Singapore. In 1908, he became the assistant manager of a rubber estate in Melaka and opened up other rubber estates in the state. He was active in public service having served as a Municipal Commissioner in Melaka, as President of the Chinese Chamber of Commerce and on several other government committees. As an unofficial member of the Straits Settlements (q.v.) Legislative Council, he was instrumental in pressing for legislation which allowed for monogamous civil marriage and remarriage among the Chinese and other non-Christians who wanted to contract such a marriage. He also fought for the admission of non-European British subjects into the Malayan Civil Service and his goal was achieved with the formation of the Straits Settlements Civil Service in the 1930s. After the Second World War, he and other Chinese community leaders established the Malaysian Chinese Association (MCA) (q.v.) and he served as the first President of the MCA. He was also the joint-Chairman of the UMNO-MCA-MIC National Council in the negotiations for independence for Malaya. He helped found the Independence of Malaya Party (q.v.) with Onn Jaafar (q.v.) because he believed that equality, cooperation and non-communalism among the various races was the only hope to a viable independent Malaya. However, when the Party foundered, he directed his energies to the MCA. In 1958, following a crisis in the MCA, he was defeated by Lim Chong Eu (q.v.) as President of the MCA. Subsequently, he played only a minor role in the MCA and devoted himself to his business and planting interests. He is well known for his use of hartal (boycott) in Malaya to achieve political ends.

TEMPLER, GERALD WALTER ROBERT (FIELD MARSHAL), SIR (1898–1979), High Commissioner of Malaya from 1952–54, is popularly known as the man who defeated the communist terrorists during the Emergency (q.v.). Templer was born in England and educated in Wellington College and Sandhurst. He had a remarkable military career which began after Dunkirk. He served in North-West Persia (now Iran) and Mesopotamia and in the European War from 1939–45. He was appointed General Officer Commander-in-Chief of the Eastern Command from 1950–52. At that time, Malaya was experiencing insurgency problems and the then High Commissioner to Malaya, Sir Henry Gurney, was killed in an ambush. Templer (then a Lieutenant-General) was appointed to replace him and to end the insurgency. When he arrived in early February 1952, he declared that his immediate objective was the formation of a united Malayan nation. Towards this goal and that of undermining and eventually destroying the CPM (q.v.), Templer introduced local elections, formed village councils and gave citizenship to over half the Chinese population, merged the War council with the Executive Council and enabled the Chinese for the first time to enter the Malayan Civil Service. In April 1954, Templer announced that an early election for the Federal Council (q.v.) would be held in 1955, thereby indicating that Malaya was drawing closer to independence. By his strategies and by involving the leaders of the main communities, Templer effectively broke the back of the communist insurrection. Three years after he left Malaya, in July 1954, he was appointed Field Marshal in 1957.

THIRTEENTH MAY INCIDENT See May 13 Incident

THIVY, JOHN ALOYSIUS (1904–) was an Indian diplomat and a leader of the Indian community in Malaya. He was born in India and educated in Madras and in the United Kingdom. During the Second World War, Thivy served as Vice-President of the Indian Independence League, Southeast Asia and was Minister in the Provisional Government of Free India. After the War, Thivy inaugurated the Malayan (later Malaysian) Indian Congress (MIC) (q.v.) in 1946 and served as its first President. The MIC was then an active political organization formed to safeguard the rights of the Indians in Malaya. Thivy was also associated with the framing of the People's Constitutional Proposals for Malaya in 1947 and elected to the Asian Relations Council. Subsequently, Thivy resigned from the MIC and in July 1947 was appointed as Indian Agent or Representative of the Government of India in Malaya, a post he held until 1950. As the Indian Agent, Thivy worked hard to improve the working conditions of the Indian workers in Malaya, and came into conflict with the local authorities and large plantation owners. In 1950 he left Malaya for India where he joined the Indian foreign service and served as an ambassador to various countries.

THURAISINGHAM, CLOUGH DATO, SIR (1898–1979), a parliamentarian and educationalist, was born in Taiping, Perak (q.v.). He was educated in Colombo and the United Kingdom where he qualified as an advocate and solicitor. He practised in Singapore and then took over the family rubber plantation in Malaya. As a planter, he was a member of the Rubber Producer's Council and served as a delegate to the Rubber Study Group in Brussels (1950) and Ottawa (1952). He also served as a member of the Malayan Advisory Council, the Selangor State Council, the Selangor Executive Council, the Federal Legislative Council and the Communities Liaison Committee to promote unity among the different communities in Malaya. He was also a member of ***Parti Negara*** (q.v.). In 1951, he was appointed First Member of Education and presided over the greatest expansion of education in Malaya with the establishment of national schools. He was also instrumental in the establishment of Malayan Teacher Training Colleges in Malaya and the United Kingdom to train teachers. Apart from his political career, he was a Ceylonese (now Sri Lankan) community leader who helped found the Ceylon Federation of Malaya and who fought for Ceylonese representation in the Federal Legislative Council.

TIMBER Timber has played a very important role in Sabah's economy ever since an experimental cargo of logs went to Australia in 1885. The timber industry grew substantially in the last decade of the nineteenth century, spurred on by the demands for rail sleepers (ties) for the railway expansion underway in China. Australia quickly rose as a major importer of Sabah timber but Hong Kong soon became the leading importer. The British Borneo Trading and Planting Company was the largest of four concerns involved in the industry. Then in 1920, a new company, formed under the aegis of the agency house of Harrisons and Crosfield was set up as the British Borneo Timber Company. It obtained monopoly rights for twenty-five years to carry out logging on state land and provided the capital necessary for the expansion of the timber industry. By 1937, timber exports totalled about 178,000 cubic meters. By 1941, Sabah was the third largest exporter of timber in the British Empire and Sandakan was one of the leading timber ports of the world. However, this expansion was achieved with very little regard for conservation and there was indiscriminate logging of the jungle. In the late 1960s and early 1970s, timber became the third most valuable of Malaysia's exports, with Japan as a leading consumer. Later in the 1970s, a drastic fall in world market prices for timber depressed the industry. At the same time, timber production in both Sarawak and Peninsular Malaysia caught up with Sabah. Today, Sarawak is the leading producer of timber and timber exports, with Sabah in second place. The government is now taking measures to control and reduce logging activities. Nevertheless, timber is a controversial export item and has resulted in protest blockades by the natives who feel that the timber companies are encroaching on their lands and destroying their livelihood.

TIN Although tin had been mined by Malays for centuries to meet the demands of India, China and Europe, production was limited and the methods used were simple and laborious. It is estimated that only about 500 tonnes annually were mined by Malays up to the middle of the nineteenth century. In the second half of the nineteenth century the Malay Peninsula became increasingly important as a source of tin. There were major discoveries of tin fields in the river valleys of Perak and Selangor. At the same time, the Industrial Revolution resulted in an increased demand for tin. This was reflected in large-scale Chinese immigration into the west coast states. The Chinese also introduced significant innovations in the tin industry and readily adopted the new techniques of hydraulic sluicing and gravel pumping which had come via Australia. By 1898, the FMS, with a total output of 40,000 tonnes, became the world's largest tin producer. Initially European participation was minor compared to Chinese participation but with the introduction of the bucket dredge in 1912, European participation increased. The large international concerns were able to obtain huge grants of mining land, and with their finance, specialized skills and international contacts soon dominated the tin industry.

The Colonial government also promoted the tin industry by providing the necessary infrastructure, conducting land surveys which contained information on tin areas and enabled leases to be accurately made. While production of tin increased, world purchases of tin did not continue to grow as rapidly. The USA has been a major market for Malaya's tin but since the 1920s its demand has remained constant at around 2,540 tonnes because of more economic use of tin and better recovery methods. Large fluctuations in world tin prices led Malaya and other tin-producing nations to adopt an international tin control scheme in 1931, which has been periodically renewed ever since. The industry was severely dislocated during the Japanese Occupation period but made a swift recovery after 1945. By 1960 production had peaked top pre-war levels, the European share in production had increased to 60 per cent and returns from the industry played a major role in helping the sterling stay afloat. High levels of production and export were maintained until the end of the 1970s, although tin's contribution to the national economy gradually declined. Depleted resources and rising costs together with plummetting prices caused a dramatic fall in production. In 1985, the London Metal Exchange suspended all dealings in tin, precipitating the collapse of the International Tin Council's buffer stock. By 1986, production dropped further and only in 1989 have production figures shown a rise. Nevertheless, Malaysia still remains the world's leading tin producer.

TRENGGANU Trengganu has long been an important area of Malay settlement. The inscription found at Kuala Brang testifies to the existence of an Islamic state in Trengganu almost a century before the rise of Melaka. Trengganu became a vassal of Melaka and subsequently of Johor. In the early part of the eighteenth century the present royal house of Trengganu was founded by a half-brother of the Sultan of Johor: his successor, Mansur Shah, played a major role in containing Bugis influence in the region. However, the main threat in the years that followed came from the Thais in the north. Although Trengganu was obliged to send tribute to Bangkok (the *bunga mas*) two strong rulers in the nineteenth century—Baginda Omar and Sultan Zainal Abidin III—

succeeded in making Thai overlordship purely nominal. However, in 1909, the forces of Western imperialism caught up with Trengganu when the British imposed their Agent on the unwilling ruler, as a result of the Anglo-Thai Treaty of Bangkok of that year. The traditional establishment did its utmost to restrict the extent of British influence in the state and to maintain its status as a center for Islamic learning and piety. During the Japanese Occupation, Trengganu was returned to Thailand. After the Japanese Occupation, Trengganu reverted to the British, then joined the Malayan Union (q.v.) and subsequently the Federation of Malaya (q.v.) in 1948.

THE TRENGGANU REBELLION The Trengganu Rebellion was a localized peasant uprising which occurred in 1928 in the northern Malay state of Trengganu (q.v.). It was organized and led by one Haji Drahman who was opposed to the Sultan's acceptance of British control and claimed that the land belonged to the people for whom infidel government was improper and unnecessary. His followers defied the authorities by refusing to pay land rent and ignoring the other controls on their economic activities. At Kuala Brang, they took over the Government office. Haji Drahman, popularly known as To' Janggut, was killed in action and the British re-established their authority only when reinforcements arrived from Kuala Lumpur.

U

UNFEDERATED MALAY STATES After Britain's *entente cordiale* with France in 1904, it was free to make advances in northern Malaya without fear of French countermoves in or against Siam. In 1909, by the Treaty of Bangkok with Siam, the four northern states of Kelantan, Trengganu, Kedah and Perlis were transferred to British rule and in time, all the Rulers accepted British advisers. In 1914, the Sultan of Johor accepted a British 'General Adviser'. These five states—Kedah, Perlis, Kelantan, Trengganu and Johor—were not included in the Federation (q.v.), and were therefore referred to as the 'Unfederated Malay States'.

UNITED MALAYS NATIONAL ORGANIZATION (UMNO) The United Malays National Organization (UMNO) is the most powerful political party in Malaysia. It was born at a rally of local Malay associations and bodies held in Kuala Lumpur in March 1946. The founder and first president was Datuk Onn bin Jaafar (q.v.) who led Malay opposition to British proposals for a Malayan Union (q.v.), in which citizenship provisions for non-Malays would be greatly liberalized. The Malays feared that they would be politically dispossessed in their own country. Having successfully fought against the Malayan Union Scheme, which was withdrawn by the British, UMNO was transformed into Malaya's largest political party and it spearheaded moves to gain independence from British rule. Onn realized that political accommodation with the other communities was necessary if the Malays were to advance towards self-government and attempted to turn UMNO into a multi-ethnic party. When the majority of the Malays would not agree to the admittance of non-Malays into the party, Onn resigned and formed a multi-ethnic party to which he hoped to attract leaders from all the communities. Onn was succeeded by Tunku Abdul Rahman (q.v.), a barrister, who became one of the driving forces behind UMNO's campaign for independence. UMNO was founded and continues to be based upon the premise that the Malays must be united and politically organized in order to safeguard their legitimate communal interests, as the indigenous population, against the challenges posed by immigrant communities of different ethnic origins. Moreover, it is believed that only when the Malays as a people receive an equitable distribution of wealth, educational and employment opportunities and feel secure in their relative position will there be lasting political stability in an environment where all ethnic communities can prosper. Tunku Abdul Rahman also became the main architect of inter-communal accommodation when he formed an alliance (q.v.) with the MCA (q.v.) in 1952 and the MIC (q.v.) in 1955 to seek independence from Britain. In 1957, Malaya achieved independence and Tunku Abdul Rahman (as leader of the Alliance government) became Prime Minister. While striving to defend Malay interests, UMNO has not been averse to cooperating with other political organizations. As the dominant political party in the country, UMNO, beginning in 1971 secured the expansion of the Alliance coalition into the much broader alignment of the National Front or ***Barisan Nasional*** (q.v.) within which were included former opposition parties as well as political parties from East Malaysia. This move was carried out with the intention of reducing divisive politicking and bringing the processes of communal bargaining within the confines of government. UMNO effectively controls the Federal Government and all state governments in Peninsular Malaysia. In recent years, largely in response to the challenge of Islamic resurgence, UMNO has increasingly sought to project itself as both a Malay nationalist party and an organization committed to universal Islamic principles. UMNO has not been without its share of internal strains. In the early 1950s, the religious section of UMNO broke away to become the Islamic Party of Malaysia (q.v.) (also known as ***Parti Islam*** or by its acronym PAS). Since then, with the exception of a brief period when PAS joined the ***Barisan Nasional*** coalition, the party and ***Semangat*** '46 have become the principal sources of Malay opposition to UMNO. Moreover, since 1987, Tengku Razaleigh Hamzah (q.v.), the man responsible for PAS being ousted from power in the State of Kalantan and once one of the top five leaders of UMNO, has become an implacable rival of Mahathir (q.v.). Razaleigh challenged Mahathir for the presidency of UMNO in 1987 and narrowly lost to him. Subsequently, UMNO was deregistered by the Court in early 1988 for violating rules governing societies, and Mahathir formed a new UMNO (***Baru***). Razaleigh and his supporters formed a splinter party (registered in 1989) called ***Semangat*** '46 (q.v.) (Spirit of 1946) after the year the original UMNO was formed. Subsequently, Razaleigh formed a pact of "cooperation and understanding" with PAS, ***Berjasa*** (q.v.) and ***Hamim*** (q.v.) (two other parties which left the ***Barisan Nasional*** coalition in 1989) called the ***Angkatan Perpaduan Ummah*** (APU) (q.v.). This pact concentrates on the common goal of unity of Malays and Muslims. Meanwhile, UMNO (***Baru***) has taken the first steps towards reconciliation with members of the splinter group with the acceptance of a six-point peace plan. Despite talk of peace, many former UMNO members have not returned to the UMNO mainstream headed by Mahathir. On

another front, UMNO's headquarters tower and the adjacent Putra World Centre (a point of contention between UMNO (***Baru***) and ***Semangat*** '46) are to be auctioned off. In January 1989, the High Court allowed an application by Bank Bumiputera Malaysia Bhd. (BBMB) to auction off the 3.6 ha of land in order to recover $M308.46 million ($US 113.17 million) owed it by UMNO. UMNO had borrowed $M200 million from BBMB in 1983 to build the centre and charged the land as security. Mahathir and two other UMNO office bearers, as the defendents, did not contest the auction order. It is suspected that BBMB will gain legal ownership of the complex at the auction, especially if the court registrar sets a sufficiently high reserve price on the property. Eventually, UMNO (***Baru***) can then buy back its headquarters without legal complications. On the political front, UMNO (***Baru***) recently lost to PAS in a by-election in Trengganu and while it has won in other by-elections, its majority has been reduced. In the 1990 General Elections, UMNO (***Baru***) lost to PAS and ***Semangat*** '46 in Kelantan and Kelantan is now an opposition state. UMNO (***Baru***) therefore now has to compete for the Malay vote with both PAS and ***Semangat*** '46 and can no longer claim that it represents all the Malays in the country.
See also: PAS; SEMANGAT '46

UNITED SABAH NATIONAL ORGANIZATION (USNO) The United Sabah National Organization (USNO) was formed in 1961 by Tun Datu Mustapha Harun (q.v.). It professed a non-communal membership policy but was heavily dependent upon Muslim support. With the exception of a brief period when he was not president of the party, Tun Datu Mustapha has dominated USNO. From 1967 to 1976, USNO and the Sabah Chinese Association constituted the ruling Sabah Alliance, with Tun Datu Mustapha Harun as Chief Minister. At the 1976 State elections, USNO was ousted by ***Berjaya*** (q.v.), a party formed by USNO dissidents. USNO became the opposition party at State level, but joined the ***Barisan Nasional*** (q.v.) coalition at the Federal level. In 1984, USNO was expelled from the ***Barisan Nasional*** after Tun Datu Mustapha Harun was accused of disloyalty to the coalition and for opposing the federal government's conversion of Labuan

into a Federal Territory. After a three-way contest between the ***Parti Bersatu Sabah*** (PBS) (q.v.), ***Berjaya*** and USNO at the 1985 State elections, PBS emerged victorious and Tun Datu Mustapha Harun failed in his attempt to form a minority USNO-***Berjaya*** government. He was sworn in as Chief Minister for several hours, but the governor subsequently revoked his commission and appointed Datuk Pairin Kitingan (q.v.) of PBS, who commanded the support of a majority of State assemblymen, as Chief Minister. Tun Datu Mustapha Harun subsequently took legal action to have his rival's appointment declared null and void. However, the High Court ruled that the governor had appointed Tun Datu Mustapha Harun under duress and confirmed Datuk Pairin Kitingan's appointment as Chief Minister. USNO rejoined the ***Barisan Nasional*** in June 1986. In May 1991, USNO was disbanded to form the Sabah UMNO chapter.
See also: BERJAYA; PARTI BERSATU SABAH

Y

YAMASHITA, TOMOYUKI, GENERAL (1885–1946), known popularly as the 'Tiger of Malaya' was the General Officer Commander-in-Chief of the Japanese 25 Army for the invasion of Malaya during the Pacific War. Yamashita was born in Osugi, Shikoku and was a graduate of the Millitary Academy and Staff College. In 1919, he was appointed military attache to Switzerland and subsequently to Germany and Vienna. He was involved in the Young Officers' Rebellion (Ni-Ni-Roku incident) in 1936 and sent to Korea. Subsequently he served in China and Manchuria. In 1941, he was appointed to lead the invasion of Malaya. After a lightning campaign, Malaya was overrun and Singapore surrendered on 15 February 1942. On 17 July 1942, Yamashita was transferred to a command in Manchuria and was promoted to General in 1943. In September 1944, he was sent to defend the Philippines which was threatened by the invasion of U.S. forces under General MacArthur. The battle for the Philippines, in which Yamashita played a major role in Northern Luzon, lasted until September

1945, shortly after the official end of the War. The Japanese army disintegrated and committed many atrocities against the civilian Filipino population. Yamashita was held responsible for these atrocities, tried for war crimes and executed on 23 February 1946.

YANG diPERTUAN AGUNG. See PARAMOUNT RULER

Z

ZAINUN BTE MUNSHI SULAIMAN, HAJAH/IBU ZAIN (1903–1989) was a prominent Malay community leader and educationalist. She was born and educated in Melaka. When her father was transferred to Johor, her education was interrupted. In Johor, she became a teacher and gradually rose to become head teacher and later supervisor of Girls' Schools in Johor. Ibu Zain was largely self-taught and a keen promoter of education among Malay girls. She set up a private religious Girls School in Johor. In 1945, at the invitation of Onn bin Jaafar (q.v.) she entered politics and sought to organize Malay Women's groups. Subsequently, she became Head of the Womens' Wing of UMNO (q.v.). She played an active role in the independence movement and in 1959 was elected member of Parliament. For her role in promoting education among girls and women's rights, she received several awards. Her literary contributions are also well known.

ZOPFAN Zone of Peace, Freedom and Neutrality. At a meeting in Kuala Lumpur, in 1971, the ASEAN (q.v.) Foreign Ministers declared the determination of their nations to "secure the recognition of, and respect for, Southeast Asia as a Zone of Peace, Freedom and Neutrality, free from any form or manner of interference by outside powers". The ZOPFAN ideal was keenly promoted as an important plank of Malaysia's foreign policy by Tun Abdul Razak (q.v.). A commitment to its ideals is still regularly asserted in Malaysian foreign policy pronouncements.
See also: ASEAN

BIBLIOGRAPHY

This bibliography includes selected major and important works on Malaysia. Priority is given to writings readily available in English, or English translations. The bibliography is divided into two parts. Part One provides the general bibliographies, general studies and indexes, directories, professional periodicals and newspapers. Part Two is divided into seven main subject headings, which are further sub-divided within each main subject heading or sub-division. The selected books, articles and manuscripts aim at a representative treatment of the historical development of Malaysia: culture, economy, history, politics, science and society. Entries are arranged alphabetically by author.

A brief note on the arrangement of Malaysian names may be useful here. Malays carry only personal names. For bibliographical purposes therefore, Malays are normally indexed by the full personal name, for example, Sharom Ahmat. Note should also be made of two insertions which frequently occur in Malay names; *bin* ('son of') and *haji* (which indicates that the person has made the pilgrimage to Mecca). Prominent Malays may also carry honorifics, notably 'Tunku', 'Tun'. For Chinese names, the family comes first, followed by the given name(s): thus *Tan* Chee Beng. Indian names in this bibliography are arranged in the same form as European names: thus *Ampalavanar*, Rajeswary.

A new spelling system has been adopted by Malaysia: thus 'Malacca' has become 'Melaka'. No attempt has been made to impose a uniform spelling on the titles in this bibliography.

PART ONE

A. Bibliographies, General Studies and Indexes

British Museum. *Catalogue of Malaysian Books in the British Museum*. London: British Museum, 1972.

Brown, Ian and Rajeswary Ampalavanar. *Malaysia*. Oxford: Clio Press, 1986. (World Bibliographical Series, Vol. 12)

Challis, Joyce. *Annotated Bibliography of Economic and Social Material West Malaysia*. Singapore: University of Singapore, Economic Research Centre, 1968.

Cheeseman, H.A.R. *Bibliography of Malaya*. London: Longmans, 1959.

Cotter, Conrad Patrick, W.G. Solheim and T.R. Williams. *North Borneo, Brunei and Sarawak: A Bibliography of English Language Historical, Administrative and Ethnographic Sources*. Hilo: University of Hawaii Peace Corps Training Center, 1963. (Mimeograph)

Cotter, Conrad Patrick. "A Guide to the Sarawak Gazette 1870–1965," (Ph.D. dissertation, Cornell University, 1967).

Crisswell, Colin N. "A Select Bibliography of Published Works in English with Relevance to Bornean History," *Borneo Research Bulletin* (East Lansing, Michigan) Vol. 4, 1972: 1–22.

Ding Choo Ming. *A Bibliography of Bibliographies on Malaysia*. Petaling Jaya: Hexagon Elite Publications, 1981.

———. "A Bibliography of Bibliographies on Malaysia: Supplement 1," *Southeast Asian Research Materials Group: Newsletter*, No. 23, 1982: 1–14.

Heussler, Robert. *British Malaya: A Bibliographical and Biographical Compendium*. New York: Garland Publishing Inc., 1981.

Human Relations Area Files, British Borneo Research Project. *Bibliography of British Borneo*. New Haven: HRAF British Borneo Research Project at the University of Chicago, 1956.

Karni, R.S. *Bibliography of Malaysia and Singapore*. Kuala Lumpur: University of Malaya Press, 1980.

Lent, John A. (ed). *Malaysian Studies: Present Knowledge and Research Trends*. DeKalb: Northern Illinois University, Center for Southeast Asian Studies, 1979. (Occasional Paper No. 7)

Lim, Beda. "Malaya, A Background Bibliography," *Journal of the Malaysian Branch Royal Asiatic Society*, Vol. 35, Parts 2 & 3, 1962: 1–199.

Lim Huck Tee and D.E.K. Wijasuriya. *Index Malaysiana*: An Index to the Journal of the Straits Branch, Royal Asiatic Society and the Journal of the Malaysian Branch, Royal Asiatic Society, 1878–1963. Kuala Lumpur: Malaysian Branch Royal Asiatic Society, 1970.

Loh Chee Yin. "A New Borneo Bibliography: II," *Sarawak Museum Journal*, Vol. 14, 1966: 350–75.

———. "Sarawak Museum Journal: An index to all the issues published from 1911 to 1979," *Sarawak Museum Journal*, Vol. 28, No. 15, 1980.

Pelzer, Karl Josef. *Selected Bibliography of the Geography of South East Asia*. New Haven: Southeast Asia Studies, Yale University Human Relations Area Files, 1949–56, Vols. 1–3.

———. *West Malaysia and Singapore: A Selected Bibliography*. New Haven: Human Relations Area Files Press, Behavior Science Bibliographies, 1971.

Ramasamy, Rajakrishnan and J. Rabindra Daniel. *Indians in Peninsular Malaysia: A Study and Bibliography*. Kuala Lumpur: University of Malaya Library, 1984.

Roff, William R. *Guide to Malay Periodicals 1876–1941 With Details of Known Holdings in Malaya*. Singapore: Eastern Universities Press, Papers on Southeast Asian Subjects No. 4, 1961.

———. *Bibliography of Malay and Arabic Periodicals Published in the Straits Settlements and Peninsular Malay States 1876–1941*. London: Oxford University Press, 1972.

———. *Southeast Asian Research Tools: Malaysia, Singapore, Brunei*. Southeast Asia Paper No. 16, Part 4, p. vii. Honolulu: Southeast Asian Program, University of Hawaii, 1979.

Rousseau, Jerome. "A Bibliography of Borneo Bibliographies," *Borneo Research Bulletin*, Vol. 2, 1970: 35–36.

———. *Central Borneo: A Bibliography*. Special Monograph No. 5. *The Sarawak Museum Journal*, Kuching, Vol. 28, No. 59 (new series), December 1988.

Subbiah, Rama. *Tamil Malaysiana: A Checklist of Tamil Books and Periodicals Published in Malaysia and Singapore*. Kuala Lumpur: University of Malaya Library (Tamil), 1969.

Tham Seong Chee. *Social Science Research in Malaysia*. Singapore: Graham Brash, 1981.

Tregonning, Kennedy Gordon (ed). *Malaysian Historical Sources*. Singapore: History Department, University of Singapore, 1962.

University of Singapore Library, Catalogue of the Singapore/Malaysia Collection. Boston: G.K. Hall, 1968.

U.S. Library of Congress, Division of Bibliography. *British Malaya and British North Borneo: A Bibliographical List*. Compiled by Florence S. Hellman. Washington, DC: Library of Congress, 1943.

U.S. Library of Congress, Orientalia Division. *Southeast Asia Subject Catalog*. Boston: G.K. Hall, 1972, 6 Vols. (Vol. 3: Laos, Malaysia)

Wijasuriya, D.E.K. and Lim Huck Tee. *Index Malaysiana*, Supplement I, An Index to the Journal of the Malaysian Branch of the Royal Asiatic Society and the JMBRAS Monographs, 1964–1973. Kuala Lumpur: Malaysian Branch Royal Asiatic Society, 1974.

———. *Index Malaysiana*, Supplement No. 2, 1974–1983. Petaling Jaya: Malaysian Branch Royal Asiatic Society, 1985.

Wong Lin Ken. "The Economic History of Malaysia: A Bibliographical Essay", *Journal of Economic History*, Vol. 25, 1965: 244–62.

———. "Twentieth-Century Malayan Economic History: A Select Bibliographic Survey," *Journal of Southeast Asian Studies*, Vol. 10, No. 1, 1979: 1–24.

B. Directories

Abdullah Zakaria Ghazali, Adnan Hj. Nawang, Krishen Jit and Lee Kam Hing. *Malaysia: Tokoh Dulu dan Kini*. Kuala Lumpur: Institute of Advanced Studies, University of Malaya and the New Straits Times, 1986.

Burkill, I.H. *A Dictionary of the Economic Products of the Malay Peninsula*. Kuala Lumpur: Ministry of Agriculture and Cooperatives, Malaysia, 1966, 2 Vols. (Originally 1935)

Dennys, N.B. *A Descriptive Dictionary of British Malaya*. London: London and China Telegraph Office, 1894.

Information Malaysia 1990 Yearbook. Kuala Lumpur: Berita Publishing, 1990. (Originally *Malay Mail Yearbook*. Kuala Lumpur: The Malay Mail, 1956–.)

Kompas Malaysia 1988. (Directory of Companies in Malaysia). Kuala Lumpur: Berita—Kompas Sdn. Bhd., 1988. (Originally *New Straits Times Directory of Companies in Malaysia, 1976–83*; then superceded by *Kompas Buku Merah*, 1984–1987.)

Official Yearbook Malaysia 1986. Kuala Lumpur: Department of Information, Ministry of Information, 1971–.

Who's Who in Malaysia and Singapore 1983–84. Petaling Jaya: Who's Who Publications, 1983 (first published 1955).

Who's Who in Malaysian Business and Directory 1985. Kuala Lumpur: Kuala Lumpur Publishing Sdn. Bhd., 1984–.

C. Professional Periodicals

Asian Survey. Berkeley: University of California Press, 1961–. Monthly

Contemporary Southeast Asia. Singapore: Institute of Southeast Asian Studies, 1979–. Quarterly

Far Eastern Economic Review. Hong Kong: Far Eastern Economic Review, 1946–. Weekly

Journal of Asian Studies. Ann Arbor: Association for Asian Studies, 1956–. Quarterly

Journal of Contemporary Asia. Stockholm: Journal of Contemporary Asia, 1970–. Quarterly

Journal of Southeast Asian History. Singapore: Department of History, University of Singapore, 1960–1969. Semi-annual

Journal of Southeast Asian Studies. Singapore: McGraw-Hill Far Eastern Publishers (1970–1977); Singapore University Press (1978), 1970–. Semi-annual

Journal of the Malaysian Branch of the Royal Asiatic Society. Kuala Lumpur: Malaysian Branch of the Royal Asiatic Society, 1923–. Semi-annual

Journal of Tropical Geography. Kuala Lumpur & Singapore: Departments of Geography, The University of Singapore and The University of Malaya, 1953–. Semi-annual. (Split into *Malaysian Journal of Tropical Geography* and *Singapore Journal of Tropical Geography* in 1980.)

Kajian Ekonomi Malaysia (Malaysian Economic Studies). Kuala Lumpur: Persatuan Ekonomi Malaysia (Malaysian Economic Association), 1964–. Semi-annual

Kajian Malaysia (Journal of Malaysian Studies). Penang: Universiti Sains Malaysia, 1983–. Semi-annual

Malaya Law Review. Singapore: Faculty of Law, The National University of Singapore, 1959–. Semi-annual

Malayan Economic Review. Singapore: Economic Society of Singapore and the Department of Economics and Statistics, The National University of Singapore, 1956–82. Semi-annual. Continued as: *The Singapore Economic Review*, 1983–.

Malayan Law Journal. Kuala Lumpur: Malayan Law Journal Pte. Ltd., 1932–. Semi-annual

Malaysian Business. Kuala Lumpur: Berita Publishing Sdn. Bhd., 1972–. Monthly

Modern Asian Studies. Cambridge: Cambridge University Press, 1967–. Quarterly

Pacific Affairs. Vancouver: University of British Columbia, 1928–. Quarterly

Sarawak Museum Journal. Kuching: The Museum, 1911–. Annual

Southeast Asian Affairs. Singapore: Institute of Southeast Asian Studies, 1974–. Annual

Southeast Asian Journal of Social Science. Singapore: Institute of Southeast Asian Studies and the Department of Sociology of the National University of Singapore, 1973–. Semi-annual

D. Major Newspapers in Malaysia

English Language

The New Straits Times
The Star
The Borneo Bulletin
The Borneo Post

Chinese Language

Nanyang Siang Pao
Sin Chiew Jit Poh

Malay Language

Berita Harian
Utusan Malaysia

Tamil Language

Tamil Nesan
Thinamani

PART TWO

GENERAL WORKS

A. Travel Accounts and Travel Guide

Atwater, Maxine. *To Malaysia with Feelings: Notes on Travel Adventure*. Kuala Lumpur: Department of Tourism, Ministry of Commerce and Industry, n.d.

Beccari, Odoardo. *Wanderings in the Great Forests of Borneo*. Introduction by the Earl of Cranbrook; Enrico H. Giglioli (trans.); rev. ed. F.H.H. Guillemard (ed). Singapore: Oxford University Press, 1986. (Originally 1904)

Bird, Isabella L. *The Golden Chersonese: Travels in Malaya in 1879*. Kuala Lumpur: Oxford University Press, 1980. (Originally 1883)

Bock, Carl Alfred. *The Headhunters of Borneo: A Narrative of Travel up the Mahakkam and Down the Barito*. London: Low, Marston, Searle and Rivington, 1881.

Fodor's Southeast Asia 1985. London: Hodder and Stoughton, 1984.

Harrisson, Barbara. *Orang-Utan*. London: Collins, 1962.

Harrisson, Tom. *World Within: A Borneo Story*. Kuala Lumpur: Oxford University Press, 1984.

——— (ed). *Borneo Jungle: An Account of the Oxford University Expedition of 1932*. Singapore: Oxford University Press, 1988. (Originally 1938)

Henderson, John et. al. *Area Handbook for Malaysia*. Washington, DC: U.S. Government Printing Office, 1970.

Hoefer, Hans. *Guide to Malaysia*. Singapore: APA Publications, 1972.

———. *Jalan-jalan: Images of Malaysia*. Kuala Lumpur: APA Publications for Tourist Development Corporation, 1981.

Hose, Charles. *Fifty Years of Romance and Research, Or a Jungle-Wallah at Large*. London: Hutchinson & Co., 1927.

———. *Natural Man: A Record from Borneo*. Introduction by Brian Durrans. Singapore: Oxford University Press, 1988. (Originally 1926)

———. *The Field-Book of a Jungle Wallah: Shore, River and Forest Life in Sarawak*. Singapore: Oxford University Press, 1985. (Originally 1929)

Insight Guides. *Malaysia*. Singapore: APA Publications, 1988.

King, Seth S. *Getting to Know Malaysia*. New York: Coward-McCann, 1964.

Kuala Lumpur. *A Guide to Kuala Lumpur*. Singapore: Donald Moore, 1957.

Lee, Arnold and Kathleen Lee. *Spotlight on Malaya*. London: Highway Press, 1962.

Lumholtz, Karl Sofus. *Through Central Borneo: An Account of Two Years' Travel in the Land of the Headhunters Between the Years 1913 and 1917*. New York: Scribner, 1920.

Malaya: A Guide for Businessmen and Visitors, 1954. Singapore: Public Relations Office and Department of Information, Federation of Malaya, 1954.

Malaysia and Sarawak. Published by authority of the Government of Sarawak. Kuching: Government Printing Office, 1962.

Malaysia in Brief. Kuala Lumpur: Government Printer, 1963.

McKie, Ronald. *Malaysia in Focus*. Sydney: Angus and Robertson, 1963.

Mohd. Fadzil Othman. *Kisah Pelayaran Muhammad Ibrahim Munsyi, Dengan Pengenalan dan Anotasi*. Kuala Lumpur: Dewan Bahasa dan Pustaka, 1980.

Moore, Wendy. *Collins Illustrated Guide to Malaysia*. London: Collins, 1989.

Nicol, Gladys. *Malaysia and Singapore*. London: B.T. Batsford, 1977.

O'Hanlon, Redmond. *Into the Heart of Borneo: An Account of a Journey Made in 1983 to the Mountains of Batu Tiban with James Fenton*. Edinburgh: Salamander Press, 1984.

Pacific Area Travel Association. PATA Patter, Malaysia 1972. Kuala Lumpur: Dept of Tourism, Ministry of Commerce and Industry, 1972.

Pillai, K. *On Malaysia*. Kuala Lumpur: Rayirath Publications, 1962.

St. John, Spenser. *Life in the Forests of the Far East: Travels in Sabah and Sarawak in the 1860s*. Introduction by Tom Harrisson (2 Vols. in 1). Singapore: Oxford University Press, 1986.

Sivaram, M. *Glimpses of Malaysia*. Petaling Jaya: V.M. Sundaram, n.d.

Vijesuria, R. *Travel in Malaysia*. Kuala Lumpur: Arena Books, 1989.

Wallace, Alfred Russel. *The Malay Archipelago*. Introduction by John Bastin. Singapore: Oxford University Press, 1986.

B. Map Collections

Fell, R.T. *Early Maps of South-East Asia*. Singapore: Oxford University Press, 1987.

C. Statistical Abstracts

Ajia Keizai Kenkyu Jo. *Bibliography of the Statistical Materials on Southeast Asia*. Tokyo: Institute of Asian Economic Affairs, 1960.

Banci Penduduk dan Perumahan Malaysia, 1980 (1980 Population and Housing Census of Malaysia). Kuala Lumpur: Department of Statistics, 1983.

Bank Negara Malaysia Quarterly Economic Bulletin. Kuala Lumpur: Bank Negara Malaysia, 1968–. Quarterly

Chiang Hai Ding. "The Statistics of the Straits Settlements Foreign Trade, 1870–1915," *Malayan Economic Review*, Vol. 10, No. 1, 1965: 73–83.

Malaysia: Buku Maklumat Perangkaan 1986. Kuala Lumpur: Government Printing Office, 1987.

Ministry of Finance, Malaysia. Economic Report. Kuala Lumpur: Ministry of Finance Malaysia, 1972–. Annual

Perangkaan Perdagangan Luar Sarawak. (Statistics of External Trade Sarawak). Kuching: Department of Statistics Malaysia (Sarawak Branch), 1964–. Annual

Rao, V.V. Bhanoji. *National Accounts of West Malaysia 1947–1971.* Singapore: Heinemann Educational Books (Asia), 1976.

Siaran Perangkaan Bulanan Semenanjung Malaysia. (Monthly Statistical Bulletin: Peninsular Malaysia). Kuala Lumpur: Department of Statistics, 1958. Monthly

Siaran Perangkaan Tahunan Sabah. (Annual Bulletin of Statistics, Sabah). Kota Kinabalu: Department of Statistics, 1964–. Annual

CULTURE

A. Archaeology and Prehistory

Bellwood, Peter. *Man's Conquest of the Pacific: The Prehistory of Southeast Asia and Oceania.* Auckland: William Collins, 1978.

———. *Prehistory of the Indo-Malaysian Archipelago.* Sydney: Academic Press, 1985.

Chêng Te-K'un. *Archaeology in Sarawak.* Cambridge: W. Heffer and Sons, University of Toronto Press, 1969.

Dunn, F.L. *Rain Forest Collectors and Traders: A Study of Resource Utilization in Modern and Ancient Malaya.* Monograph No. 5. Malaysian Branch Royal Asiatic Society: Kuala Lumpur, 1975.

———and B.A.V. Peacock. "An Annotated Bibliography of Malayan (West Malaysian) Archeology: 1962–1969," *Asian Perspectives*, Vol. 14, 1971: 43–48.

Evans, Ivor H.N. *Papers on the Ethnology and Archaeology of the Malay Peninsula.* Cambridge: Cambridge University Press, 1927.

Hall, K.R. and J.K. Whitmore (eds). *Explorations in Early Southeast Asia History: The Origins of Southeast Asian Statecraft.* Ann Arbor: University of Michigan, 1976.

Harrisson, Tom. "The Caves of Niah: A History of Prehistory," *Sarawak Museum Journal*, n.s., Vol. 8, No. 12, 1958: 549–95.

———. "The Prehistory of Borneo," *Asian Perspectives*, Vol. 13, 1970: 17–45.

———. *The Prehistory of Sabah.* Kota Kinabalu: Sabah Society, 1971.

Kuak, Monica Sim Joo and Che Puteh binti Ismail. *Archaeology in Malaysia: A Bibliography.* Kuala Lumpur: Perpustakaan Universiti Malaya, 1980.

Lamb, Alastair. "Report on the Excavation and Reconstruction of Chandi Bukit Batu Pahat, Central Kedah," *Federation Museums Journal*, n.s., Vol. 5, 1960.

———. "Miscellaneous Papers on Early Hindu and Buddhist Settlement in Northern Malaya and Southern Thailand," *Federation Museums Journal*, n.s., Vol. 6, 1961.

Leong Sau Heng. "A Study of Ceramic Deposits from Pengkalan Bujang, Kedah," (MA thesis, University of Malaya, 1974).

———. "Lembah Bujang", (the Bujang Valley), *Malaysia Dari Segi Sejarah* (Journal of the Malaysian Historical Society), No. 8, 1979: 45–51. (Also published in *Lembah Bujang*. Compiled by J. Chandran and Jazamuddin Baharuddin. Kuala Lumpur: Malaysian Historical Society, 1980: 5–11.)

Medway, G., Lord. "The Niah Excavations and An Assessment of the Impact of Early Man on Mammals in Borneo," *Asian Perspectives*, Vol. 20, No. 1, 1977: 51–69.

Peacock, B.A.V. "Short Description of Malayan Prehistoric Pottery," *Asian Perspectives*, Vol. 3, No. 2, 1959: 121–56.

———. *The Later Prehistory of the Malay Peninsula*, in: *Early South East Asia, Essays in Archaeology, History and Historical Geography*, R.B. Smith and W. Watson (eds). New York: Oxford University Press, 1979: 199–214.

——— and F.L. Dunn. "Recent Archaeological Discoveries in Malaysia, 1967," *Journal of the Malaysian Branch Royal Asiatic Society*, Vol. 41, No. 1, 1968: 171–79.

Quaritch Wales, H.G. "Archaeological Research on Ancient Indian Colonization in Malaya," *Journal of the Malayan Branch Royal Asiatic Society*, Vol. 18, Part 1, 1940: 1–85.

———. *The Malay Peninsula in Hindu Times*. London: Bernard Quaritch, 1976.

Sandhu, Kernail Singh. *Early Malaysia: Some Observations on the Nature of Indian Contacts with Pre-British Malaya*. Singapore: University Education Press, 1973.

Sieveking, G. de G. "The Iron Age Collections of Malaya," *Journal of the Malayan Branch Royal Asiatic Society*, Vol. 29, No. 2, 1956: 79–138.

Solheim, Wilhelm G. II. "The Present Status of the Palaeolithic in Borneo," *Asian Perspectives*, Vol. 2, No. 2, 1958: 83–90.

———. "Borneo Archaeology, Past and Future," *Sabah Society Journal*, Vol. 6, No. 1, 1973–74: 27–37.

——— and Barbara Jensen. "Tom Harrisson—Bibliography of Publications Concerning Southeast Asian Prehistory," *Asian Perspectives*, Vol. 20, No. 1, 1977: 13–20.

Tweedie, M.W.F. "The Stone Age in Malaya," Monographs on Malay Subjects, No. 1, *Journal of the Malayan Branch Royal Asiatic Society*, Vol. 26, No. 2, 1953: 1–90.

———. *Prehistoric Malaya*. Singapore: Eastern University Press, 1965.

Wheatley, Paul. *The Golden Khersonese: Studies in the Historical Geography of the Malay Peninsula before A.D. 1500*. Kuala Lumpur: University of Malaya Press, 1961.

———. *Impressions of the Malay Peninsula in Ancient Times*. Singapore: Donald Moore for Eastern Universities Press, 1964.

B. Architecture

Dumarcay, Jacques. *The House in South-East Asia*. Translated and edited by Michael Smithies. Singapore: Oxford University Press, 1987.

Edwards, Norman. *The Singapore House and Residential Life 1819–1939*. Singapore: Oxford University Press, 1989.

Gibbs, Philip. *Building a Malay House*. Singapore: Oxford University Press, 1987.

C. Arts

Brandon, James R. *Theatre in Southeast Asia*. Cambridge: Harvard University Press, 1967.

———. *Brandon's Guide to Theatre in Asia*. Honolulu: University of Hawaii Press, 1976.

Brown, Roxanna M. *The Ceramics of South East Asia: their dating and identification*. Singapore: Oxford University Press, 1989.

Chin, Lucas. *Cultural Heritage of Sarawak*. Kuching: Sarawak Museum, 1980.

Frey, Edward. *The Kris: Mystic Weapon of the Malay World*. Singapore: Oxford University Press, 1988.

Guy, John S. *Ceramic Traditions of South-East Asia*. Singapore: Oxford University Press, 1989.

Harrisson, Barbara. *Pusaka: Heirloom Jars of Borneo*. Singapore: Oxford University Press, 1986.

Ho Wing Meng. *Straits Chinese Silver: A Collector's Guide*. Singapore: Times Books International, 1984.

Ku Ahmad bin Ku Mustaffa and Wong Kiew Kit. *Silat Melayu: The Malay art of attack and defence*. Kuala Lumpur: Oxford University Press, 1978.

Mohd Taib Osman (ed). *Traditional drama and music of Southeast Asia*. Kuala Lumpur: Dewan Bahasa dan Pustaka, 1974.

Munan, Heidi. *Sarawak Crafts: Methods, Materials and Motifs*. Singapore: Oxford University Press, 1989.

Rahmah Bujang. *Boria: A Form of Malay Theatre*. Singapore: Institute of Southeast Asian Studies, 1987.

Roth, Henry Ling. *Oriental Silverwork: Malay and Chinese, A Handbook for Connoisseurs, Collectors, Students and Silversmiths*. Kuala Lumpur: University of Malaya Press, 1966.

Sabapathy, T.K. *Modern Artists of Malaysia*. Kuala Lumpur: Dewan Bahasa dan Pustaka, 1983.

Selvanayagam, Grace. *Malaysian Songket*. Singapore: Oxford University Press, 1989.

Sheppard, Mubin. *Living Crafts of Malaysia*. Singapore: Times Books International, 1978.

———. *Taman Saujana: Dance, drama, music and magic in Malaya long and not-so-long ago*. Petaling Jaya: International Book Service, 1983.

———. *A Royal Pleasure Ground: Malay Decorative Arts and Pastimes*. Singapore: Oxford University Press, 1986.

Southeast Asian Ceramic Society. *A Ceramic Legacy of Asia's Maritime Trade: Song Dynasty Guangdang wares and other 11th-19th Century Trade Ceramics found on Tioman Island, Malaysia*. Singapore: Oxford University Press, 1985. (Published in Association with the Southeast Asian Ceramic Society.)

Studies in Malaysian Oral and Musical Traditions. Ann Arbor: University of Michigan, Center for South and Southeast Asian Studies, 1974. (Michigan papers on South and Southeast Asia, No. 8.)

Sweeney, Amin. *Malay Shadow Puppets: The Wayang Siam of Kelantan*. London: Trustees of the British Museum, 1972.

———. *The Ramayana and the Malay Shadow Play*. Kuala Lumpur: Universiti Kebangsaan Malaysia Press, 1972.

Taylor, Eric. *Musical Instruments of Southeast Asia*. Singapore: Oxford University Press, 1989.

D. Language and Dictionaries

Asmah Haji Omar. *Language and Society in Malaysia*. Kuala Lumpur: Dewan Bahasa dan Pustaka, 1982.

———. *The Malay Peoples of Malaysia and their Languages*. Kuala Lumpur: Dewan Bahasa dan Pustaka, 1983.

Kamus Dwibahasa: Bahasa Inggeris—Bahasa Malaysia. Kuala Lumpur: Dewan Bahasa dan Pustaka, 1981.

Marsden, William. *A Dictionary and Grammar of the Malayan Language*. Singapore: Oxford University Press, 1984.

Noss, Richard B. (ed). *An Overview of Language Issues in Southeast Asia 1950–1980*. Singapore: Oxford University Press, 1984.

Richards, A.J.N. *An Iban—English Dictionary*. Kuala Lumpur: Oxford University Press, 1981.

Winstedt, R.O. *An Unabridged Malay-English Dictionary*. Singapore: Marican & Sons, 1957.

E. Literature

A. Samad Said. *Salina*. Translated by Harry Aveling. Kuala Lumpur: Dewan Bahasa dan Pustaka, 1975.

Abdullah bin Abdul Kadir. *The Hikayat Abdullah*. With an annotated translation by A.H. Hill. Kuala Lumpur: Oxford University Press, 1970.

Alias Ali. *Crisis*. Translated by Barclay M. Newman. Kuala Lumpur: Dewan Bahasa dan Pustaka, Malaysia, 1980.

Bennet, Bruce, Ee Tiang Hong and Ron Shepherd (eds). *The Writer's Sense of the Contemporary: Papers in Southeast Asian and Australian Literature*. Nedlands: Center for Studies in Australian Literature, University of Western Australia, 1982.

Burgess, Anthony. *Maugham's Malaysian Stories*. Kuala Lumpur: Heinemann Educational Books (Asia), 1969.

———. *The Malayan Trilogy*. Harmondsworth: Penguin Books, 1972.

Chapman, F. Spencer. *The Jungle Is Neutral*. London: Chatto and Windus, 1949.

Chin Kee Onn. *Ma-Rai-Ee*. Singapore: Eastern Universities Press, 1981.

Conrad, Joseph. *Lord Jim*. Harmondsworth: Penguin Books, 1957.

D' Alpuget, Blanche. *Turtle Beach*. Ringwood: Penguin Books, 1981.

de Freitas, G.V. *Maugham's Borneo Stories*. Singapore: Heinemann Educational Books (Asia), 1976.

Ding, Choo Ming. *Bibliografi sastera kreatif Melayu: A Bibliography of Malay Creative Writings 1920–1980. Vol. l: Brunei, Malaysia, Singapore*. Bangi: Perpustakaan Universiti Kebangsaan Malaysia, 1980.

Dossier: Litterature Malaysienne (Dossier: Malaysian Literature). *Archipel*, No. 19, 1980: 169–296.

Fang Xiu. *Notes on the History of Malayan Chinese New Literature 1920–1942*. Translated by Angus W. McDonald. Tokyo: Center for East Asian Cultural Studies, 1977. (East Asian Cultural Studies Series No. 18)

Fauconnier, Henri. *The Soul of Malaya*. Kuala Lumpur: Oxford University Press, 1965.

Fernando, Lloyd. *Twenty-two Malaysian Stories: An Anthology of Writing in English*. Singapore: Heinemann Educational Books (Asia), 1968.

———. *Scorpion Orchid*. Kuala Lumpur: Heinemann Educational Books (Asia), 1976.

———. "The Relation of the Sectional Literatures to the National Literature," *Tenggara*, Vol. 6, 1973: 121–27.

——— (ed). *New Drama One by Edward Dorall, K. Das and Lee Joo For*. Kuala Lumpur: Oxford University Press, 1972.

Glaskin, Gerald. *The Beach of Passionate Love*. London: Barrie & Rockliff, 1961.

Han Suyin. *And the Rain My Drink*. Frogmore: Panther Books, 1973.

Herbert, P. and Anthony Milner. *Southeast Asia. Languages and Literature: A Select Guide*. Honolulu: University of Hawaii Press, 1988.

Ishak Haji Muhammad. *The Prince of Mount Tahan*. Translated by Harry Aveling. Kuala Lumpur: Heinemann Educational Books (Asia), 1980.

Ismail Hamid. *The Malay Islamic Hikayat*. Bangi: Universiti Kebangsaan Malaysia Press, 1983.

Ismail Hussein. *Bibliography of Works and Articles on Traditional Malay Literature*. Kuala Lumpur: n.d. (Mimeograph)

———. *The Study of Traditional Malay Literature, with a Selected Bibliography*. Kuala Lumpur: Dewan Bahasa dan Pustaka, 1974.

Journal of Contemporary Literature. (Oxford) publishes an annual bibliography of Literature in English from Malaysia and Singapore.

Kassim Ahmad. *Hikayat Hang Tuah*. Kuala Lumpur: Dewan Bahasa dan Pustaka, 1964.

Keith, Agnes. *Three Came Home*. Boston: Little Brown, 1947.

Keris Mas. *Blood and Tears*. Translated by Harry Aveling with an Introduction by Syed Husin Ali. Petaling Jaya: Oxford University Press, 1984.

Kirkup, James. *Tropic Temper: A Memoir of Malaya*. London: Collins, 1963.

Knappert, Jan. *Malay Myths and Legends*. Kuala Lumpur: Heinemann Educational Books (Asia), 1980.

Lee Kok Liang. *Flowers in the Sky*. Kuala Lumpur: Heinemann Educational Books (Asia), 1981.

Li Chuan Siu. *A Bird's-Eye-View of the Development of Modern Malay Literature, 1921–1941*. Kuala Lumpur: Penerbitan Pustaka Antara, 1970.

———. *An Introduction to the Promotion and Development of Modern Malay Literature 1942–1962*. Yogyakarta: Penerbitan Yayasan Kanisius, 1975.

Ly Singko. *Reunion and Other Stories*. Singapore: Heinemann Educational Books (Asia), 1980.

——— and Leon Comber. *An Anthology of Modern Malaysian Chinese Stories*. Hong Kong: Heinemann Educational Books (Asia), 1967.

Maniam, K.S. *The Return*. Kuala Lumpur: Heinemann Educational Books (Asia), 1981.

Matheson, Virginia. "Concepts of Malay Ethos in Indigenous Malay Writings," *Journal of Southeast Asian Studies*, Vol. 10, No. 2, 1979: 351–71.

Modern Malaysian Stories II. Kuala Lumpur: Dewan Bahasa dan Pustaka, 1983.

Mohd. Taib Osman. "Trends in Modern Malay Literature", in: *Malaysia: A Survey*, Wang Gungwu (ed). Singapore: Donald Moore, 1964: 210–24.

———. "Towards the Development of Malaysia's National Literature," *Tenggara*, Vol. 66, 1973: 105–20.

———. *An Introduction to the development of modern Malay language and literature* (revised edition). Singapore: Times Books International, 1986.

Monique Zaini-Lajoubert. "The Evolution of the Malay Short Story: From its Origins to the Present Day," in: *The Short Story in South East Asia. Aspects of a Genre*, J.H.C.S. Davidson and Helen Cordell (eds). London: School of Oriental and African Studies, 1982.

Muhammad Haji Salleh. *The Travel Journals of Si Tenggang II*. Translated by the Poet, Kuala Lumpur: Dewan Bahasa dan Pustaka, 1979.

Newmann, Barclay M. *Modern Malaysian Stories*. Kuala Lumpur: Dewan Bahasa dan Pustaka, 1977.

———. *Modern Malaysian Poetry*. Kuala Lumpur: Dewan Bahasa dan Pustaka, 1980.

Palia Dorai. pseud. [i.e. Frederick William Knocker]. *A Malayan Miscellany*. Kuala Lumpur: Huxley Palmer, 1924. (Notes and jottings, reminiscences and anecdotes, stories and essays from the scrap-books of an Englishman resident in British Malaya.)

Roff, William R. *Stories by Sir Hugh Clifford.* Kuala Lumpur: Oxford University Press, 1966.

———. *Stories and Sketches by Sir Frank Swettenham.* Kuala Lumpur: Oxford University Press, 1967.

———. "English-language Fiction relating to Malaysia, Singapore and Brunei," *Journal of the Malaysian Branch Royal Asiatic Society*, Vol. 55, Part 1, 1982: 62–77.

Shahnon Ahmad. *No Harvest But a Thorn.* Translated and Introduced by Adibah Amin. Kuala Lumpur: Oxford University Press, 1972.

———. *Srengenge: A Novel From Malaysia.* Translated by Harry Aveling. Kuala Lumpur: Heinemann Educational Books (Asia), 1979.

Sweeney, Amin. *Authors and Audiences in Traditional Malay Literature.* Berkeley: University of California, Center for South and Southeast Asia Studies, 1980. (Monograph Series No. 20)

———. *A Full Hearing. Orality and Literacy in the Malay World.* Berkeley: University of California Press, 1987.

——— and Nigel Phillips. *The Voyages of Mohamed Ibrahim Munshi.* Kuala Lumpur: Oxford University Press, 1975.

Syed Naguib Al-Attas. *The Origin of the Malay Sha'ir.* Kuala Lumpur: Dewan Bahasa dan Pustaka, 1968.

Theroux, Paul. *The Consul's File.* Harmondsworth: Penguin Books, 1978.

Thomas, Leslie. *The Virgin Soldiers.* London: Pan Books, 1967.

Thumboo, Edwin. *The Second Tongue: An Anthology of Poetry from Malaysia and Singapore.* Singapore: Heinemann Educational Books (Asia), 1976.

Wignesan, T. (ed). *Bunga Emas: An Anthology of Contemporary Malaysian Literature (1930–1963)*. London: Anthony Blond with Rayirath (Raybooks) Publications Malaysia, 1964.

Wilkinson, R.J. *Malay Literature*. Kuala Lumpur: FMS Government Printing Office, 1907.

Winstedt, Sir Richard. *A History of Classical Malay Literature*. Kuala Lumpur: Oxford University Press, 1969.

Zieseniss, Alexander. *The Rama Saga in Malaysia: Its Origin and Development*. Translated by P.W. Burch. Singapore: Malaysian Sociological Research Institute, 1963.

F. Mass Media

Adhikarya, Ronny, Woon Ai Leng, Wong Hock Seng, and Khor Yoke Lim. *Broadcasting in Peninsular Malaysia*. London: Routledge & Kegan Paul, 1977.

Advertisers Association, The. *A Review of Advertising in Singapore and Malaysia During Early Times*. Singapore: Federal Publications Sdn. Bhd., 1970.

Ampalavanar, Rajeswary. "Tamil Journalism and the Indian Community in Malaya 1920–1941," *Journal of Tamil Studies*, Vol. 2, 1970: 1–17.

Betts, Russel. *The Mass Media of Malaya and Singapore as of 1965*. Cambridge: Massachusetts Institute of Technology, Center for International Studies, 1969. (Mimeograph)

Blackburn, Paul P. "Mass Communications Systems of Burma, Malaysia, and Thailand: A Comparative Analysis," in: *Asian Communication: Research, Training, Planning*, Daniel Lerner (ed). Honolulu: East-West Communication Institute, 1976: 57–76.

British Broadcasting Corporation (BBC). *Overseas Audience Research Report: Survey of Listening in Singapore and Malaya, 1959*. Singapore: Malayan Research Services, 1959.

Bureau of Social Science Research, American University. *Communications and Public Opinion in Malaya: A Survey of Selected Sources*. Washington: American University Press, 1954.

Coats, Howard and Frances Dyer. *The Print and Broadcasting Media in Malaysia*. Kuala Lumpur: South East Asian Press Centre, 1972. (Mimeograph)

Glattbach, Jack. *The State of the Press in East Malaysia: A Short Survey for the South East Asia Press Centre, Kuala Lumpur, and the Press Foundation of Asia*. Kuala Lumpur: South East Asian Press Centre, 1970.

——— and Mike Anderson. *The Print and Broadcasting Media in Malaysia*. Kuala Lumpur: South East Asian Press Centre, 1971. (Mimeograph)

Grenfell, Newell. *Switch On: Switch Off. Mass Media Audiences in Malaysia*. Kuala Lumpur: Oxford University Press, 1979.

Lent, John A. *Asian Mass Communications: A Comprehensive Bibliography, 1977 Supplement*. Philadelphia: Temple University, School of Communications and Theater, 1978.

———. "Malaysian Chinese and Their Mass Media: History and Survey," *Asian Profile*, Vol. 2, 1974: 397–412.

———. "Malaysian Broadcasting: Guided Media in Operation," in: *Pacific Nations Broadcasting III and Bibliography*, Benjamin Draper (ed). San Francisco: San Francisco State University, 1974: 19–24.

———. "Malaysian Indians and Their Mass Media," *South East Asian Studies* (Kyoto, Japan), Vol. 12, 1974: 344–49.

———. "Asian Mass Communications: Selected Information Sources," *Journal of Broadcasting*, Vol. 19, 1975: 321–40.

———. "The Motion Picture in Malaysia: History and Problems," *Asian Profile*, Vol. 4, 1976: 261–70.

———. "Television in Malaysia," *Television Quarterly*, Vol. 13, 1976: 51–55.

———. "The Mass Media in Malaysia," in: *Cultural Pluralism in Malaysia*, John A. Lent (ed). DeKalb: Northern Illinois University, Special Report No. 14, 1977: 32–42.

——— (ed). *Newspapers in Asia: Contemporary Trends and Problems*. Hong Kong: Heinemann Educational Books (Asia), 1982.

Lim Huck Tee. *Mass Communication in Malaysia: An Annotated Bibliography*. Singapore: Asian Mass Communications Research and Information Centre, 1975.

Lim, Pui Huen, P. "Malaysian Newspapers Currently Published," *Perpustakaan Malaysia*, Vol. 1, 1965: 56–61.

Nik Ahmad bin Nik Hassan. "The Malay Press," *Journal of the Malayan Branch Royal Asiatic Society*, Vol. 36, 1963: 37–78.

Roff, William R. "Malay Newspapers," in: *Malaysian Historical Sources*, K.G. Tregonning (ed). Singapore: University of Singapore, History Department, 1962: 95–97.

Singapore University Library. *Malay and Arabic Newspapers*. Singapore, 1966.

Singapore University Library. *English Newspapers Published in Malaysia, Singapore and Brunei*. Singapore, 1966.

Singapore University Library. *Chinese Newspapers on Microfilm*. Singapore, 1968.

Stevenson, Rex. "Cinemas and Censorship in Colonial Malaysia," *Journal of Southeast Asian Studies*, Vol. 5, No. 2, 1974: 209–24.

Subbiah, Rama. *History of Tamil Journalism in Malaysia*. Kuala Lumpur: National Union of Plantation Workers, n.d.

Zainal Abidin b. Ahmad. "Malay Journalism in Malaya," *Journal of the Royal Asiatic Society Malayan Branch*, Vol. 19, 1941: 244–55.

ECONOMY

A. General

Allen, George Cyril and A.G. Donnithorne. *Western Enterprise in Indonesia and Malaya: A Study in Economic Development*. London: Allen & Unwin, 1957.

International Bank for Reconstruction and Development. *The Economic Development of Malaya*. Baltimore: Johns Hopkins University Press, 1955.

Jomo, K.S. *Growth and Structural Change in the Malaysian Economy*. London: Macmillan, 1990.

Kanapathy, V. *The Malaysian Economy: Problems and Prospects*. Singapore: Donald Moore, 1970.

Lim Chong Yah. *Economic Development of Modern Malaya*. Kuala Lumpur: Oxford University Press, 1967.

———. *Economic Structure and Organization*. Singapore: Oxford University Press, 1973.

Lim, David (ed). *Readings on Malaysian Economic Development*. Kuala Lumpur: Oxford University Press, 1975.

———. *Further Readings on Malaysian Economic Development*. Kuala Lumpur: Oxford University Press, 1983.

Lim Lin Lean and Chee Peng Lim (eds). *The Malaysian Economy at the Crossroads: Policy Adjustment or Structural Transformation*. Kuala Lumpur: Malaysian Economic Association and Organizational Resources Sdn. Bhd., 1984.

MALAYSIA; Report on Finance, Commerce, Industry. Kuala Lumpur: Prepared and published by Marketing and P.R. Consultants (Asia) Sdn. Bhd. in Association with A.M. Lederer & Co. Incorp., 1971.

Silcock, T.H. (ed). *Readings in Malayan Economics*. Singapore: Eastern Universities Press, 1961.

Tan Tat Wai. *Income Distribution and Determination in West Malaysia*. Kuala Lumpur: Oxford University Press, 1982.

Wong, John. *ASEAN Economies in Perspective: A Comparative Study of Indonesia, Malaysia, the Philippines, Singapore and Thailand*. London: Macmillan, 1979.

Young, Kevin, William C.C. Bussink and Parvez Hasan. *Malaysia: Growth and Equality in a Multi-Racial Society*. Baltimore: Johns Hopkins University Press for the World Bank, 1980.

B. Agriculture and Natural Resources

General

Agricultural Bulletin/Journal. "Classified List of the Principal Original Articles Published in the *Agricultural Bulletin* of the *FMS* and *SS* and the *Malayan Agricultural Journal* for the periods 1913 to 1930," Vols. 1–18. Kuala Lumpur: Caxton Press for the SS. Dept. of Agriculture, 1931.

Bailey, Conner L. *The Sociology of Production in Rural Malay Society*. Kuala Lumpur: Oxford University Press, 1983.

Fatimah Halim. "Differentiation of the Peasantry: A Study of the Rural Communities in West Malaysia," *Journal of Contemporary Asia*, Vol. 10, No. 4, 1980: 400–22.

Gibbons, David, Rudolph de Konick and Ibrahim Hassan. *Agricultural Modernization: Poverty and Inequality*. London: Saxon Press, 1980.

Graham, Edgar and Ingrid Floering. *The Modern Plantation in the Third World*. London: Croom Helm, 1984.

Ho, Robert. *Farmers of Central Malaya*. Department of Geography Publications No. G/4. Canberra: Australian National University Press, 1967.

Hong, Evelyn. "Trade, Crops and Land: The Impact of Colonialism and Modernization in Sarawak," *Sarawak Museum Journal*, Vol. 25, No. 46, 1977: 55–65.

Jackson, James C. *Planters and Speculators: Chinese and European Agricultural Enterprise in Malaya, 1786–1921*. Kuala Lumpur: University of Malaya Press, 1968.

Lim Teck Ghee. *Origins of a Colonial Economy: Land and Agriculture in Perak, 1874–1897*. Penang: Universiti Sains Malaysia Press, 1976.

———. *Peasants and Their Agricultural Economy in Colonial Malaya 1874–1941*. Kuala Lumpur: Oxford University Press, 1977.

Selvadurai, S. *Agriculture in Peninsular Malaysia*, Ministry of Agriculture Bulletin No. 148. Kuala Lumpur: Ministry of Agriculture, 1979.

Senftleben, W. *Backgrounds to Agricultural Land Policy in Malaysia*. Weisbaden: Otto Harrassowitz, 1978.

Forest Resources

Goh, K.C. "Forest Resource Exploitation in Malaysia," *Kajian Malaysia*, Vol. 1, No. 1, 1983: 116–31.

John, David. "The Timber Industry and Forest Administration in Sabah Under Chartered Company Rule," *Journal of Southeast Asian Studies*, Vol. 5, No. 1, 1974: 55–81.

Kumar, Raj. *The Forest Resources of Malaysia: Their Economics and Development*. Singapore: Oxford University Press, 1986.

Oil Palm

Khera, Harcharan Singh. *The Oil Palm Industry in West Malaysia: An Economic Study*. Kuala Lumpur: University of Malaya Press, 1976.

Ng Siew Kee. "Soil Suitability for Oil Palms in West Malaysia," in: *Oil Palm Developments in Malaysia*. Proceedings of the First Oil

Palm Conference, Malaysia organized by the Incorporated Society of Planters, Kuala Lumpur, 1968.

Olie J.J. and T.D. Tjeng. *The Extraction of Palm Oil.* Kuala Lumpur: The Incorporated Society of Planters, 1974.

Williams, C.N. and Y.C. Hsu. *Oil Palm Cultivation in Malaysia: Technical and Economic Aspects.* Kuala Lumpur: University of Malaya Press, 1970.

Petroleum

Harper, G.C. "The Miri Field 1910–1972," *Sarawak Museum Journal*, Vol. 20, Nos. 40–41, 1972: 21–30.

Siddayao, Carazon Morales. *The Off-Shore Petroleum Resources of South-East Asia. Potential Conflict Situations and Related Economic Considerations.* Kuala Lumpur: Oxford University Press, under the auspices of the Institute of Southeast Asian Studies, Singapore, 1978.

Valencia, Mark J. *South-East Asian Seas: Oil Under Troubled Waters. Hydrocarbon Potential Jurisdictional Issues and International Relations.* Singapore: Oxford University Press, 1985.

Rice

Cheng Siok Hwa. "The Rice Industry of Malaya: An Historical Survey", *Journal of the Malaysian Branch Royal Asiatic Society*, Vol. 42, No. 2, 1969: 130–44.

Ding Eing Tan Soo Hai. *The Rice Industry in Malaya, 1920–1940.* Singapore: Malaya Publishing House, 1963.

Doering, Otto Charles III. "Malaysian Rice Policy and the Muda River Irrigation Project," (Ph.D. dissertation, Cornell University, 1973).

Fredericks, L.J. and R.J.G. Wells. *Rice Processing in Peninsular Malaysia: An Economic and Technical Analysis.* Kuala Lumpur: Oxford University Press, 1983.

Fujimoto, Akimi. *Income-Sharing Among Malay Peasants: A Study of Land Tenure and Rice Production*. Singapore: Singapore University Press, 1983.

Grist, Donald Honey. *Rice*. London: Longmans, Green & Co., 1953.

Habsah Hj. Ibrahim and Zainab Awang Ngah. *Bibliografi Aspek-aspek Sosio-Budaya Penanaman dan Penggunaan Padi di Malaysia*. Kuala Lumpur: University of Malaya Library, 1981.

Hill, R.D. *Rice in Malaya: A Study in Historical Geography*. Kuala Lumpur: Oxford University Press, 1977.

Horii, Kenzo. *Rice Economy and Land Tenure in West Malaysia: A Comparative Study of Eight Villages*. Tokyo: Institute of Developing Economies, 1981.

Kratoska, Paul H. "Rice Cultivation and the Ethnic Division of Labour in British Malaya," *Comparative Studies in Society and History*, Vol. 24, No. 2, 1982: 280–314.

Kuchiba, Masuo', Yoshihiro Tsubouchi and Narifumi Maeda. *Three Malay Villages: A Sociology of Padi Growers in West Malaysia*. Honolulu: University of Hawaii Press, 1979. (Monograph of the Center for Southeast Asian Studies, Kyoto University, No. 14)

Lai, K.C. "Income Distribution Among Farm Households in the Muda Irrigation Scheme: A Developmental Perspective," *Kajian Ekonomi Malaysia*, Vol. 15, No. 1, 1978: 38–57.

Purcal, John T. *Rice Economy Employment and Income in Malaysia*. Honolulu: University of Hawaii Press, 1972.

Rubber

Barlow, Colin. *The Natural Rubber Industry: Its Development, Technology, and Economy in Malaysia*. Kuala Lumpur: Oxford University Press, 1978.

Bauer, Peter Tamas. *The Rubber Industry: A Study of Competition and Monopoly*. London: Longmans Green for the London School of Economics and Political Science, 1948.

Coates, Austin. *The Commerce in Rubber: The First 250 Years*. Singapore: Oxford University Press, 1987.

Drabble, J.H. "Investment in the Rubber Industry in Malaya in 1900–1922," *Journal of Southeast Asian Studies*, Vol. 3, No. 2, 1972: 247–61.

———. *Rubber in Malaya 1876–1922: the Genesis of the Industry*. Kuala Lumpur: Oxford University Press, 1973.

———. "Peasant Smallholders in the Malayan Economy: An Historical Study with Special Reference to the Rubber Industry," in: *Issues in Malaysian Development*, James C. Jackson and Martin Rudner (eds). Singapore: Heinemann Educational Books (Asia) for the Asian Studies Association of Australia, 1979: 69–99.

———. *Malayan Rubber: The Interwar Years*. London: Macmillan, 1991.

Reksopoetranto S. and G.S. Tan (eds). *The Progress and Development of Rubber Smallholders: Proceedings of the Third Seminar 1977*. Kuala Lumpur: Association of the Natural Rubber Countries, 1979.

Rudner, Martin. "Rubber Strategy for Post-War Malaya, 1945–48," *Journal of Southeast Asian Studies*, Vol. 1, No. 1, 1970: 23–36.

———. "Development Policies and Patterns of Agrarian Dominance in the Malaysian Rubber Export Economy," *Modern Asian Studies*, Vol. 15, Part 1, 1981: 83–105.

Voon Phin Keong. *Western Rubber Planting Enterprise in Southeast Asia 1876–1921*. Kuala Lumpur: University of Malaya Press, 1976.

Sago

Tan Koon Lin. *The Swamp-Sago Industry in West Malaysia: A Study of the Sungei Batu Pahat Floodplain*. Singapore: Institute of Southeast Asian Studies, 1983.

Tapioca

Jackson, James C. "Tapioca: A Plantation Crop which preceded Rubber in Malaya," *Malaysia in History*, Vol. 10, 1967.

Tobacco

John, David and James C. Jackson. "The Tobacco Industry of North Borneo: A Distinctive Form of Plantation Agriculture," *Journal of Southeast Asian Studies*, Vol. 4, No.1, 1973: 88–106.

C. Mineral Resources

Harris, Henry G.B. and E.S. Willbourn. *Mining in Malaya*. London: Malayan Information Agency, 1940.

Jomo, K.S. (ed). *Undermining Tin: The decline of Malaysian pre-eminence*. Sydney: Transnational Corporations Research Project, 1990.

Kaur, Amarjit. "Hewers and Haulers: A History of Coal Miners and Coal Mining in Malaya," *Modern Asian Studies*, Vol. 24, No. 1, 1990: 75–113.

Krause, Lawrence B. and Hugh Patrick (eds). *Mineral Resources in the Pacific Area: Papers and Proceedings of the Ninth Pacific Trade and Development Conference, San Francisco, August 1977*. San Francisco: Federal Research Bank of San Francisco, 1978.

Robertson, William. *Tin: Its Production and Marketing*. London: Croom Helm, 1982.

Thoburn, John. "Commodity Prices and Appropriate Technology—Some Lessons from Tin Mining," *Journal of Development Studies*, Vol. 14, No. 1, 1977: 35–52.

———. *Multinationals, Mining and Development: A Study of the Tin Industry*. Farnborough: Gower Publishing, 1981.

Wong Lin Ken. *The Malayan Tin Industry to 1914*. Tucson: University of Arizona Press, 1965.

Yip Yat Hoong. *The Development of the Tin Mining Industry of Malaya*. Kuala Lumpur: University of Malaya Press, 1969.

D. Business and Trade

Brown, C.P. *Primary Commodity Control.* Kuala Lumpur: Oxford University Press, 1975.

Bumiputra Trade Directory of Malaysia. Kuala Lumpur: Berita Publishing Sdn. Bhd., 1978.

The Chartered Bank, Malaysia. *Malaysia, the Businessman's Guide.* Kuala Lumpur: The Chartered Bank, 1973.

Chew Fook Yew, Alan. *The Malaysian Balance of Payments 1960–1970*. Kuala Lumpur: University of Malaya Press, 1975.

Cunyngham-Brown, Sjovald. *The Traders: A Story of Britain's South-East Asian Commercial Adventure*. London: Newman Neame Ltd. for Guthrie and Company, 1971.

Doing Business in Malaysia, March 1975. Kuala Lumpur: SGV-Kassim Chan Sdn. Bhd., 1975.

Edwards, C.T. *Public Finances in Malaysia and Singapore*. Canberra: Australian National University Press, 1970.

Gale, Bruce. *Politics and Business: A Study of Multi-purpose Holdings Berhad*. Petaling Jaya: Eastern Universities Press, 1985.

Jesudasan, James V. *Ethnicity and the Economy: The State, Chinese Business and Multinationals in Malaysia*. Singapore: Oxford University Press, 1989.

K.A. Mohamed Ariff. *Export Trade and the West Malaysian Economy—An Enquiry into the Economic Implications of Export Instability*. Kuala Lumpur: Faculty of Economics and Administration, University of Malaya, 1972. (Monograph Series on Malaysian Economic Affairs)

Khor Kok Peng. *Recession and the Malaysian Economy*. Penang: Institut Masyarakat, 1983.

Lee, Edwin. *The Towkays of Sabah*. Singapore: Singapore University Press, 1976.

Lim, David. "Export Instability and Economic Development in West Malaysia 1947–1968," *Malayan Economic Review*, Vol. 17, No. 2, 1972: 99–113.

Lim Mah Hui. *Ownership and Control of the One Hundred Largest Corporations in Malaysia*. Kuala Lumpur: Oxford University Press, 1981.

Schmitt-Rink, Gerhard (ed). *Malaysia's Foreign Trade 1968–80, Trends and Structures*. Bochum: Studienverlag Brockmeyer, 1982.

Sritua Arief and K.S. Jomo (eds). *The Malaysian Economy and Finance*. Sydney: Rosecons, 1983.

Stahl, Kathleen Mary. *The Metropolitan Organization of British Colonial Trade*. London: Faber, 1951.

Thoburn, John T. *Primary Commodity Exports and Economic Development: Theory, Evidence and a Study of Malaysia*. London: John Wiley & Sons, 1977.

Wong Lin Ken. "The Trade of Singapore, 1819–1869," *Journal of the Malayan Branch Royal Asiatic Society*, Vol. 33, No. 4, 1960.

E. Development

Abdul Aziz bin Abdul Hamid, Ungku. *Footprints on the Sands of Time—The Malay Poverty Concept over 50 Years from Za'ba to Aziz and the Second Malaysia Plan*. Kuala Lumpur: Persatuan Ekonomi Malaysia, 1974.

Afifuddin Haji Omar. *Peasants, Institutions and Development in West Malaysia: The Political Economy of Development in the Muda Region*. Alor Setar: Muda Agriculture Development Authority, 1978.

Anand, Sudhir. *Inequality and Poverty in Malaysia: Measurement and Decomposition*. New York: Oxford University Press for the World Bank, 1983.

Carlson, Sevinc. *Malaysia: A Search for National Unity and Economic Growth*. Beverly Hills: Sage Publications, 1975.

Chandler, Glenn, Norma Sullivan and Jan Branson. *Development and Displacement: Women in Southeast Asia*. Monash: Center of Southeast Asian Studies, Monash University, 1988. (Monash Papers on Southeast Asia, No. 18)

Chee Peng Lim, Stephen. *Rural Local Government and Rural Development in Malaysia*. Ithaca: Cornell University Press, 1974. (Special Series on Rural Local Government No. 9)

——— and Khoo Siew Mun (eds). *Malaysian Economic Development and Policies*. Kuala Lumpur: Malaysian Economic Association, 1975.

Chee Peng Lim, Stephen, M.C. Puthucheary and Donald Lee. *A Study of Small Entrepreneurs and Entrepreneurial Development Programmes in Malaysia*. Kuala Lumpur: University of Malaya Press, 1979.

Cheema, G. Shabbir et al. *Rural Organization and Rural Development in Selected Malaysian Villages*. Kuala Lumpur: Asian and Pacific Development Administration Centre, 1978. (Rural Organization Series No. 2)

Cheong Kee Cheok, Khoo Siew Mun and R. Thillainathan (eds). *Malaysia: Some Contemporary Issues in Socioeconomic Development*. Kuala Lumpur: Malaysian Economic Association, 1979.

Cramb, R.A. and R.H.W. Reece. *Development in Sarawak: Historical and Contemporary Perspectives*. Monash: Center of Southeast Asian Studies, Monash University, 1988. (Monash Papers on Southeast Asia, No. 17).

Fifth Malaysia Plan, 1986–1990. Kuala Lumpur: Government Printing Office, 1986.

Fisk, Ernest Kelvin and Osman Rani (eds). *The Political Economy of Malaysia*. Kuala Lumpur: Oxford University Press, 1982.

Golay, Frank H., Ralph Anspach, M. Ruth Pfanner and Eliezer B. Ayal. *Underdevelopment and Economic Nationalism in Southeast Asia*. Ithaca: Cornell University Press, 1969.

Guyot, James F. *The Two Cultures and Malaysia's Development Revolution*. Philadelphia: Association for Asian Studies, 1968.

Jackson, James C. and Martin Rudner (eds). *Issues in Malaysian Development*. Singapore: Heinemann Educational Books (Asia), 1979. (Asian Studies Association of Australia, Southeast Asia Publications Series, No. 3)

Jomo, K.S. *A Question of Class: Capital, the State and Uneven Development in Malaya*. Singapore: Oxford University Press, 1986.

———. *Mahathir's Economic Policies*. Kuala Lumpur: Insan, 1989.

Kaspar, Wolfgang. *Malaysia: A Study of Successful Economic Development*. Washington: American Enterprise Institute for Public Research, 1974.

Lee Soo Ann. *Economic Growth and the Public Sector in Malaya and Singapore 1948–1960*. Kuala Lumpur: Oxford University Press, 1974.

Leigh, Michael. "Is There Development in Sarawak? Political Goals and Practice," in: *Issues in Malaysian Development*, James C. Jackson and Martin Rudner (eds). Singapore: Heinemann Educational Books (Asia) for the Asian Studies Association of Australia, 1979: 339–74.

Li Dun Jen. *British Malaya: An Economic Analysis*. Petaling Jaya: Insan, 1982. (Originally 1955)

Lim, David. *Economic Growth and Development in West Malaysia, 1947–1970*. Kuala Lumpur: Oxford University Press, 1973.

Lim Mah Hui. "Multinational Corporations and Development in Malaysia," *Southeast Asian Journal of Social Science*, Vol. 4, No. 1, 1975: 53–76.

——— and William Canak. "The Political Economy of State Policies in Malaysia," *Journal of Contemporary Asia*, Vol. 11, No. 2, 1981: 208–24.

Manderson, Lenore. "A Woman's Place: Malay Women and Development in Peninsular Malaysia," in: *Issues in Malaysian Development*, James C. Jackson and Martin Rudner (eds). Singapore: Heinemann Educational Books (Asia), for the Asian Studies Association of Australia, 1979: 233–71.

Mills, Lennox A. *Malaya: A Political and Economic Appraisal*. Minneapolis: University of Minnesota Press, 1958.

Milne, R.S. "The Politics of Malaysia's New Economic Policy," *Pacific Affairs*, Vol. 49, No. 2, 1976: 235–62.

Mohd. Shahari Ahmad Jabar. "Rural Poverty and the Malay Peasant: Politics of Survival," (Ph.D. dissertation, University of Hawaii, 1978).

Mokhzani Abdul Rahim and Khoo Siew Mun (eds). *Some Case Studies on Poverty in Malaysia. Essays Presented to Professor Ungku A. Aziz*. Kuala Lumpur: Persatuan Ekonomi Malaysia (Malaysian Economic Association), 1977.

Ness, Gayl D. *Bureaucracy and Rural Development in Malaysia: A Study of Complex Organizations in Stimulating Economic Development in New States*. Berkeley: University of California Press, 1967.

Ozay Mehmet. "Colonialism, Dualistic Growth and the Distribution of Economic Benefits in Malaysia," *Southeast Asian Journal of Social Science*, Vol. 5, Nos. 1–2, 1977: 1–21.

———. *Development in Malaysia: Poverty, Wealth and Trusteeship*. London: Croom Helm, 1986.

Parkinson, Brian K. "Non-economic Factors in the Economic Retardation of the Rural Malays," *Modern Asian Studies*, Vol. 1, Part I, 1967: 31–46.

———. "The Economic Retardation of the Malays—A Rejoinder," *Modern Asian Studies*, Vol. 2, Part 3, 1968: 267–72.

Pauker, Guy J., Frank H. Golay and Cynthia H. Enlow. *Diversity and Development in Southeast Asia: The Coming Decade*. New York: McGraw-Hill, 1977.

Rao, V.V. Bhanoji. *Malaysia: Development Pattern and Policy, 1947–1971*. Singapore: Singapore University Press, 1980.

Rudner, Martin. *Nationalism, Planning and Economic Modernization in Malaysia: The Politics of Beginning Development*. London: Sage Publications, 1975.

Shamsul Amri Baharuddin. "The Development of the Underdevelopment of the Malaysian Peasantry," *Journal of Contemporary Asia*, Vol. 9, No. 4, 1979: 434–54.

———. *From British to Bumiputera Rule: Local Politics and Rural Development in Peninsular Malaysia*. Singapore: Institute of Southeast Asian Studies, 1986.

Short, David Eric. "Some Aspects of the Role of Irrigation in Rural Development in Malaya," (Ph.D. dissertation, University of Hull, 1971).

Silcock, T.H. and Ungku Abdul Aziz. *The Political Economy of Independent Malaya: A Case Study in Development*. Berkeley: University of California Press, 1963.

Snodgrass, Donald R. *Inequality and Economic Development in Malaysia*. Kuala Lumpur: Oxford University Press, 1980.

——— and R.J.G. Wells (eds). *The Fourth Malaysia Plan: Economic Perspectives*. Kuala Lumpur: Persatuan Ekonomi Malaysia, 1983.

Syed Husin Ali. *Poverty and Landlessness in Kelantan, Malaysia*. Saarbrucken: Breitenbach, 1983. (Bielefeld Studies on the Sociology of Development, Vol. 20)

——— (ed). *Ethnicity, Class and Development, Malaysia*. Kuala Lumpur: Persatuan Sains Sosial Malaysia, 1984.

——— (co-ordinator). *Bibliography on Poverty in Malaysia*. Kuala Lumpur: University of Malaya Library, 1986.

Tan, Gerald. "Multinational Corporations and Development in Malaysia: A Comment," *Southeast Asian Journal of Social Science*, Vol. 6, Nos. 1–2, 1978: 27–36.

Thillainathan, R. "The Second Malaysia Plan. Notes on the Objectives of Balanced Distribution of Wealth and Employment," *Kajian Ekonomi Malaysia*, Vol. 7, No. 2, 1970: 57–71.

Ungku A. Aziz. "Poverty and Rural Development in Malaysia," *Kajian Ekonomi Malaysia*, Vol. 1, No. 1, 1964: 70–105.

F. Finance

Chee Peng Lim, Phang Siew Nooi and Margaret Boh. "The History and Development of the Hongkong and Shanghai Banking Corporation in Peninsular Malaysia," in: *Eastern Banking: Essays on the History of the Hongkong and Shanghai Banking Corporation*, Frank H.H. King (ed). London: Athlone Press, 1983: 350–91.

Drake, P.J. *Financial Development in Malaya and Singapore*. Canberra: Australian National University Press, 1969.

Edwards, C.T. *Public Finances in Malaya and Singapore*. Canberra: Australian National University Press, 1970.

Firth, Raymond and B.S. Yanney (eds). *Capital, Saving and Credit in Peasant Societies: Studies from Asia, Oceania, the Caribbean and Middle America*. London: Allen & Unwin, 1964.

Lee Sheng Yi. *The Monetary and Banking Development of Malaysia and Singapore*. Singapore: Singapore University Press, 1974.

Lee Soo Ann. "Fiscal Policy and Political Transition: The Case of Malaya, 1948–1960," *Journal of Southeast Asian Studies*, Vol. 5, No. 1, 1974: 102–14.

Lim Mah Hui. *Ownership and Control of the One Hundred Largest Corporations in Malaysia*. Kuala Lumpur: Oxford University Press, 1981.

Mann, Lewis. "Some Effects of Foreign Investment: The Case of Malaysia," *Bulletin of Concerned Asian Scholars*, Vol. 9, No. 4, 1977: 2–14.

Meerman, Jacob. *Public Expenditure in Malaysia: Who Benefits and Why*. New York: Oxford University Press for the World Bank, 1979.

Popenoe, Oliver. "Malay Entrepreneurs," (Ph.D. dissertation, London School of Economics, 1970).

Puthucheary, J.J. *Ownership and Control in the Malayan Economy*. Singapore: Eastern Universities Press, 1960.

Shome, Parthasarthi (ed). *Fiscal Issues in South-East Asia*. Singapore: Oxford University Press, 1985.

Singh, Supriya. *Bank Negara Malaysia: The First 25 Years 1959–1984*. Kuala Lumpur: Bank Negara Malaysia, 1984.

Skully, Michael T. (ed). *Financial Institutions and Markets in Southeast Asia: A Study of Brunei, Indonesia, Malaysia, Philippines, Singapore and Thailand*. London: Macmillan, 1984.

———. *Merchant Banking in ASEAN: A Regional Examination of its Development and Operations*. Singapore: Oxford University Press, 1985.

Yoshihara Kunio. *The Rise of Ersatz Capitalism in South-East Asia*. Singapore: Oxford University Press, 1988.

Zeti Akhtar Aziz. "Financial Institutions and Markets in Malaysia," in: *Financial Institutions and Markets in Southeast Asia: A Study of Brunei, Indonesia, Malaysia, Philippines, Singapore and Thailand*, Michael T. Skully (ed). London: Macmillan, 1984: 110–66.

G. Industry

Bell, Philip W. *Industrial Growth and Economic Development in Malaysia*. Penang: Universiti Sains Malaysia Press, 1977.

Edwards, Christopher, B. "Protection, Profits and Policy—An Analysis of Industrialization in Malaysia," (Ph.D. dissertation, University of East Anglia, 1975).

Fong Chan Onn. *Technological Leap: Malaysian Industry in Transition*. Singapore: Oxford University Press, 1985.

Gale, Bruce. *Politics and Public Enterprise in Malaysia*. Singapore: Eastern Universities Press, 1981.

Hirschman, Charles. "Industrial and Occupational Change in Peninsular Malaysia, 1947–70," *Journal of Southeast Asian Studies*, Vol. 13, No. 1, 1982: 9–32.

Hoffman, Lutz and Tan Siew Ee. *Industrial Growth, Employment and Foreign Investment in Peninsular Malaysia*. Kuala Lumpur: Oxford University Press, 1980.

Junid Saham. *British Industrial Investment in Malaysia 1963–1971*. Kuala Lumpur: Oxford University Press, 1980.

Spinanger, Dean. *Industrialization Policies and Regional Economic Development in Malaysia*. Singapore: Oxford University Press, 1986.

Suriyamongkol, Majorie L. *Politics of ASEAN Economic Co-operation: The Case of ASEAN Industrial Projects*. Singapore: Oxford University Press, 1988.

Tan, Gerald. "Foreign Investment and Employment Generation in Malaysia," *Kajian Ekonomi Malaysia*, Vol. 15, No. 1, 1978: 19–24.

Von der Mehden, Fred R. "Communalism, Industrial Policy and Income Distribution in Malaysia," *Asian Survey*, Vol. 15, No. 3, 1975: 247–61.

Wheelright, Edward Lawrence. *Industrialization in Malaysia*. Melbourne: Melbourne University Press, 1975.

H. Labor and Trade Unions

Awberry, A.S. and F.W. Dalley. *Labour and Trade Union Organization in the Federation of Malaya and Singapore*. Kuala Lumpur: Government Printing Office, 1948.

Blythe, W.L. "Historical Sketch of Chinese Labour in Malaya," *Journal of the Malayan Branch Royal Asiatic Society*, Vol. 20, No. 1, 1947: 13–25.

Fatimah Halim. "Rural Labour Force and Industrial Conflict in West Malaysia," *Journal of Contemporary Asia*, Vol. II, No. 3, 1981: 271–96.

———. "Capital, Labour and the State: The West Malaysian Case," *Journal of Contemporary Asia*, Vol. 12, No. 3, 1982: 259–80.

———. "Workers' Resistance and Management Control: A Comparative Case Study of Male and Female Workers in West Malaysia," *Journal of Contemporary Asia*, Vol. 13, No. 2, 1983: 131–50.

Gamba, Charles. *Labour Law in Malaya*. Singapore: Donald Moore, 1955.

———. *The Origins of Trade Unionism in Malaya: A Study in Colonial Labour Unrest*. Singapore: Eastern Universities Press, 1962.

———. *The National Union of Plantation Workers. The History of the Plantation Workers of Malaya 1946–1958*. Singapore: Donald Moore for Eastern Universities Press, 1962.

Gilman, E.W.F. *Labour in British Malaya*. Singapore: Fraser and Neave, 1923.

Hing Ai Yun. "Women and Work in West Malaysia," *Journal of Contemporary Asia*, Vol. 14, No. 2, 1984: 204–18.

——— and Rokiah Talib (eds). *Women and Employment in Malaysia*. Kuala Lumpur: Department of Anthropology and Sociology, University of Malaya, 1986.

Hirschman, Charles. "A Note on Labour Underutilization in Peninsular Malaysia, 1970," *Malayan Economic Review*, Vol. 24, No. 2, 1979: 89–104.

——— and Akbar Aghajanian. "Women's Labour Force Participation and Socio-economic Development: The Case of Peninsular Malaysia, 1957–1970," *Journal of Southeast Asian Studies*, Vol. 11, No. 1, 1980: 30–49.

Jackson, Robert Nicholas. *Immigrant Labour and the Development of Malaya, 1786–1920*. Kuala Lumpur: Government Printing Office, 1961.

Jain, R.K. *South Indians on the Plantation Frontier in Malaya*. New Haven: Yale University Press, 1970.

Kaur, Amarjit. "Women at Work in Malaysia," in: *Women and Employment in Malaysia*, Hing Ai Yun and Rokiah Talib (eds). Kuala Lumpur: Dept. of Anthropology and Sociology, University of Malaya, 1986: 1–16.

———. "Working on the Railway: Indian Workers in Malaya 1880–1957," in: *Pullers, Planters, Plantation Workers . . . The Underside of Malaysian History*, Peter Rimmer and Lisa Allen (eds). Singapore: Singapore University Press, 1990: 99–127.

Mazumdar, Dipak. *The Urban Labor Market and Income Distribution: A Study of Malaysia*. New York: Oxford University Press for the World Bank, 1981.

Neelakandha Aiyer, K.A. *Indian Problems in Malaya*. Kuala Lumpur: Indian Office, 1938.

Parmer, J.N. *Colonial Labor Policy and Administration: A History of Labor in the Rubber Plantation Industry in Malaya, c. 1910–1941*. Locust Valley: J.J. Augustin for the Association for Asian Studies, 1960.

Rudner, Martin. "Malayan Labour in Transition. Labour Policy and Trade Unionism, 1955–63," *Modern Asian Studies*, Vol. 7, Part 1, 1973: 21–45.

Shimaoka, Helene R. (comp.). *Selected Bibliographies on Labor and Industrial Relations in Burma, Indonesia, Korea, Malaya, Singapore, Thailand*. Honolulu: University of Hawaii Press, 1962.

Snodgrass, Donald R. "Growth and Utilization of Malaysian Labour Supply," *Philippine Economic Journal*, No. 30, Vol. 15, Nos. 1–2, 1976: 273–313.

Stenson, Michael. *Industrial Conflict in Malaya: Prelude to the Communist Revolt of 1948*. London: Oxford University Press, 1970.

Thillainathan, R. "Inter-racial Balance in Malaysian Employment and Wealth: An Evaluation of Distributional Targets," *The Developing Economies* (Tokyo), Vol. 14, No. 3, 1976: 239–60.

———. "The Twenty-year Plan for Restructuring Employment in Peninsular Malaysia: A Quarterly Assessment," *Kajian Ekonomi Malaysia*, Vol. 14, No. 2, 1977: 49–62.

Thompson, Virginia McLean. *Notes on Labor Problems in Malaya*. New York: Institute of Pacific Relations, 1945.

Tinker, Hugh. *A New System of Slavery: The Export of Indian Labour Overseas 1830–1920*. London: Oxford University Press, 1974.

Zaidi, S.J.H. *Malaysian Trades Union Congress 1949–1974*. Petaling Jaya: Malaysian Trades Union Congress, 1975.

I. Land and Land Settlement Schemes

Ahmad Nazri Abdullah. *Melayu dan Tanah*. Petaling Jaya: Media Intelek, 1985.

Das, Sudhir Kumar. *The Torrens System in Malaya*. Singapore: Malayan Law Journal, 1963.

Ho, Robert. "Land Settlement Projects in Malaya: An Assessment of the Role of the Federal Land Development Authority," *The Journal of Tropical Geography*, Vol. 20, 1965: 1–15.

———. "Land Ownership and Economic Prospects of Malayan Peasants," *Modern Asian Studies*, Vol. 4, Part 1, 1970: 83–92.

Kratoska, Paul H. "Ends that We Cannot Foresee: Malay Reservations in British Malaya," *Journal of Southeast Asian Studies*, Vol. 14, 1983.

Lim Sow Ching. *Land Development Schemes in Peninsular Malaysia: A Study of Benefits and Costs*. Kuala Lumpur: Rubber Research Institute of Malaysia, 1976.

MacAndrews, Colin. *Mobility and Modernisation: The Federal Land Development Authority and Its Role in Modernising the Rural Malay*. Yogyakarta: Gadjah Mada University Press, 1977.

Porter, A.F. *Land Administration in Sarawak, 1841–1967*. Kuching: Government Printing Office, 1967.

Tunku Shamsul Bahrin and P.D.A. Perera. *FELDA—21 Years of Land Development*. Kuala Lumpur: Federal Land Development Authority, 1977.

———, ——— and Lim Heng Kow. *Land Development and Resettlement in Malaysia*. Kuala Lumpur: Department of Geography, University of Malaya, 1979.

Wong, David. *Tenure and Land Dealings in the Malay States*. Singapore: Singapore University Press, 1975.

J. Transport and Communications

Asian Development Bank. *Southeast Asian Regional Transport Survey*. Singapore: Straits Times Press, 1972–3.

Kaur, Amarjit. "The Impact of Railroads on the Malayan Economy, 1874–1941," *Journal of Asian Studies*, Vol. 39, No. 4, 1980: 693–710.

———. *Bridge and Barrier: Transport and Communications in Colonial Malaya 1870–1957*. Singapore: Oxford University Press, 1985.

———. *Seabad Keretapi di Malaysia* (A Century of Railways in Malaysia). Kuala Lumpur: Persatuan Muzium Malaysia, 1985.

Leinbach, T.R. "Transportation and Modernization in Malaya," (Ph.D. dissertation, Pennsylvania State University, 1971).

——— and Chia Lin Sien. *South-East Asian Transport Issues in Development*. Singapore: Oxford University Press, 1989.

Pendakur, V. Setty. *Urban Transport in South and Southeast Asia. An Annotated Bibliography*. Singapore: Institute of Southeast Asian Studies, Library Bulletin, No. 15, 1984.

HISTORY AND HISTORIOGRAPHY

A. Historiography

Cowan, C.D. and O.W. Wolters (eds). *Southeast Asian History and Historiography: Essays Presented to D.G.E. Hall*. Ithaca: Cornell University Press, 1976.

Drake, P.J. "The Economic Development of British Malaya to 1914: An Essay in Historiography with Some Questions for Historians," *Journal of Southeast Asian Studies*, Vol. 10, No. 2, 1979: 262–90.

Khoo Kay Kim. "Recent Malaysian Historiography," *Journal of Southeast Asian Studies*, Vol. 10, No. 2, 1979: 247–61.

———. "Local Historians and the Writing of Malaysian History in the Twentieth Century," in: *Perceptions of the Past in Southeast Asia*, Anthony Reid and David Marr (eds). Singapore: Heinemann Educational Books (Asia), 1979.

Muhammad Yusoff Hashim. *Persejarahan Melayu Nusantara*. Kuala Lumpur: Teks Publishers, 1988.

Stockwell, A.J. "The Historiography of Malaysia: Recent Writings in English on the History of the Area Since 1874," *Journal of Imperial and Commonwealth History*, Vol. 5, No. 1, 1976: 82–110.

Sullivan, Patrick. "A Critical Appraisal of Historians of Malaya: The Theory of Society Implicit in Their Work," in: *Southeast Asia: Essays in the Political Economy of Structural Change*, Richard Higgot and Richard Robison (eds). London: Routledge & Kegan Paul, 1985: 65–92.

B. History

The Malay Peninsula and Borneo Prior to British Colonial Rule (up to 1874)

Andaya, Barbara Watson. *Perak: The Abode of Grace—A Study of An Eighteenth Century Malay State*. Kuala Lumpur: Oxford University Press, 1979.

Andaya, Leonard Y. *The Kingdom of Johor 1641–1728: Economic and Political Developments*. Kuala Lumpur: Oxford University Press, 1975.

Bonney, R. *Kedah, 1771–1821: The Search for Security and Independence*. Kuala Lumpur: Oxford University Press, 1971.

Brown, C.C. *Sejarah Melayu, Malay Annals. Journal of the Malayan Branch Royal Asiatic Society*, Vol. 25, Parts 2 and 3, 1952.

Crawford, John. *History of the Indian Archipelago: Containing An Account of the Manners, Arts, Languages, Religions, Institutions and Commerce of Its Inhabitants*. Edinburgh: Constable, 1820.

de Sa' de Meneses, Francisco. *The Conquest of Malacca*. Translated by Edgar C. Knowlton. Kuala Lumpur: University of Malaya Press, 1970.

Gullick, J.M. *Indigenous Political Systems of Western Malaya*. London: Athlone Press, 1958.

Hall, K.R. *Maritime Trade and State Development in Early Southeast Asia*. Honolulu: University of Hawaii Press, 1985.

Irwin, Graham. *Nineteenth Century Borneo: A Study of Diplomatic Rivalry*. Singapore: Donald Moore, 1955.

Meilink-Roelofz, M.A.P. *Asian Trade and European Influence in the Indonesian Archipelago between 1500 and about 1630*. The Hague: Martinus Nijhoff, 1962.

Milner, A.C. *Kerajaan: Malay Political Culture on the eve of colonial rule*. Tucson: University of Arizona Press, 1982.

Muhammad Yusoff Hashim. *Kesultanan Melayu Melaka*. Kuala Lumpur: Dewan Bahasa dan Pustaka, 1989.

Raja Ali Haji Ibn. Ahmad. *The Precious Gift* (Tuhfat al-Nafis) (an annotated translation by Virginia Matheson and Barbara Watson Andaya). Kuala Lumpur: Oxford University Press, 1982.

Reid, Anthony J.S. *Southeast Asia in the Age of Commerce 1450–1680. Vol. 1. The Lands below the Winds*. New Haven: Yale University Press, 1988.

——— and J. Brewster (eds). *Slavery, Bondage and Dependency in Southeast Asia*. St. Lucia: Queensland University Press, 1983.

——— and Lance Castles (eds). *Pre-Colonial State Systems in Southeast Asia*. Monograph No. 6, Malaysian Branch Royal Asiatic Society. Kuala Lumpur, 1975.

Rubin, Alfred P. *The International Personality of the Malay Peninsula: A Study of the International Law of Imperialism*. Kuala Lumpur: University of Malaya Press, 1974.

Sardesai, D.R. "The Portugese Administration in Malacca, 1511–1641," *Journal of Southeast Asian History*, Vol. 10, No. 3, 1969: 501–12.

Sharon Ahmat. *Tradition and Change in a Malay State: A Study of the Economic and Political Development of Kedah 1878–1923*. Monograph No. 12, Malaysian Branch Royal Asiatic Society. Kuala Lumpur, 1984.

Sullivan, Patrick. *Social Relations of Dependence in a Malay State: Nineteenth Century Perak*. Monograph No. 10, Malaysian Branch Royal Asiatic Society. Kuala Lumpur, 1982.

Trocki, Carl. *Prince of Pirates: the Temenggongs and the Development of Johor and Singapore, 1784–1885*. Singapore: Singapore University Press, 1979.

Wake, Christopher H. "Malacca's Early Kings and the reception of Islam," *Journal of Southeast Asian History*, Vol. 5, No. 2, 1964: 104–28.

Wang, Gungwu. The Opening of Relations Between China and Malacca, 1403–5. Oxford: Clarendon Press, 1964.

Wheatley, Paul. *The Golden Khersonese.* Kuala Lumpur: University of Malaya Press, 1961.

———. *Impressions of the Malay Peninsula in Ancient Times.* Singapore: Eastern Universities Press, 1964.

Wolters, O.W. *The Fall of Srivijaya in Malay History.* Kuala Lumpur: Oxford University Press, 1970.

Peninsular Malaya, Sabah and Sarawak during the Period of Colonial Rule to 1941

Allen, Charles and Michael Mason. *Tales from the South China Seas. Images of the British, in South-East Asia in the twentieth century.* London: Andre Deutsch and the British Broadcasting Corporation, 1983.

Arasaratnam, Sinnappah. *Indians in Malaysia and Singapore.* Kuala Lumpur: Oxford University Press, 1979.

Baker, Michael H. *Sabah: The First Ten Years as a Colony, 1946–1956.* Singapore: University of Singapore Press, 1965.

Baring-Gould, S. and Bampfylde, C.A. *A History of Sarawak under its Two White Rajahs.* Introduction by Nicholas Tarling. Singapore: Oxford University Press, 1989. (Originally 1909)

Barr, Pat. *Taming the jungle. The men who made British Malaya.* London: Secker & Warburg, 1977.

Bhar, Supriya. "Sandakan. Gun-running village to timber centre, 1879–1979," *Journal of the Malaysian Branch Royal Asiatic Society*, Vol. 53, No. 1, 1980: 120–49.

Black, Ian. *A Gambling Style of Government: The Establishment of Chartered Company Rule in Sabah, 1878–1915.* Kuala Lumpur: Oxford University Press, 1983.

Brimmell, J.H. *Communism in Southeast Asia: A Political Analysis.* London: Oxford University Press for the Royal Institute of International Affairs, 1959.

British Association of Malaya. *Documents and Papers Received from the British Association of Malaya History Archives (up to 9th February, 1962)*. London: 1962–. (Documents deposited in the Library of the Royal Commonwealth Society)

Brooke, Charles. *Ten Years in Sarawak*. London: Tinsley, 1866.

Brooke, Margaret. *My Life in Sarawak*. Singapore: Oxford University Press, 1986. (Originally 1913)

Brownfoot, Janice N. "Memsahibs in Colonial Malaya: A Study of European wives in a British colony and protectorate 1900–1940," in: *The Incorporated Wife*, Hilary Callen and Shirley Ardener (eds). London: Croom Helm, 1984: 186–210.

Buckley, C.B. *An Anecdotal History of Old Times in Singapore*. Singapore: University of Malaya Press, 1965.

Burns, P.L. (ed). *The Journals of J.W.W. Birch, First British Resident to Perak 1874–1875*. Kuala Lumpur: Oxford University Press, 1976.

——— and C.D. Cowan (eds). *Swettenham's Malayan Journals 1874–1876*. Kuala Lumpur: Oxford University Press, 1975.

Butcher, John. *The British in Malaya 1880–1941*. Kuala Lumpur: Oxford University Press, 1971.

———. "The Demise of the Revenue Farm System in the Federated Malay States," *Modern Asian Studies*, Vol. 17, Part 3, 1983: 387–412.

Cant, R.G. *An Historical Geography of Pahang*. Monograph No. 4, Malaysian Branch Royal Asiatic Society. Kuala Lumpur, 1973.

Chai Hon Chan. *The Development of British Malaya 1896–1909*. Kuala Lumpur: Oxford University Press, 1967.

Cheah Boon Kheng. *The Peasant Robbers of Kedah 1900–1929: Historical and Folk Perceptions*. Singapore: Oxford University Press, 1988.

Chew, Daniel. *Chinese Pioneers on the Sarawak Frontier 1841–1941*. Singapore: Oxford University Press, 1989.

Chew, Ernest. "Sir Frank Swettenham and the Federation of the Malay States," *Modern Asian Studies*, Vol. 2, Part 1, 1968: 51–69.

Chin, J.M. *The Sarawak Chinese*. Kuala Lumpur: Oxford University Press, 1981.

Cloake, John. *Templer, Tiger of Malaya: The Life of Field Marshal Sir Gerald Templer*. London: Harrap, 1985.

Cowan, C.D. *Nineteenth century Malaya: Origins of British Political Control*. London: Oxford University Press, 1967.

Crisswell, Colin. *Rajah Charles Brooke: Monarch of All He Surveyed*. Kuala Lumpur: Oxford University Press, 1978.

Cunyngham-Brown, Sjovald. *The Traders: A Story of Britain's South-East Asian Commercial Adventure*. London: Newman Neame for Guthrie & Company, 1971.

Dalton, Clive (pseud.) [i.e. Frederick Stephen Clark]. *Men of Malaya*. London: Eldon Press, 1942.

Drabble, J.H. "Some thoughts on the economic development of Malaya under British administration," *Journal of Southeast Asian Studies*, Vol. 5, No. 2, 1974: 199–208.

——— and P.J. Drake. "The British Agency Houses in Malaysia: Survival in a changing world," *Journal of Southeast Asian Studies*, Vol. 12, No. 2, 1981: 297–328.

Emerson, Rupert. *Malaysia: A Study of Direct and Indirect Rule*. Kuala Lumpur: University of Malaya Press, 1966.

Gullick, J.M. *The Story of Kuala Lumpur (1857–1939)*. Singapore: Eastern Universities Press, 1983.

———. *Malay Society in the Late Nineteenth Century: The Beginnings of Change*. Singapore: Oxford University Press, 1987.

——— and Gerald Hawkins. *Malayan Pioneers*. Singapore: Eastern Universities Press, 1958.

Hahn, Emily. *James Brooke of Sarawak*. London: Arthur Barker, 1953.

Innes, Emily. *The Chersonese with the gilding off*. Introduction by Khoo Kay Kim. Kuala Lumpur: Oxford University Press, 1974.

Kennedy, J. *A History of Malaya: AD 1400–1959*. Kuala Lumpur: Macmillan, 1965.

Khasnor, Johan. *The Emergence of the Modern Malay Administrative Elite*. Singapore: Oxford University Press, 1984.

Khoo Kay Kim. "The Origin of British Administration in Malaya," *Journal of the Malaysian Branch Royal Asiatic Society*, Vol. 39, Part 1, 1966: 52–91.

———. *The Western Malay States 1850–1873: The Effects of Commercial Development on Malay Politics*. Kuala Lumpur: Oxford University Press, 1972.

———. "Malay Society, 1874–1920s," *Journal of Southeast Asian Studies*, Vol. 5, No. 2, 1974: 179–98.

Kratoska, Paul H. *The Chettiar and the Yeoman: British cultural categories and rural indebtedness in Malaya*. Singapore: Institute of Southeast Asian Studies, 1975. (Occasional Paper No. 32)

Lee Poh Ping. *Chinese Society in Nineteenth Century Singapore*. Kuala Lumpur: Oxford University Press, 1978.

Leigh, Michael. *The Chinese Community of Sarawak*. Singapore: Singapore University Press, 1964.

Leong, Cecilia. *Sabah, The First l00 Years*. Kuala Lumpur: Nan Yang Muda, 1982.

Leong, Stephen. "The Kuomintang—Communist united front in Malaya during the National Salvation period 1937–1941," *Journal of Southeast Asian Studies*, Vol. 8, No. 1, 1977: 31–47.

Lim Teck Ghee. *Origins of a Colonial Economy: Land and Agriculture in Perak 1874–1897*. Penang: Universiti Sains Malaysia Press, 1976.

———. *Peasants and their Agricultural Economy in Colonial Malaya 1874–1941*. Kuala Lumpur: Oxford University Press, 1977.

———. "British colonial administration and the ethnic division of labour in Malaysia," *Kajian Malaysia* (Journal of Malaysian Studies), Vol. 2, No. 2, 1984: 28–66.

Lockard, Craig A. "Leadership and power within the Chinese community of Sarawak: A historical survey," *Journal of Southeast Asian Studies*, Vol. 2, No. 2, 1971: 195–217.

Loh Fook Seng, Philip. *The Malay States 1877–1895: Political Change and Social Policy*. Kuala Lumpur: Oxford University Press, 1969.

Low, Hugh. *Sarawak*. Introduction by R.H.W. Reece. Singapore: Oxford University Press, 1988. (Originally 1848)

MacIntyre, D. "Britain's Intervention in Malaya: The origin of Lord Kimberley's instructions to Sir Andrew Clarke in 1873," *Journal of Southeast Asian History*, Vol. 2, No. 3, 1961: 47–69.

Middlebrook, S.M. and J.M. Gullick. "Yap Ah Loy (1837–1885)," *Journal of the Malayan Branch Royal Asiatic Society*, Vol. 24, No. 2, 1951: 1–127.

Mills, Lennox A. *British Malaya 1824–1867*. Kuala Lumpur: Oxford University Press, 1966.

Mohamed Amin (pseud.) and Malcolm Caldwell (eds). *Malaya—The Making of a Neo-Colony*. Nottingham: Spokesman, 1977.

Newbold, T.J. *Political and Statistical Accounts of the British Settlements in the Straits of Malacca*. London: J. Murray, 1839; Reprinted Kuala Lumpur: Oxford University Press, 1971.

Parkinson, Ann and Cyril Northcote Parkinson. *Heroes of Malaya*. Singapore: Donald Moore, 1956.

Parkinson, Cyril Northcote. *British Intervention in Malaya 1867–1877*. Singapore: University of Malaya Press, 1960.

Payne, Robert. *The White Rajahs of Sarawak*. Singapore: Oxford University Press, 1986.

Png Poh Seng. "The Kuomintang in Malaya, 1912–1941," *Journal of Southeast Asian History*, Vol. 2, No. 1, 1961: 1–32.

Pollard, Elizabeth. *Kuching Past and Present*. Kuching: Borneo Literature Bureau, 1972.

Pringle, Robert M. *Rajahs and Rebels: The Ibans of Sarawak Under Brooke rule, 1841–1941*. Ithaca: Cornell University Press, 1970.

Purcell, Victor. *The Chinese in Malaya*. Kuala Lumpur: Oxford University Press, 1967.

Reece, Robert. *The Name of Brooke: The End of White Rajah Rule in Sarawak*. Kuala Lumpur: Oxford University Press, 1982.

Runciman, Steven. *The White Rajahs: A History of Sarawak from 1841–1941*. Cambridge: Cambridge University Press, 1960.

Sadka, Emily. *The Protected Malay States 1874–1895*. Kuala Lumpur: University of Malaya Press, 1968.

Saint, Max. *A flourish for the Bishop, Brooke's friend Grant: Two Studies in Sarawak History, 1848–1868*. Braunton: Merlin Books, 1985.

Sandhu, K.S. and Paul Wheatley (eds). *Melaka: Transformation of a Malay Capital 1400–1980*, 2 volumes. Kuala Lumpur: Oxford University Press, 1982.

Sardesai, D.R. *British Trade and Expansion in Southeast Asia 1830–1914*. New Delhi: Allied Publishers, 1977.

Shaharil Talib. "Voices from the Kelantan Desa 1900–1940," *Modern Asian Studies*, Vol. 17, Part 2, 1983: 177–95.

———. *After Its Own Image: The Trengganu Experience 1881–1941*. Singapore: Oxford University Press, 1984.

Sidhu, Jagjit Singh. *Administration in the Federated Malay States 1896–1920*. Kuala Lumpur: Oxford University Press, 1980.

Singh, I.J. Bahadur (ed). *Indians in Southeast Asia*. New Delhi: Sterling Publishers, 1982.

Singh, Ranjit. "The Development of Indigenous Society and Administration in Sabah, 1865–1941," (Ph. D. dissertation, University of Malaya, 1986).

Stenson, Michael. *Industrial Conflict in Malaya: Prelude to the Communist Revolt in 1948*. London: Oxford University Press, 1970.

———. *Class, Caste and Conflict among the Indians in Colonial Malaya*. St. Lucia: University of Queensland Press, 1980.

Stockwell, A.J. "The white man's burden and brown humanity: colonialism and ethnicity in British Malaya," *Southeast Asian Journal of Social Science*, Vol. 10, No. 1, 1982: 44–68.

Sullivan, A. and C. Leong (eds). *Commemorative History of Sabah, 1881–1981*. Kota Kinabalu: Sabah State Government, Centenary Publications Committee, 1981.

Swettenham, Sir Frank Athelstone. *British Malaya: An Account of the Origin and Progress of British Influence in Malaya*. London: John Lane, 1906, 2nd rev. ed. with a new chapter entitled: *Twenty Five Years After*. London, 1929.

———. *Stories and Sketches*. W.R. Roff (ed). Kuala Lumpur: Oxford University Press, 1967.

Tarling, Nicholas. *Piracy and Politics in the Malay World: A Study of British Imperialism in Nineteenth-Century South-East Asia*. Melbourne: F.W. Cheshire, 1963.

———. *British Policy in the Malay Peninsula and Archipelago, 1824–1871*. Monograph, Malaysian Branch Royal Asiatic Society. Kuala Lumpur, 1969.

———. *Britain, The Brookes, and Brunei*. London: Oxford University Press, 1971.

———. *Sulu and Sabah: A Study of British Policy Towards the Philippines and North Borneo From the Late Eighteenth Century*. Kuala Lumpur: Oxford University Press, 1978.

———. *The Burthen, the Risk, and the Glory: A Biography of Sir James Brooke*. Kuala Lumpur: Oxford University Press, 1982.

Thio, Eunice. *British Policy in the Malay Peninsula 1880–1910*. 2 Vols. Kuala Lumpur: University of Malaya Press, 1969.

Tregonning, K.G. *The British in Malaya, 1786–1826*. Tucson: University of Arizona Press, 1965.

———. *A History of Modern Sabah, 1881–1963*. Singapore: University of Malaya Press, 1965.

———. *Home Port Singapore: A History of Straits Steamship Company Limited 1890–1965*. Singapore: Oxford University Press, 1967.

Turnbull, C.M. *The Straits Settlements 1826–67: Indian Presidency to Crown Colony*. London: Athlone Press, 1972.

———. *A History of Singapore 1819–1975*. Kuala Lumpur: Oxford University Press, 1977.

Warren, James. *The North Borneo Chartered Company's Administration of the Bajau, 1878–1909*. Ohio: Ohio University Center for International Studies, Southeast Asia Programme, 1971.

———. *The Sulu Zone 1768–1898: The Dynamics of External Trade, Slavery and Ethnicity in the Transformation of a Southeast Asian Maritime State*. Singapore: Singapore University Press, 1981.

———. *Rickshaw Coolie: A People's History of Singapore (1880–1940)*. Singapore: Oxford University Press, 1987.

Whelan, F.G. *A History of Sabah*. London: Macmillan, 1970.

Winstedt, R.O. *The Malays: A Cultural History*. Singapore: Kelly & Walsh, 1947.

———. *Malaya and its History*. London: Hutchinson's University Library, 1966. (7th ed.)

Wong Lin Ken. *The Malaysian Tin Industry to 1914 with special reference to the states of Perak, Selangor, Negeri Sembilan and Pahang*. Tucson: University of Arizona Press, 1965.

Wright, Arnold and Thomas H. Reid. *The Malay Peninsula: A record of British progess in the Middle East*. London: Fisher Unwin, 1912.

——— and H. Cartwright (eds). *Twentieth century impressions of British Malaya: Its history, people, commerce, industries and resources*. London: Lloyds' Greater British Publishing Company, 1908.

Wright, Leigh. *The Origins of British Borneo*. Hong Kong: Hong Kong University Press, 1970.

Yen Ching Hwang. "Overseas Chinese Nationalism in Singapore and Malaya 1877–1912," *Modern Asian Studies*, Vol. 16, Part 3, 1982: 397–425.

———. *A Social History of the Chinese in Singapore and Malaya*. Kuala Lumpur: Oxford University Press, 1986.

Yeo Kim Wah. "The grooming of an elite: Malay administrators in the Federated Malay States, 1903–1941," *Journal of Southeast Asian Studies*, Vol. 11, No. 2, 1980: 287–319.

———. *The Politics of Decentralization: Colonial controversy in Malaya 1920–1929*. Kuala Lumpur: Oxford University Press, 1982.

Yip Yat Hoong. *The Development of the Tin Mining Industry of Malaya*. Kuala Lumpur: University of Malaya Press, 1969.

Yong C.F. and R.B. McKenna. *The Kuomintang Movement in British Malaya 1912–1949*. Singapore: Singapore University Press, 1990.

Yuen Choy Leng. "Japanese rubber and iron investments in Malaya, 1900–1941," *Journal of Southeast Asian Studies*, Vol. 5, No. 1, 1974: 18–36.

———. "The Japanese Community in Malaya before the Pacific War: Its genesis and growth", *Journal of Southeast Asian Studies*, Vol. 9, No. 2, 1978: 163–79.

The Japanese Occupation, the Emergency and the Independence Campaign (1942–1957)

Akashi, Yoji. "Japanese Policy Towards the Malayan Chinese 1941–1945," *Journal of Southeast Asian Studies*, Vol. 1, No. 2, 1970: 61–89.

Allen, James de Vere. *The Malayan Union*. New Haven: Yale University Press, 1967. (Yale University Southeast Asia Monograph No. 10)

Allen, Richard. *Malaysia: Prospect and Retrospect. The impact and aftermath of colonial rule*. London: Oxford University Press, 1968.

Ampalavanar Rajeswary. *The Indian Minority and Political Change in Malaya 1945–1957*. Kuala Lumpur: Oxford University Press, 1981.

Arasaratnam, S. "Indian Society of Malaysia and its Leaders: Trends in Leadership and Ideology among Malaysian Indians, 1945–60," *Journal of Southeast Asian Studies*, Vol. 13, No. 2, 1982: 236–51.

Barber, Noel. *The War of the Running Dogs: How Malaya Defeated the Communist Guerillas, 1948–60*. London: Collins, 1971.

Cheah Boon Kheng. *The Masked Comrades: A Study of the Communist United Front in Malaya, 1945–48*. Singapore: Times Books, 1979.

———. *Red Star Over Malaya: Resistance and Social Conflict During and After the Japanese Occupation of Malaya, 1941–1946*. Singapore: Singapore University Press, 1983.

Chin Kee Onn. *Malaya Upside Down*. Kuala Lumpur: Federal Publications, 1976.

Clutterbuck, Richard. *Riot and Revolution in Singapore and Malaya 1945–1963*. London: Faber & Faber, 1973.

Cruickshank, Charles. *SDE in the Far East*. Oxford: Oxford University Press, 1983.

Halinah Bamadhaj. "The Impact of the Japanese Occupation of Malaya on Malay Society and Politics, 1941–1945," (MA dissertation, University of Auckland, 1975).

Hanrahan, Gene Z. *The Communist Struggle in Malaya*. Kuala Lumpur: University of Malaya Press, 1971.

Lebra, Joyce C. *Japanese-trained Armies in Southeast Asia, Independence and Volunteer Forces in World War II.* Hong Kong: Heinemann Educational Books (Asia), 1977.

Miller, Harry. *Jungle War in Malaya: The Campaign Against Communism 1948–60.* London: Arthur Barker, 1972.

Mohamed Noordin Sopiee. "The Advocacy of Malaya—Before 1961," *Modern Asian Studies*, Vol. 7, Part 4, 1973: 717–32.

———. *From Malayan Union to Singapore Separation: Political Unification in the Malaysia Region 1945–65.* Kuala Lumpur: University of Malaya Press, 1974.

O'Ballance, Edgar. *Malaya: The Communist Insurgent War, 1948–60.* London: Faber & Faber, 1966.

Ongkili, James P. "The British and Malayan Nationalism, 1946–1957," *Journal of Southeast Asian Studies*, Vol. 5, No. 2, 1974: 255–77.

———. *The Borneo Response to Malaysia, 1961–1963.* Singapore: Donald Moore, 1967.

Roff, Margaret Clarke. *The Politics of Belonging: Political Change in Sabah and Sarawak.* Kuala Lumpur: Oxford University Press, 1974.

Roff, William Robert. *The Origins of Malay Nationalism.* Kuala Lumpur: University of Malaya Press, 1967.

Rudner, Martin. "The Organization of the British Military Administration in Malaya, 1946–48," *Journal of Southeast Asian History*, Vol. 9, No. 1, 1968: 95–106.

Short, Anthony. *The Communist Insurrection in Malaya, 1948–60.* London: Muller, 1975.

Silcock, Thomas Henry. *Towards A Malayan Nation.* Singapore: Donald Moore for Eastern Universities Press, 1961.

——— and Ungku Abdul Aziz. "Nationalism in Malaya," in: *Asian Nationalism and the West*, William L. Holland (ed). New York: Macmillan, 1953.

Simandjuntak, B.. *Malayan Federalism 1945–1963. A Study of Federal Problems in a Plural Society*. Kuala Lumpur: Oxford University Press, 1969.

Smith, E.D. *Counter-Insurgency Operations: 1. Malaya and Borneo*. London: Ian Allan, 1985.

Soenarno, Radin. "Malay Nationalism," *Journal of Southeast Asian History*, Vol. 1, No. 1, 1960: 1–28.

Stenson, Michael. "The Ethnic and Urban Bases of Communist Revolt in Malaya," in: *Peasant Rebellion and Communist Revolution in Asia*, John Wilson Lewis (ed). Stanford: Stanford University Press, 1974.

Stockwell, Anthony J. *British Policy and Malay Politics during the Malayan Union Experiment, 1942–1948*. Monograph No. 8, Malaysian Branch Royal Asiatic Society. Kuala Lumpur, 1979.

———. "British imperial policy and decolonization in Malaya, 1942–52," *Journal of Imperial and Commonwealth History*, Vol. 13, No. 1, 1984: 68–87.

Stubbs, Richard. "The United Malays National Organization, the Malayan Chinese Association, and the early years of the Malayan Emergency, 1948–1955," *Journal of Southeast Asian Studies*, Vol. 10, No. 1, 1979: 77–88.

———. *Hearts and Minds in Guerilla Warfare: The Malayan Emergency 1948–1960*. Singapore: Oxford University Press, 1989.

Thompson, Virginia McLean (ed). *Government and Nationalism in Southeast Asia*. New York: Institute of Pacific Relations, 1942.

———. *Postmortem in Malaya*. New York: Macmillan, 1943.

——— and Richard Adloff. *The Left Wing in South East Asia*. New York: William Sloan Associates, 1950.

Trenowden, Ian. *Operations Most Secret. SOE: the Malayan Theatre*. London: William Kimber, 1978.

Turnbull, C.M. "British Planning for Post-War Malaya," *Journal of Southeast Asian Studies*, Vol. 5, No. 2, 1974: 239–54.

Yeo Kim Wah. "The Anti-Federation Movement in Malaya, 1946–48," *Journal of Southeast Asian Studies*, Vol. 4, No. 1, 1973: 31–51.

Malaysia–General

Andaya, Barbara Watson and Leonard Andaya. *A History of Malaysia*. London: Macmillan, 1982.

Bastin, John S. and Robin Winks. *Malaysia: Selected Historical Readings*. Kuala Lumpur: Oxford University Press, 1966.

Gullick, J.M. *Malaysia and Its Neighbours*. London: Routledge & Kegan Paul, 1967. (World Study Series)

———. *Malaysia: Economic Expansion and National Unity*. London & Boulder: Earnest Benn & Westview Press, 1981.

Hanna, Willard Anderson. *The Formation of Malaysia*. New York: American Universities Field Staff, 1964.

Lee Poh Ping. "Report on Malaysian and Southeast Asian Studies: Origins, Issues and Trends," in: *Oriental and Asian Studies in the Contemporary World: Problems and Trends*. East Asian Cultural Studies (special issue, March 1980): 21–58.

McKie, Ronald Cecil Hamlyn. *The Emergence of Malaysia*. New York: Harcourt, Brace & World, 1963.

Nazareth, Philip N. *The Story of Malaysia*. Singapore: La Salle Publications, 1964.

Rimmer, Peter and Lisa M. Allen (eds). *Pullers, Planters, Plantation Workers . . . The Underside of Malaysian History*. Singapore: Singapore University Press, 1990.

Smith, Thomas Edward and John Bastin. *Malaysia*. London: Oxford University Press, 1967.

Steinberg, David Joel, et al. *In Search of South-East Asia: A Modern History*. Singapore: Oxford University Press, 1972.

Wang Gungwu (ed). *Malaysia: A Survey*. London: Pall Mall, 1964.

POLITICS

A. Law and Constitution

Allen, J. de V., A.J. Stockwell and L.R. Wright (eds). *A Collection of Treaties and Other Documents Affecting the States of Malaysia, 1761–1963*. London: Oceana Publications, 1981.

Bradell, Sir Roland St. John. *The Legal Status of the Malay States*. Singapore: Malaya Publishing House, 1931.

———. *The Laws of the Straits Settlements: A Commentary*. Introduction by M.B. Hooker. Kuala Lumpur: Oxford University Press, 1982.

Federation of Malaya. *An Introduction to the Federal Constitution*. Kuala Lumpur: Federation of Malaya Information Services, 1960.

Gibson, W.S. *The Laws of the Federated Malay States in Force on December 31, 1934*. 4 Vols. London: Roworth, 1935.

Haji Mokhtar bin H. Mohamed Dom. *Malaysian Customary Laws and Usage*. Kuala Lumpur: Federal Publications, 1979.

Hashim Yeop A. Sani. *Perlembagaan Kita*. Kuala Lumpur: Malaysian Law Publishers, 1983.

Hickling, R.H. *An Introduction to the Federal Constitution*. Kuala Lumpur: Federation of Malaya Information Services, 1960.

Hooker, M.B. *The Personal Laws of Malaysia: An Introduction*. Kuala Lumpur: Oxford University Press, 1976.

———. *A Concise Legal History of South-East Asia*. Oxford: Clarendon Press, 1978.

———. *Islamic Law in South-East Asia*. Singapore: Oxford University Press, 1984.

Maxwell, Sir W. George and W.S. Gibson. *Treaties and Engagements Affecting the Malay States and Borneo*. London: James Truscott, 1924.

Mills, J.V.G. *The Chronological Table of Straits Settlements Laws*. Singapore: Government Printing Office, 1926.

Mohamed Salleh bin Abas. *Constitution, Law and Judiciary*. Kuala Lumpur: Malaysia Law Publishers, 1985.

Mohammad Suffian bin Hashim, Tan Sri. *Malaysian Citizenship*. Kuala Lumpur: Jabatan Penerangan, 1970.

———, H.P. Lee and F.A. Trinidad (eds). *The Constitution of Malaysia: Its Development 1957–1977*. Kuala Lumpur: Oxford University Press, 1978.

Sheridan, Lionel Ashton and Harry E. Groves. *The Constitution of Malaysia*. Singapore: Malayan Law Journal (Pte.), 1979.

Sinnadurai, Visu. *The Law of Contract in Malaysia and Singapore: Cases and Commentary*. Kuala Lumpur: Oxford University Press, 1979.

Tan Chee Beng (ed). *Reflections on the Malaysian Constitution*. A Compilation of papers presented at a conference on "Reflections on the Malaysian Constitution: 30 years after Merdeka". Penang: Aliran Kesedaran Negara, 1987.

Wu Min Aun. *An Introduction to the Malaysian Legal System*. Kuala Lumpur: Heinemann Educational Books (Asia), 1982.

——— and Beatrix Vohrah. *The Commercial Law of Malaysia*. Kuala Lumpur: Heinemann Educational Books (Asia), 1979.

B. Politics–General

Abdul Ghani Ismail. *Razaleigh Lawan Musa: Pusingan Kedua 1984*. Kuala Lumpur: IJS Communications, 1983.

Alias Muhammad. *The Trial of Mokhtar Hashim.* Kuala Lumpur: Insular Publishing House, 1983.

Andersen, Robert Allan. "The Separation of Singapore from Malaysia: A Study in Political Involution," (Ph.D. dissertation, The American University, 1973).

Barraclough, Simon. *A Dictionary of Malaysian Politics.* Singapore: Heinemann Educational Books (Asia), 1988.

———. "The Dynamics of Coercion in the Malaysian Political Process," *Modern Asian Studies*, Vol. 19, Part 4, 1985: 792–822.

Bedlington, Stanley S. *Malaysia and Singapore: The Building of New States.* Ithaca: Cornell University Press, 1978.

Burns, Peter L. *Peasantry and National Integration in Peninsular Malaysia.* Center for Asian Studies, Working Paper No. 13, University of Adelaide, 1983.

Dancz, Virgina, H. *Women and Party Politics in Peninsular Malaysia.* Singapore: Oxford University Press, 1987.

Datar, Kiran Kapur. *Malaysia: Quest for a Politics of Consensus.* New Delhi: Vikas Publishing House, 1983.

Fisk, E.K. and H. Osman Rani. *The Political Economy of Malaysia.* Kuala Lumpur: Oxford University Press, 1982.

Gale, Bruce (ed). *Readings in Malaysian Politics.* Kuala Lumpur: Pelanduk Publications, 1986.

Gullick, J. and Bruce Gale. *Malaysia: Its Political and Economic Development.* Kuala Lumpur: Pelanduk Publications, 1986.

Kershaw, Roger. "The 'East Coast' in Malayan Politics: Episodes of Resistance and Integration in Kelantan and Trengganu," *Modern Asian Studies*, Vol. 11, Part 4, 1977: 515–41.

Khoo Yoke Kuan (ed). *Whither Democracy? An Analysis of the Malaysian Experience.* Penang: Aliran Kesedaran Malaysia, 1978.

Leigh, Michael. *The Rising Moon: Political Change in Sarawak*. Sydney: Sydney University Press, 1974.

Leong, Stephen. "The Malayan Overseas Chinese and the Sino-Japanese War, 1937–1941," *Journal of Southeast Asian Studies*, Vol. 10, No. 2, 1979: 293–320.

Lim Joo Jock and S. Vani. *Armed Communist Movements in Southeast Asia*. Aldershot: Gower Publishing, 1984.

Lim Kit Siang. *Time Bombs in Malaysia: Problems of Nation-Building in Malaysia*. Petaling Jaya: Democratic Action Party, 1972.

Mayerchak, Patrick Martin. "An Analysis of the Distribution of Rewards in the Malaysian Alliance Coalition (1959–1973)," (Ph.D. dissertation, The American University, 1975).

Means, Gordon P. *Malaysian Politics*. New York: New York University Press, 1970.

———. *Malaysian Politics, The Second Generation*. Singapore: Oxford University Press, 1990.

Milne, R.S. *Government and Politics in Malaysia*. Boston: Houghton Mifflin, 1967.

——— and Diane K. Mauzy. *Politics and Government in Malaysia*. Singapore: Federal Publications under the auspices of the Institute of Southeast Asian Studies, 1978.

——— and K.L. Ratnam. *Malaysia: New States in a New Nation*. London: Frank Cass, 1974.

Muhammad Ghazali bin Shafie, Tan Sri. *The New Malaysians*. Kuala Lumpur: Jabatan Penerangan, 1971.

Mullard, Chris and Martin Brennan. "The Malaysian Predicament: Towards a New Theoretical Frontier," *Journal of Contemporary Asia*, Vol. 8, No. 3, 1978: 341–54.

Parkinson, Cyril Northcote. *Marxism for Malaysia*. Singapore: Donald Moore, 1956.

Pye, Lucian Wilmot. *Guerilla Communism in Malaya: Its Social and Political Meaning*. Princeton: Princeton University Press, 1956.

Rao, Chandriah Appa, Bruce Ross-Larson, Noordin Sopiee and Tjoa Hock Guan. *Issues in Contemporary Malaysia*. Kuala Lumpur: Heinemann Educational Books (Asia), 1977.

Regan, Daniel. "Intellectuals, Religion, and Politics in a Divided Society: Malaysia," (Ph.D. dissertation, Yale University, 1977).

Roff, William R. (ed). *Kelantan: Religion, Society and Politics in a Malay State*. Kuala Lumpur: Oxford University Press 1974.

Tan Chee Khoon. *Without Fear or Favour*. Singapore: Eastern Universities Press, 1984.

Tunku Abdul Rahman Putra Al-Haj. *Looking Back: Monday Musings and Memories*. Kuala Lumpur: Pustaka Antara, 1977.

———. *As a Matter of Interest*. Kuala Lumpur: Heinemann Educational Books (Asia), 1981.

———. *Lest We Forget: Further Candid Reminiscences*. Singapore: Eastern Universities Press, 1983.

———. *Contemporary Issues in Malaysian Politics*. Petaling Jaya: Pelanduk Publications, 1984.

Van der Kroef, Justuz M. *Communism in Malaysia and Singapore: A Contemporary Survey*. The Hague: Martinus Nijhoff, 1967.

Winzeler, Robert. "Malay Religion, Society and Politics in Kelantan," (Ph.D. dissertation, University of Chicago, 1970).

Zakaria Hj. Ahmad (ed). *Government and Politics of Malaysia*. Kuala Lumpur: Oxford University Press, 1987.

C. Government and Administration

Abdullah Sanusi Ahmad. "The District Office as an Institution of Development," (Ph.D. dissertation, University of Southern California, 1977).

———. "Administrative Reforms for Development in Malaysia's Focus on Grass-Root Organization," in: *Administrative Reforms for Decentralised Development*, A.P. Saxena (ed). Kuala Lumpur: The Asia and Pacific Development Center, 1980.

Allen, J. de Vere. "Malayan Civil Service, 1874–1941: Colonial Bureaucracy/Malayan Elite," *Comparative Studies in Society and History*, Vol. 12, No. 2, 1970: 149–78.

Beaglehole, J.H. *The District: A Study in Decentralization in West Malaysia*. London: Oxford University Press, 1976. (University of Hull Monographs on Southeast Asia No. 6)

Braun, W.K. "The Introduction of Representative Institutions into Malaya," (Ph.D. dissertation, University of Cincinnati, 1956).

Doering, Otto. "Government in Sarawak Under Charles Brooke," *Journal of the Malaysian Branch Royal Asiatic Society*, Vol. 39, No. 2, 1966: 95–107.

Esman, Milton J. *Administration and Development in Malaysia: Institution Building and Reform in a Plural Society*. Ithaca: Cornell University Press, 1972.

Gale, Bruce. *Politics and Public Enterprise in Malaysia*. Kuala Lumpur: Eastern Universities Press, 1981.

Harrisson, Tom et al. *Council Negri Centenary, 1867–1967*. Kuching: Borneo Literature Bureau, 1967.

Heussler, Robert. *British Rule in Malaya: The Malayan Civil Service and Its Predecessors, 1867–1942*. Oxford: Clio Press, 1981.

———. *Completing a Stewardship: The Malayan Civil Service, 1942–1957*. Westport: Greenwood Press, 1983.

Jones, S.W. *Public Administration in Malaya*. London: Oxford University Press, 1953.

Lockard, Craig A. "The Evolution of Urban Government in Southeast Asian Cities: Kuching Under the Brookes," *Modern Asian Studies*, Vol. 12, No. 2, 1978: 245–67.

Means, Gordon P. " 'Special Rights' as a Strategy for Development: The Case of Malaysia," *Comparative Politics*, Vol. 5, No. 1, 1972: 29–61.

Meerman, Jacob. *Public Expenditure in Malaysia: Who Benefits and Why*. New York: Oxford University Press, 1979.

Ness, Gayl D. *Bureaucracy and Rural Development in Malaysia: A Study of Organizations in Stimulating Economic Development in New States*. Berkeley: University of California Press, 1967.

Norris, M.W. *Local Government in Peninsular Malaysia*. Westmead: Gower Publishing Company, 1980.

Ongkili, James P. *Modernization in East Malaysia, 1960–1970*. Kuala Lumpur: Oxford University Press, 1972.

Puthucheary, Mavis. *The Politics of Administration: The Malaysian Experience*. Kuala Lumpur: Oxford University Press, 1978.

Rudner, Martin. *Nationalism, Planning and Economic Modernization: The Politics of Beginning Development*. London: Sage Publications, 1975.

Salem, T. "Capitalist Development and the Formation of the Bureaucratic Bourgeoisie in Peninsular Malaysia," *Kajian Malaysia*, Vol. 1, No. 2, 1983: 71–104.

Scott, James C. *Political Ideology in Malaysia: Reality and the Beliefs of An Elite*. New Haven: Yale University Press, 1968.

Tilman, R.O. *Bureaucratic Transition in Malaya*. Durham: Duke University Press, 1964.

D. Political Parties

Aziz Ahmad. *UMNO: Falsafah dan Perjuangannya*. Kuala Lumpur: Amir Enterprise, 1980.

Brimmel, Jack Henry. *Short History of the Malayan Communist Party*. Singapore: Donald Moore, 1956.

Clark, M.F. "The Malayan Alliance and Its Accommodation of Communal Pressures, 1952–1962," (MA thesis, University of Malaya, 1964).

The Communist Party of Malaya: Selected Documents. Published by the South East Asia Documentation Group, 1979.

Funston, John. "The Origins of Parti Islam Se Malaysia," *Journal of Southeast Asian Studies*, Vol. 7, No. 1, 1976: 58–73.

———. *Malay Politics in Malaysia: A Study of UMNO and PAS*. Kuala Lumpur: Heinemann Educational Books (Asia), 1980.

Heng Pek Koon. "The Social and Ideological Origins of the Malayan Chinese Association," *Journal of Southeast Asian Studies*, No. 14, No. 2, 1983: 290–311.

———. *Chinese Politics in Malaysia: A History of the Malaysian Chinese Association*. Singapore: Oxford University Press, 1988.

Manderson, Lenore. *Women, Politics and Change: The Kaum Ibu UMNO, Malaysia, 1945–1972*. Kuala Lumpur: Oxford University Press, 1980.

Mauzy, Diane K. *Barisan Nasional: Coalition Government in Malaysia*. Kuala Lumpur: Marican, 1983.

Milne, R.S. "Political Parties in Sarawak and Sabah," *Journal of Southeast Asian History*, Vol. 6, No. 2, 1965: 104–17.

Ramlah, Adam. *UMNO: Organisasi dan Kegiatan 1945–1951*. Kota Bharu: Mohd. Nawi Bookstore, 1978.

Roff, Margaret. "The Malayan Chinese Association, 1948–65," *Journal of Southeast Asian History*, Vol. 6, No. 2, 1965: 40–53.

Safie Ibrahim. *The Islamic Party of Malaysia: Its Formative Stage and Ideology*. Kelantan: Nuawai Ismail, 1981.

Stockwell, A.J. "The Formation and First Years of the United Malays National Organization (UMNO) 1946–1948," *Modern Asian Studies*, Vol. 11, Part 4, 1977: 481–513.

Vasil, Raj. K. *Politics in a Plural Society: A Study of Non-Communal Political Parties in West Malaysia*. Kuala Lumpur: Oxford University Press, 1971.

Zakry Abadi. *UMNO: Jalan Seribu Liku*. Kuala Lumpur: Penerbitan Gatra Jaya, 1983.

E. Ethnicity and Politics

Brennan, Martin. "Class, Politics and Race in Modern Malaysia," *Journal of Contemporary Asia*, Vol. 12, No. 2, 1982: 188–215.

Cham, B.N. "Class and Communal Conflict in Malaysia," *Journal of Contemporary Asia*, Vol. 5, No. 4, 1975: 446–61.

Chandra Muzaffar. *Islamic Resurgence in Malaysia*. Petaling Jaya: Penerbit Fajar Bakti, 1987.

Chew Huat Hock. "Some Observations on Coalition Politics in Penang," *Modern Asian Studies*, Vol. 19, Part 1, 1985: 125–46.

Comber, Leon. *13 May 1969: A Historical Survey of Sino-Malay Relations*. Kuala Lumpur: Heinemann Educational Books (Asia), 1983.

Enloe, Cynthia E. *Multi-Ethnic Politics: The Case of Malaysia*. Berkeley: University of California Press, 1970. (Research Monograph No. 2)

Freedman, Maurice. "The Growth of a Plural Society in Malaya," *Pacific Affairs*, Vol. 33, No. 2, 1960: 158–68.

Gagliano, Felix V. *Communal Violence in Malaysia 1969: The Political Aftermath*. Athens: Ohio University, 1970. (Southeast Asia Series No. 13)

Goh, Cheng Teik. *The May Thirteenth Incident and Democracy and Malaysia*. Kuala Lumpur: Oxford University Press, 1971.

Hua Wu Yin. *Class and Communalism in Malaysia: Politics in a Dependent Capitalist State*. London: Zed Books, 1983.

Hussein Mutalib. *Islam and Ethnicity in Malay Politics*. Singapore: Oxford University Press, 1989.

Ibrahim Mahmood. *Sejarah Perjuangan Bangsa Melayu*. Kuala Lumpur: Pustaka Antara, 1981.

Kershaw, Roger. "Of Race, Class and Clientship in Malaysia," *Journal of Commonwealth and Comparative Politics*, Vol. 14, No. 3, 1976: 299–303.

Kessler, Clive S. "Muslim Identity and Political Behaviour in Kelantan," in: *Kelantan: Religion, Society and Politics in a Malay State*, William R. Roff (ed). Kuala Lumpur: Oxford University Press, 1974.

———. *Islam and Politics in a Malay State: Kelantan 1838–1969*. Ithaca: Cornell University Press, 1978.

Lee, Edwin. "The Emergence of Towkay Leaders in Party Politics in Sabah," *Journal of Southeast Asian History*, Vol. 9, No. 2, 1968: 306–24.

———. *The Towkays of Sabah: Chinese Leadership and Indigenous Challenge in the Last Phase of British rule*. Singapore: Singapore University Press, 1976.

Leigh, Michael. *The Chinese Community of Sarawak: A Study of Communal Relations*. Singapore: Malaysia Publishing House, 1964.

Lim Mah Hui. "Ethnic and Class Relations in Malaysia," *Journal of Contemporary Asia*, Vol. 10, Nos. 1 & 2, 1980: 130–54.

Lockard, Craig A. "Parties, Personalities and Crisis Politics in Sarawak," *Journal of Southeast Asian History*, Vol. 8, No. 1, 1967: 111–21.

Loh Kok Wah. *The Politics of Chinese Unity in Malaysia: Reform and Conflict in the Malaysian Chinese Association 1971–73*. Singapore: Maruzen Asia, 1982.

Mauzy, Diane K. and R.S. Milne. "The Mahathir Administration in Malaysia: Discipline Through Islam," *Pacific Affairs*, Vol. 56, No. 4, 1983–84: 617–48.

The May 13 Tragedy. A Report. Kuala Lumpur: National Operations Council, 1969.

Milne, R.S. "The Politics of Malaysia's New Economic Policy," *Pacific Affairs*, Vol. 49, No. 2, 1976: 235–62.

Mohamad Abu Bakar. "Islam and Nationalism in Contemporary Malay Society," in: *Islam and Society in Southeast Asia*, S. Siddique (ed). Singapore: Institute of Southeast Asian Studies, 1986.

Rabushka, Alvin. *Race and Politics in Urban Malaya*. Stanford: Hoover Institution Press, 1973.

Ratnam, K.J. *Communalism and the Political Process in Malaya*. Kuala Lumpur: Oxford University Press, 1965.

Reid, Anthony. "The Kuala Lumpur Riots and the Malaysian Political System," *Australian Outlook*, Vol. 23, 1969: 258–78.

Roff, Margaret Clarke. "The Rise and Demise of Kadazan Nationalism," *Journal of Southeast Asian History*, Vol. 10, No. 2, 1969: 326–43.

Rogers, Marvin L. "The Politicization of Malay Villagers: National Integration or Disintegration?," *Comparative Politics*, Vol. 7, No. 2, 1975: 205–25.

Sanib, Said. *Malay Politics in Sarawak, 1946–1966*. Singapore: Oxford University Press, 1985.

Searle, Peter. *Politics in Sarawak 1970–1976: The Iban Perspective*. Singapore: Oxford University Press, 1983.

Slimming, John. *Malaysia: Death of a Democracy*. Don Mills: Longmans, 1969.

Stenson, Michael. "Class and Race in West Malaysia," *Bulletin of Concerned Asian Scholars*, Vol. 8, No. 2, 1976: 45–54.

———. *Class, Race and Colonialism in West Malaysia*. St. Lucia: University of Queensland Press, 1980.

Strauch, Judith. "Multiple Ethnicities in Malaysia: The Shifting Relevance of Alternative Chinese Categories," *Modern Asian Studies*, Vol. 15, Part 2, 1981: 235–60.

———. *Chinese Village Politics in the Malaysian State*. Cambridge: Harvard University Press, 1981.

Syed Husin Ali. *The Malays: Their Problem and Future*. Kuala Lumpur: Heinemann Educational Books (Asia), 1981.

Thompson, Virginia Mclean and Richard Adloff. *Minority Problems in Southeast Asia*. Stanford: Stanford University Press, 1955.

Tunku Abdul Rahman. *May 13– Before and After*. Kuala Lumpur: Utusan Melayu Press Ltd., 1969.

Vasil, R.K. *Ethnic Politics in Malaysia*. New Delhi: Radiant Publishers, 1980.

Von Vorys, Karl. *Democracy Without Concensus: Communalism and Political Stability in Malaysia*. Princeton: Princeton University Press, 1975.

Wan Hashim. *Race Relations in Malaysia*. Kuala Lumpur: Heinemann Educational Books (Asia), 1983.

Wang Gungwu. "Traditional Leadership in a New Nation: The Chinese in Malaya and Singapore," in: *Leadership and Authority. A Symposium*, Gehan Wijeyewardene (ed). Singapore: University of Malaya Press, for the Center for Southeast Asian Studies in the Social Sciences, University of Singapore, 1968: 208–22; and, in: *Community and Nation: Essays on Southeast Asia and the Chinese,* Wang Gungwu (ed). Singapore: Heinemann Educational Books (Asia), for the Asian Studies Association of Australia, 1981: 159–72.

Winzeler, Robert R. *Ethnic Relations in Kelantan: A Study of the Chinese and Thai as Ethnic Minorities in a Malay State*. Singapore: Oxford University Press, 1985.

F. Elections

Chandra Muzaffar. "Pilihanraya Umum 1982: Satu Analisa," *Aliran Quarterly*, Vol. 2, 1982.

Crouch, Harold, et al. (eds). *Malaysian Politics and the 1978 Elections*. Kuala Lumpur: Oxford University Press, 1980.

———. *Malaysia's 1982 General Election*. Singapore: Institute of Southeast Asian Studies, 1982. (Research Notes and Discussion Paper No. 34.)

Ismail Kassim. *Race, Politics and Moderation: A Study of Malaysian Electoral Process*. Singapore: Times International, 1979.

Milne, R.S. and K.J. Ratnam. "The Sarawak Elections of 1970: An Analysis of the Vote," *Journal of Southeast Asian Studies*, Vol. 3, No. 1, 1972: 111–122.

Moore, Daniel E. "The United Malays National Organization and the 1959 Elections: A Study of a Political Party in Action in a Newly Independent Plural Society," (Ph.D. dissertation, University of California, 1960).

Pillay Chandrasekaran (Chandra Muzaffar). *The 1974 General Election in Malaysia: A Post-Mortem*. Singapore: Institute of Southeast Asian Studies, 1974. (Occasional Paper No. 25)

Ratnam, K.J. and R.S. Milne. *The Malayan Parliamentary Election of 1964*. Singapore: University of Malaya Press, 1967.

———. "The 1969 Parliamentary Election in West Malaysia," *Pacific Affairs*, Vol. 43, No. 2, 1970: 203–26.

Vasil, Raj K. *The Malayan General Election of 1969*. Kuala Lumpur: Oxford University Press, 1971.

G. Biography of Political Leaders

Adshead, Robin. *Mahathir of Malaysia: Statesman and Leader*. London: Hibiscus Publications, 1989.

Ahmad Boestamam (pseud.). *Dr. Burhanuddin: Putera Setia Melayu Raya*. Kuala Lumpur: Pustaka Kejora, 1972.

Ahmad Bujang. *Bapa Pembangunan, Tun Razak*. Petaling Jaya: International Book Service, 1985.

Anwar Abdullah. *Dato Onn Jaafar*. Kuala Lumpur: Pustaka Nusantara, 1966.

Campbell, Bill (ed). *Sabah under Harris: A collection of speeches by Datuk Harris bin Mohd. Salleh as Chief Minister of Sabah 1976–1985*. Kuala Lumpur: Penerbit Warisan, 1986.

Durai Raja Singam, Sabapathipillai (ed). *Tribute to Tunku Abdul Rahman (on his 60th birthday)*. Kuala Lumpur: The Editor, 1963.

Gale, Bruce. *Musa Hitam: A Political Biography*. Petaling Jaya: Eastern Universities Press, 1982.

Gullick, John Michael and Gerald Hawkins. *Malaysian Pioneers*. Singapore: Eastern Universities Press, 1968.

Healy, A.M. *Tunku Abdul Rahman*. St. Lucia: University of Queensland Press, 1982.

Hussein, Abdullah. *Tun Datu Mustapha: Bapa Kemerdekaan Sabah*. Kuala Lumpur: M.F.I., 1976.

Ishak bin Tadin. "Dato Onn and Malay Nationalism 1946–1951," *Journal of Southeast Asian History*, Vol. 1, No. 1, 1960: 56–88.

Kamaruddin Jaafar. *Dr. Burhanuddin Al-Helmy: Politik Melayu dan Islam*. Kuala Lumpur: Yayasan Anda, 1980.

Miller, Harry. *Prince and Premier: A Biography of Tunku Abdul Rahman Putra al-Haj. First Prime Minister of the Federation of Malaya*. London: George G. Harrap, in association with Donald Moore, 1959.

Morais, Victor J. *Tun Tan: Potrait of a Statesman*. Singapore: Quins, 1981.

———. *Hussein Onn: A Tryst With Destiny*. Singapore: Times Books International, 1981.

———. *Mahathir: A Profile in Courage*. Petaling Jaya: Eastern Universities Press, 1982.

———. *Anwar Ibrahim: Resolute in Leadership*. Kuala Lumpur: Arenabuku, 1984.

Roff, W.R. *Autobiography and Biography in Malay Historical Studies*. Singapore: Institute of Southeast Asian Studies, 1972.

Ross-Larson, Bruce. *The Politics of Federalism: Syed Kechik in East Malaysia*. Singapore: Bruce Ross-Larson, 1976.

Shahrom Husein. *Biografi Perjuangan Politik Dato Onn bin Jaafar*. Kuala Lumpur: Penerbit Fajar Bakti, 1985.

Shaw, William. *Tun Razak: His Life and Times*. Kuala Lumpur: Longmans Malaysia, 1976.

Sheppard, Mubin, Tan Sri Dato'. *Tunku: A pictorial biography, 1957–1987*. Petaling Jaya: Pelanduk Publications, 1987.

Soh Eng Lim. "Tan Cheng Lock: His Leadership of the Malayan Chinese," *Journal of Southeast Asian History*, Vol. 1, No. 1, 1960: 29–55.

Syed Ibrahim bin Syed Abdullah. *Tun Fuad: Memories in Brief*. Kota Kinabalu, n.d.

Vasil, R.K. *Dr. Tan Chee Khoon: An Elder Statesman*. Kuala Lumpur: Pelanduk Publications, 1987.

H. International Relations and Defence

Ariff, M.O. *The Philippines' Claim to Sabah: Its Historical, Legal and Political Implications*. Kuala Lumpur: Oxford University Press, 1970.

Boyce, Peter. *Malaysia and Singapore in International Diplomacy: Documents and Commentaries*. Sydney: Sydney University Press, 1968.

Chandran Mohandas Jeshurun. *The Growth of the Malaysian Armed Forces, 1963–73: Some Foreign Press Reactions*. Singapore: Institute of Southeast Asian Studies, 1975.

———. *Malaysian Defence Policy: A Study in Parliamentary Attitudes 1963–1973*. Kuala Lumpur: University of Malaya Press, under the auspices of the Institute of Southeast Asian Studies, Singapore, 1980.

Chin Kin Wah. *The Defence of Malaysia and Singapore: The Transformation of a Security System 1957–1971*. Cambridge: Cambridge University Press, 1983.

Fletcher, Nancy McHenry. *The Separation of Singapore from Malaysia*. Ithaca: Cornell University Press, 1969. (Southeast Asia Program, Data Paper No. 73.)

Gould, James W. *The United States and Malaysia*. Cambridge: Harvard University Press, 1969.

Hawkins, David. *The Defense of Malaysia and Singapore: From AMDA to ANZUK*. London: Royal United Services Institute for Defence Studies, 1972.

James, Harold and Denis Sheil-Small. *The Undeclared War: The Story of the Indonesian Confrontation 1962–1966*. Kuala Lumpur: University of Malaya Cooperative Bookshop, 1979.

Lau Teik Soon. "Malaysia-Singapore Relations: Crisis of Adjustment, 1965–68," *Journal of Southeast Asian History*, Vol. 10, No. 1, 1969: 155–76.

Leifer, Michael. *The Philippine Claim to Sabah*. Hull: University of Hull, Centre for South-East Asian Studies, 1968. (Hull Monographs on South-East Asia, No. 1.)

———. *Malacca, Singapore and Indonesia*. Alphen aan den Rijn: Sijthoff & Noordhoff, 1978. (Series: International Straits of the World, No. 2.)

Mackie, J.A.C. *Konfrontasi—The Indonesia-Malaysia Dispute 1963–1966*. Kuala Lumpur: Oxford University Press, 1974.

McDougall, Derek. "The Wilson Government and the British Defence Commitment in Malaysia-Singapore," *Journal of Southeast Asian Studies*, Vol. 4, No. 2, 1973: 229–40.

Noble, Lela Garner. *Philippine Policy Towards Sabah: A Claim to Independence*. Tucson: University of Arizona Press, 1977.

Osborne, Milton E. *Singapore and Malaysia*. Ithaca: Cornell University Press, 1964. (Southeast Asia Program, Data Paper No. 53.)

Saravanamuttu, J. *The Dilemma of Independence: Two Decades of Malaysia's Foreign Policy 1957–1977*. Penang: Universiti Sains Malaysia Press, 1983.

Stubbs, Richard. *ASEAN at Twenty: The Search for a New Consensus*. Toronto: Canadian Institute of International Affairs, 1988.

Van der Kroef, Justus M. "The Sarawak-Indonesian Border Insurgency," *Modern Asian Studies*, Vol. 2, Part 3, 1968: 245–65.

Wong, John. *The Political Economy of Malaysia's Trade Relations with China*. Singapore: Institute of Southeast Asian Studies, 1974.

Zakariah Haji Ahmed and Harold Crouch (eds). *Military-Civilian Relations in South-East Asia*. Singapore: Oxford University Press, 1985.

I. Human Rights

Aliran. *Dialogue on Democracy*. Collection of Speeches made by leaders of various political parties and public interest societies in connection with the Third Dialogue of Concern on Parliamentary Democracy. Penang: Aliran Kesedaran Negara, 1985.

Aliran. *Freedom in Fetters: An Analysis of the State of Democracy in Malaysia*, Chandra Muzaffar (ed). Penang: Aliran Kesedaran Negara, 1986.

Aliran. *Nation on Trial*. Penang: Aliran Kesedaran Negara, 1989.

Amnesty International Malaysia. *"Operation Lallang": Detention without Trial under the Internal Security Act*. London: International Secretariat, 1988.

Colchester, Marcus. *Pirates, Squatters and Poachers: The Political Ecology of Dispossession of the Native Peoples of Sarawak*. London: Survival International, 1989.

Lent, John A. "Human Rights in Malaysia," *Journal of Contemporary Asia*, Vol. 14, No. 4, 1984: 442–58.

Logging Against the Natives of Sarawak. Kuala Lumpur: Institute of Social Analysis, 1989.

The Report of the International Mission of Lawyers to Malaysia. London: Marram Books, 1983.

Tangled Web—Dissent, Deterrence and the 27 October 1987 Crackdown in Malaysia. Kuala Lumpur: Committee Against Repression in the Pacific and Asia, 1988.

SCIENCES

A. Geography

General

Aiken, S. Robert, Colin H. Leigh, Thomas R. Leinbach and Michael R. Moss. *Development and Environment in Peninsular Malaysia*. Singapore: McGraw-Hill, 1982.

Courtney, P.P. *A Geography of Trade and Development in Malaya*. London: G. Bell, 1972.

Dale, W.L. "The Rainfall of Malaya, Part 1," *Journal of Tropical Geography*, Vol. 13, 1959: 23–37.

Dobby, E.G. *Southeast Asia*. London: London University Press, 1950.

Fisher, Charles A. *South-East Asia: A Social, Economic and Political Geography*. London: Methuen, 1966.

Frank, M. LeBar (ed). *Ethnic Groups of Insular Southeast Asia*. New Haven: Human Relations Area Files Press, 1972.

Fryer, Donald W. *Emerging Southeast Asia: A Study in Growth and Stagnation*. London: George Philip & Son, 1979.

Hamzah Sendut. "Patterns of Urbanization in Malaya," *Journal of Tropical Geography*, Vol. 16, 1962: 114–30.

Hill, R.D. *South-East Asia: A Systematic Geography*. Kuala Lumpur: Oxford University Press, 1979.

Hodder, B.W. *Man in Malaya*. London: University of London Press, 1959.

Holshausen, C.G. *Climatic Data of the Main Towns in Malaysia*. Singapore: Singapore Polytechnic, 1963.

Jackson, James C. *Sarawak: A Geographical Survey of a Developing State*. London: University of London Press, 1968.

Macdonald, Malcolm. *Borneo People*. London: Jonathan Cape, 1956.

McTaggart, W.D. and D. Stormont. *Mapping Ethnic Groups in Malaysia*. Tucson: Center for Asian Studies, University of Arizona, 1974. (Occasional Paper No. 5)

Ooi Jin Bee. *Land, People and Economy in Malaya*. London: Longmans, 1963.

———. *Peninsular Malaysia*. London: Longmans, 1976.

———. and Chia Lin Sien. *The Climate of West Malaysia and Singapore*. Singapore: Oxford University Press, 1974.

Rimmer, Peter et al. (eds). *Food, Shelter and Transport in Southeast Asia and the Pacific*. Canberra: Australian National University Press, 1978.

Sham Sani. *The Climate of Kuala Lumpur—Petaling Jaya Area Malaysia: A Study of the Impact of Urbanization on Local Climate Within the Humid Tropics*. Bangi: Universiti Kebangsaan Malaysia Press, 1980. (Monograph No. 1)

Takahashi, K. and H. Arakawa. *Climates of Southern and Western Asia*. Amsterdam: Elsevier Scientific Publishing Company, 1981. (World Survey of Climatography, Vol. 9.)

Population, Demography and Settlement

Alexander, Garth. *Silent Invasion: The Chinese in Southeast Asia*. London: Macdonald, 1973.

Alliston, Cyril. *Threatened Paradise: North Borneo and Its Peoples*. London: Robert Hale, 1966.

Arasaratnam, Sinnappah. *Indians in Malaysia and Singapore*. Kuala Lumpur: Oxford University Press, 1979.

Caldwell, John Charles. "The Population of Malaya," (Ph.D. dissertation, Australian National University, 1962).

———. "Some Implications of Past Population Growth and Likely Future Trends in Malaya," *Population Review*, Vol. 7, No. 2, 1963: 43–52.

———. "New and Old Malaya: Aspects of Demographic Change in a High Growth Rate Multiracial Society," *Population Review*, Vol. 8, No. 2, 1964: 29–36.

Carey, Iskandar. *Orang Asli: The Aboriginal Tribes of Peninsular Malaysia*. Kuala Lumpur: Oxford University Press, 1976.

Cheong Kee Cheok and Lim Lin Lean. *Demographic Impact on Socio-Economic Development: The Malaysian Experience*. Canberra: Australian National University Press, 1982. (Development Studies Centre, Monograph No. 29.)

Chin, John M. *The Sarawak Chinese*. Kuala Lumpur: Oxford University Press, 1981.

Crabb, Charles Harry. *Malaya's Eurasians—an opinion*. Singapore: Donald Moore for Eastern Universities Press, 1960.

Cushman, Jennifer and Wang Gungwu (eds). *Changing Identities of the Southeast Asian Chinese since World War II*. Hong Kong: Hong Kong University Press, 1988

Denton, Robert Knox. *The Semai: A Non-Violent People of Malaya*. New York: Holt, Rinehart & Winston, 1968.

Drakakis-Smith, D.W. "The Role of the Private Sector in Housing the Urban Poor in Peninsular Malaysia," in: *Issues in Malaysia Development*, James C. Jackson and Martin Rudner (eds). Singapore: Heinemann Educational Books (Asia) for the Asian Studies Association of Australia, 1979.

Goh Ban Lee and Hans-Dieter Evers. "Urban Development and Land Ownership in Butterworth, Malaysia," *Journal of Southeast Asian Studies*, Vol. 9, No. 1, 1978: 28–49.

Guyot, James F. "Creeping Urbanism and Political Development in Malaysia," in: *Comparative Urban Research*, Robert T. Daland (ed). Beverly Hills: Sage Publications, 1969: 124–61.

Han Sin-Fong. "Hailam Chinese in Sabah: A Study of Occupational Patterns and Changes," *Journal of Southeast Asian Studies*, Vol. 6, No. 1, 1975: 25–37.

———. *The Chinese in Sabah, East Malaysia*. Taipei: Orient Culture Service, 1975. (Asian Folklore and Social Life Monograph, No. 67)

Harrisson, Tom (ed). *The Peoples of Sarawak*. Kuching: Sarawak Museum, 1959.

———. *The Peoples of North and West Borneo*, in: *Malaysia: A Survey*, Wang Gungwu (ed). Singapore: Donald Moore, 1964.

———. *The Malays of South-West Sarawak Before Malaysia: A Socioecological Survey*. London: Macmillan, 1970.

Jain, Ravindra K. *South Indians on the Plantation Frontier in Malaya*. Sydney: University of New England Press, 1970.

Johnstone, Michael. "The Evolution of Squatter Settlements in Peninsular Malaysian Cities," *Journal of Southeast Asian Studies*, Vol. 12, No. 2, 1981: 364–80.

Jones, L.W. *The Population of Borneo: A Study of the Peoples of Sarawak, Sabah and Brunei*. London: Athlone Press, 1966.

Kaur, Amarjit. "North Indians in Malaya: A Study of their Economic, Social and Political Activities with Special Reference to Selangor, 1870s–1940s," (MA thesis, University of Malaya, 1974).

Koentjaraningrat, R.M. *Introduction to the Peoples and Cultures of Indonesia and Malaysia*. Menlo Park: Cummings Publishing Company, 1975.

Lee Boon Thong. "Malay Urbanization and the Ethnic Profile of Urban Centres in Peninsular Malaysia," *Journal of Southeast Asian Studies*, Vol. 8, No. 2, 1977: 224–34.

Lee, Yong Leng. *North Borneo: A Study in Settlement Geography*. Singapore: Eastern Universities Press, 1965.

———. *Population and Settlement in Sarawak*. Singapore: Donald Moore for Asia Pacific Press, 1970.

Lim Heng Kow. *The Evolution of the Urban System in Malaya*. Kuala Lumpur: University of Malaya Press, 1978.

Lim Lin Lean. *Population and Development: Theory and Empirical Evidence. The Malaysian Case*. Petaling Jaya: International Book Service, 1983.

Lim, Linda Y.C. and L.A. Peter Gosling. *The Chinese in Southeast Asia*. Singapore: Maruzen Asia, 1983.

Lockard, Craig A. *From Kampong to City: A Social History of Kuching, Malaysia, 1820–1970*. Athens: Ohio University, 1987. (Monographs in International Studies, Southeast Asia Series, No. 75)

Mahajani, Usha. *The Role of Indian Minorities in Burma and Malaya*. Bombay: Vora & Company, 1960. Issued under the auspices of the Institute of Pacific Relations, New York.

McGee, T.G. *The Southeast Asian City: A Social Geography of the Primate Cities of Southeast Asia*. London: G. Bell & Sons, 1967.

———. "Malays in Kuala Lumpur: A Geographical Study in the Process of Urbanization," (Ph.D. dissertation, Victoria University, 1968).

———. (ed). *The Urbanization Process in the Third World*. London: G. Bell & Sons, 1971.

Newell, William H. *Treacherous River: A Study of Rural Chinese in North Malaya*. Kuala Lumpur: University of Malaya Press, 1962.

Nyce, Ray. *Chinese New Villages in Malaya: A Community Study*, Shirle Gordon (ed). Singapore: Malaysian Sociological Research Institute, 1973.

Ooi, Jin Bee. "Urbanization and the Urban Population in Peninsular Malaysia, 1970," *Journal of Tropical Geography*, Vol. 40, 1975: 40–47.

Padoch, Christine. *Migration and its alternatives among the Iban of Sarawak*. The Hague: Martinus Nijhoff for Koninklijk Instituut voor Taal-, Land-, en Volkenkunde, Leiden, No. 98, 1982.

Pryor, Robin J. "The Changing Settlement System of West Malaysia," *Journal of Tropical Geography*, Vol. 37, 1973: 53–67.

———. *Migration and Development in Southeast Asia: A Demographic Perspective*. Kuala Lumpur: Oxford University Press, 1979.

Purcell, V. *The Chinese in Malaya*. Kuala Lumpur: Oxford University Press, 1948.

———. *The Chinese in Southeast Asia*. London: Oxford University Press, under the auspices of the Royal Institute of International Affairs, 1965.

Rimmer, Peter J. and George C. H. Cho. "Urbanization of the Malays since Independence: Evidence from West Malaysia 1957 and 1970," *Journal of Southeast Asian Studies*, Vol. 12, No. 2, 1981: 249–63.

Sandhu, Kernail Singh. "Emergency Resettlement in Malaya," *Journal of Tropical Geography*, Vol. 18, 1964: 157–83.

———. *Indians in Malaya: Immigration and Settlement, 1786–1957*. Cambridge: Cambridge University Press, 1969.

Saw Swee Hock. "Patterns of Urbanization in West Malaysia, 1911–1970," *Malayan Economic Review*, Vol. 17, No. 2, 1972: 114–20.

———. *The Demography of Malaysia, Singapore and Brunei: A Bibliography*. Hong Kong: University of Hong Kong Press, 1970.

——— and Cheng Siok Hwa. *A Bibliography of the Demography of Malaysia and Brunei*. Singapore: University Education Press, 1975.

Sidhu, Manjit Singh and Gavin W. Jones. *Population Dynamics in a Plural Society: Peninsular Malaysia*. Kuala Lumpur: University of Malaya Cooperative Bookshop, 1981.

Siew Mee Kan. *Population of Southeast Asia: A Bibliography*. Wellington: Library School, National Library Service, 1964.

Smith, T.E. *Population Growth in Malaya: An Analysis of Recent Trends*. London: Royal Institute of International Affairs, 1952.

———. *The Background to Malaysia*. London: Royal Institute of International Affairs, 1963.

———. "Immigration and Permanent Settlement of Chinese and Indians in Malaya: and the future growth of the Malay and Chinese Communities," in: *The Economic Development of South-East Asia: Studies in Economic History and Political Economy*, C.D. Cowan (ed). London: Allen & Unwin, 1984.

Tunku Shamsul Bahrin. "The Indonesians in Malaya: A Study of the Pattern of Migration into Malaya," (MA thesis, University of Sheffield, 1964).

———. "The Pattern of Indonesian Migration and Settlement in Malaya," *Asian Studies* Vol. 5, No. 2, 1967: 233–57.

Vlieland, C.A. "The Population of the Malay Peninsula: A Study in Human Migration," *Geographical Review*, Vol. XXIV, 1934: 61–78.

Wegelin, Emiel A. *Urban Low-income Housing and Development: A Case Study in Peninsular Malaysia*. Leiden: Martinus Nijhoff,

Social Sciences Division, 1978. (Studies in Development and Planning, Vol. 6)

Yeung, Y.M. and C.P. Lo (eds). *Changing South-East Asian Cities: Readings on Urbanization*. Singapore: Oxford University Press, 1976.

Zahrah bte. Haji Mahmud. "The Period and Nature of Traditional Settlement in the Malayan Peninsula," *Journal of the Malaysian Branch Royal Asiatic Society*, Vol. 43, No. 2, 1970: 81–113.

B. Geology

Bradford, E.F. "The Occurrence of Tin and Tungsten in Malaya," *Proceedings of the Ninth Pacific Science Congress*, Vol. 12, 1961: 378–98.

Burton, C.K. "Wrench Faulting in Malaya," *Journal of Geology*, Vol. 73, 1965: 781–98.

Geological Society of Malaysia. *Bulletins* 1–22 (1967–1988). (Contains numerous papers on the Geology of Peninsular Malaysia, Sabah and Sarawak.)

Geological Survey of Malaysia. *Annual Reports for Peninsular Malaysia, Sabah and Sarawak*. (Memoirs on various areas in Malaysia, Geological Maps of Peninsular Malaysia, Sabah and Sarawak.)

Gobbett, D.J. "Bibliography and Index of the Geology of West Malaysia and Singapore," *Geological Society Malaysia Bulletin*, No. 2, 1968: 1–152.

———. "Bibliography and Index of the Geology of West Malaysia and Singapore," Supplement 1968. *Geological Society Malaysia Bulletin*, No. 3, 1970: 115–29.

——— and C.S. Hutchison (eds). *Geology of the Malay Peninsula* (West Malaysia and Singapore). New York: Wiley-Interscience, 1973.

Haile, N.S. "Geosynclinal Theory and the Organisational Pattern of the North-West Borneo Geosyncline," *Quarterly Journal of the Geological Society of London*, Vol. 124, 1969: 171–95.

Hamilton, W. *Tectonics of the Indonesian Region*. United States Geological Survey Professional Paper #1078, Washington, DC: Government Printing Office, 1979.

Hess, F.L. and E. Hess. "Bibliography of the Geology and Mineralogy of Tin," *Smithsonian Miscellaneous Collection*, Vol. 58, No. 2, 1912: 1–408.

Hutchison, C.S. *Geological Evolution of South-East Asia*. Oxford: Oxford University Press, 1989.

Jones, C.R., D.J. Gobbett and T. Kobayashi. "Summary of fossil record in Malaya and Singapore 1900–1965," *Geology and Palaeontology of Southeast Asia*, Vol. 2, 1966: 301–59.

Kobayashi, T., R. Toriyama and W. Hashimoto (eds). *Geology and Palaeontology of Southeast Asia*. Vols. 1–25, 1964–1984. (Mainly Stratigraphical and Palaeontological Papers on Peninsular Malaysia)

Liechti, P., F.W. Roe, and N.S. Haile. "The Geology of Sarawak, Brunei and the Western Part of North Borneo," *British Borneo Geological Survey Bulletin*, No. 3, 1960.

Metcalfe, Ian. "Origin and Assembly of South-East Asian Continental Terranes," in: *Gondwana and Tethys*, M.G. Audley-Charles and A. Hallam (eds). Oxford: Oxford University Press, 1988: 101–18. (Geological Society London, Special Publication No. 37)

Nutalaya, P. (ed). *Stratigraphic correlation of Thailand and Malaysia. Volume 1: Technical Papers*. Geological Society Thailand/ Geological Society Malaysia Special Publication, 1983.

Reinhard M. and E. Wenk. "The Geology of the Colony of North Borneo," *British Borneo Geological Survey Bulletin*, No. 1. London: His Majesty's Stationery Office, 1951.

Scrivenor, J.B. *The Geology of Malayan Ore-Deposits*. London: Macmillan, 1928.

———. *The Geology of Malaya*. London: Macmillan, 1931.

Tan, D.N.K., C.H. Kho, and V. Hon. "Regional Geology: Sarawak," *Geological Survey Malaysia*, Annual Report for 1979: 97–118.

Wilford, G.E. "The Geology and Mineral Resources of Brunei and adjacent parts of Sarawak," *British Borneo Geological Survey*, Memoir 10. Brunei: Government Printer, 1961.

C. Medicine

Gimlette, John Desmond. *A Dictionary of Malayan Medicine*. Edited and completed by H.W. Thomson. New York: Oxford University Press, 1939.

Institute for Medical Research. *1900–1950: Fifty Years of Medical Research in Malaya*. Kuala Lumpur: Institute for Medical Research, 1951.

Khoo Oon Chor and M.S. Muir. *Bibliography of Medical Research at the University of Singapore 1955–1964*.

D. Flora and Fauna (Zoology, Botany)

Allen, B. Molesworth. *Common Malaysian Fruits*. Kuala Lumpur: Longmans Malaysia, 1968.

Barlow, H.S. *An Introduction to the Moths of South-East Asia*. Kuala Lumpur: Malayan Nature Society, 1982.

Berry, P.Y. *The Amphibian Fauna of Peninsular Malaysia*. Kuala Lumpur: Tropical Press, 1975.

Brockway, Lucille H. *Science and Colonial Expansion: The Role of the British Royal Botanic Gardens*. New York: Academic Press, 1979.

Corbet, A. Steven and H.M. Pendlebury. *The Butterflies of the Malayan Peninsula*. Kuala Lumpur: Malayan Nature Society, 1978.

Corner, E.J.H. *Wayside Trees of Malaya.* Singapore: Government Printing Office, 1952.

Fleming, W.A. *Butterflies of West Malaysia and Singapore.* Kuala Lumpur: Longmans Malaysia, 1975.

Gilliland, H.B. *A Revised Flora of Malaya. Vol. 3: Grasses of Malaya.* Singapore: Government Printing Office, 1971.

Glenister, A.G. *The Birds of the Malay Peninsula, Singapore and Penang: An Account of all the Malayan Species, with a note of their occurence in Sumatra, Borneo, and Java and a list of the birds of those islands.* Kuala Lumpur: Oxford University Press, 1971.

Hanbury-Tenison, Robin. *Mulu: The Rain Forest.* London: Weidenfeld & Nicholson, 1980.

Harrison, John. *An Introduction to the Mammals of Sabah.* Kota Kinabalu: The Sabah Society, 1973.

Henderson, M.R. *Common Malayan Wildflowers.* Kuala Lumpur: Longmans Malaysia, 1961.

Holttum, R.E. *Gardening in the Lowlands of Malaya.* Singapore: Straits Times Press (Malaya), 1953.

———. *Plant Life in Malaya.* Kuala Lumpur: Longmans Malaysia, 1954.

Hsuan Keng. *Orders and families of Malayan seed plants: Synopsis of orders and families of Malayan gymnosperms, dicotyledons and monocotyledons.* Singapore: Singapore University Press, 1978.

Johnson, Anne. *Mosses of Singapore and Malaysia.* Singapore: Singapore University Press, 1980.

Lim Boo Liat. *Poisonous Snakes of Peninsular Malaysia.* Kuala Lumpur: Malayan Nature Society, in association with the Institute for Medical Research, Kuala Lumpur, 1982.

Luping, Margaret Chin Wen and E. Richard Dingley (eds). *Kinabalu: Summit of Borneo.* Kota Kinabalu: The Sabah Society, 1978.

Macdonald, David. *Expedition to Borneo: The search for proboscis monkeys and other creatures*. London: J.M. Dent & Sons, 1982.

MacKinnon, John. *Borneo*. Amsterdam: Time-Life International (Nederland) B.V., 1975.

Medway, Lord. "The fauna of Malaysia in general," in: *Malaysia, A Survey*, Wang Gungwu (ed). London: Pall Mall, 1964: 55–66.

———. *Mammals of Borneo: Field keys and an annotated checklist*. Kuala Lumpur: Malaysian Branch Royal Asiatic Society, 1977. (Monograph No. 7)

———. *The Wild Mammals of Malaya (Peninsular Malaysia) and Singapore*. Kuala Lumpur: Oxford University Press, 1978.

——— and David R. Wells. *The Birds of the Malay peninsula: A general account of the birds inhabiting the region from the Isthmus of Kra to Singapore with the adjacent islands*, Volume V: *Conclusion, and survey of every species*. London: H.F. & G. Witherby; Kuala Lumpur: University of Malaya Press, 1976.

Morell, R. *Common Malayan Butterflies*. London: Longmans Green, 1960.

Nutter-Chasen, Frederick. *A handlist of Malaysian Mammals: A systematic list of the mammals of the Malay Peninsula, Sumatra, Borneo and Java, including the adjacent small islands*. Singapore: Government Printing Office, 1940. (Bulletin of the Raffles Museum, Singapore, No. 15)

Shuttleworth, Charles. *Malaysia's Green and Timeless World: An account of the Flora, Fauna and Indigenous People of the Forests of Malaysia*. Kuala Lumpur: Heinemann Educational Books (Asia), 1981.

Smythies, Bertram E. *The Birds of Borneo*. (Revised by the Earl of Cranbrook [Lord Medway]). Kota Kinabalu: The Sabah Society with the Malayan Nature Society, 1981.

Tung, W.W.Y. *Common Malayan Beetles*. Kuala Lumpur: Longmans Malaysia, 1983.

Tweedie, M.W.F. *Poisonous Animals of Malaya*. Singapore: Malaya Publishing House, 1941.

———. *The Snakes of Malaya*. Singapore: National Printers, 1983.

———. *Malayan Naturalist*. Singapore: Eastern Universities Press, 1957.

———. *Common Birds of the Malay Peninsula*. Kuala Lumpur: Longmans Malaysia, 1970.

——— and John L. Harrison. *Malayan Animal Life*. Kuala Lumpur: Longmans Malaysia, 1970.

Wallace, Alfred Russell. *Island life; or the phenomena and causes of insular faunas and floras, including a revision and attempted solution of the problem of geological climates*. London: Macmillan, 1880.

———. *The Malay Archipelago*. Singapore: Oxford University Press, 1986. (Originally 1869)

Whitmore, T.C. *Palms of Malaya*. Kuala Lumpur: Oxford University Press, 1973.

——— and F.S.P. Ng. *Tree Flora of Malaysia*. 3 Vols. Kuala Lumpur: Longmans Malaysia, 1978.

Yong Hoi Sen. *Magnificent Plants*. Kuala Lumpur: The Tropical Press, 1981.

———. *Malaysian Butterflies—An Introduction*. Kuala Lumpur: The Tropical Press, 1983.

E. Environment

Chuah, Donald G.S. and S.L. Lee. *Solar Radiation in Malaysia: A study on availability and distribution of solar energy in Malaysia*. Singapore: Oxford University Press, 1984.

Environment, Development and Natural Resource Crisis in Asia and the Pacific. Penang: Sahabat Alam Malaysia (Friends of the Earth Malaysia), 1984.

Lee, David. *The Sinking Ark: Environmental Problems in Malaysia and Southeast Asia*. Kuala Lumpur: Heinemann Educational Books (Asia), 1980.

Marshall, Adrian G. "Man and Nature in Malaysia: Attitudes to wildlife and conservation," in: *Nature and Man in South East Asia*, P.A. Stott (ed). London: School of Oriental and African Studies, 1978: 23–33.

Proceedings of the Conference on Forest Resources Crisis in the Third World, 6–8 September 1986. Penang: Sahabat Alam Malaysia, 1986.

The State of the Malaysian Environment 1983/84: Towards Greater Environment Awareness. Penang: Sahabat Alam Malaysia, 1983.

World Rainforest Movement and Sahabat Alam Malaysia. *The Battle for Sarawak's Forests*. Penang: World Rainforest Movement and Sahabat Alam Malaysia, 1990.

SOCIETY

A. Social Anthropology

Appell, George. "A Survey of the Social and Medical Anthropology of Sabah: Retrospect and Prospect," *Behavior Science Notes*, Vol. 3, 1968: 1–54.

———. (ed). *Studies in Borneo Societies: Social Process and Anthropological Explanation*. DeKalb: Center for Southeast Asian Studies, Northern Illinois University, 1976. (Special Report No. 12)

Arasaratnam, Sinnappah. *Indian Festivals in Malaya*. Kuala Lumpur: University of Malaya Press, 1966.

Azizah Kassim. "Some Aspects of Temuan Beliefs," *Federation Museum Journal*, National Museum, Vol. 21, new series, 1976: 53–67.

———. "A Matrilineal Society in the Context of Development," *Federation Museum Journal*, National Museum, Vol. 21, new series, 1976: 41–57.

Banks, David J. *Malay Kinship*. Philadelphia: Institute for the Study of Human Issues, 1983.

Dickson, Mora. *Longhouse in Sarawak*. London: Victor Gollancz, 1971.

Endicott, Kirk. *Batek Negrito Religion: The world-view and rituals of a hunting and gathering people of Peninsular Malaysia*. Oxford: Clarendon Press, 1979.

———. *An Analysis of Malay Magic*. Singapore: Oxford University Press, 1981.

Evans, I.H.N. *The Religion of the Tempasuk: Dusuns of North Borneo*. Cambridge: Cambridge University Press, 1953.

Firth, Raymond William. *Malay Fishermen: Their Peasant Economy*. London: Routledge & Kegan Paul, 1966.

———. "Faith and Scepticism in Kelantan Village Magic," in: *Kelantan: Religion, Society and Politics in a Malay State*, William R. Roff (ed). Kuala Lumpur: Oxford University Press, 1974: 190–224.

Firth, Rosemary. *Housekeeping Among Malay Peasants*. London: Athlone Press, 1966. (London School of Economics Monograph on Social Anthropology No. 7)

Fisk, E.K. "The Economics of the Handloom Industry of the North Eastern Malay States," *Journal of the Malayan Branch Royal Asiatic Society*, Vol. 32, Part 4, 1959: 1–70.

Freeman, J.D. "The Family System of the Iban of Borneo," in: *The Developmental Cycle in Domestic Groups*, Jack Goody (ed). Cambridge: Cambridge University Press, 1958: 15–52.

———. "The Iban of Western Borneo," in: *Social Structure in Southeast Asia*, George Peter Murdock (ed). Chicago: Quadrangle Books; London: Tavistock Publications, 1960.

Furness, William Henry. *The Home-Life of Borneo Head-hunters: Its Festivals and Folklore.* New York: AMS Press, 1979. (Originally 1902)

Geddes, W.R. *Nine Dayak Nights.* Singapore: Oxford University Press, 1985.

Gimlette, John D. *Malay Poisons and Charm Cures.* Kuala Lumpur: Oxford University Press, 1971.

Gullick, J.M. *Indigenous Political Systems of Western Malaya.* London: Athlone Press, 1958.

Haddon, Alfred C. *Head-hunters: Black, White and Brown.* New York: AMS Press, 1978. (Originally 1901)

Haji Mokhtar bin Haji Mohammed Dom. *Traditions and Taboos.* Kuala Lumpur: Federal Publications, 1979.

———. *Malay Superstitions and Beliefs.* Kuala Lumpur: Federal Publications, 1979.

———. *Malay Wedding Customs.* Kuala Lumpur: Federal Publications, 1979.

———. *The Bomoh and the Hantu.* Kuala Lumpur: Federal Publications, 1979.

Howell, Signe. *Chewong Myths and Legends.* Kuala Lumpur: Malaysian Branch Royal Asiatic Society, 1982. (Monograph No. 11)

———. *Society and Cosmos: Chewong of Peninsular Malaysia.* Singapore: Oxford University Press, 1984.

Jensen, Erik. *The Iban and Their Religion.* Oxford: Clarendon Press, 1974.

King, Victor T. "Ethnicity in Borneo: An Anthropological Problem," *Southern Asian Journal of Social Science*, Vol. 10, No. 1, 1982: 23–43.

LeBar, Frank M., Gerald C. Hickey and John K. Musgrave. *Ethnic Groups of Mainland Southeast Asia.* New Haven: Human Relations Area Files Press, 1964.

Lim Boo Liat. *Orang Asli Animal Tales*. Singapore: Eastern Universities Press, 1981.

Metcalf, Peter. *A Borneo journey into death: Berawan eschatology from its rituals*. Philadelphia: University of Pennsylvania Press, 1982.

Mohd. Taib Osman. *Malay Folk Beliefs*. Kuala Lumpur: Dewan Bahasa dan Pustaka, 1989.

Nagata, Judith A. "Kinship and Social Mobility Among the Malays," *Man*, new series, Vol. 11, No. 2, 1976: 400–9.

Roth, Henry Ling. *The Natives of Sarawak and British North Borneo*. London: Truslove & Hanson, 1896.

Rutter, Owen. *British North Borneo: An Account of Its History, Resources and Native Tribes*. London: Constable & Co. Ltd., 1922.

———. *The Pagans of North Borneo*. London: Hutchinson & Company, 1929.

Sandin, Benedict. *The Sea Dayaks of Borneo before White Rajah Rule*. London: Macmillan, 1967.

———. *Iban Adat and Augury*. Penang: Universiti Sains Malaysia Press, 1980.

Schneeberger, W.F. *Contributions to the Ethnology of Central Northeast Borneo (parts of Kalimantan, Sarawak and Sabah)*. Berne: University of Berne, 1979.

Sheppard, Mubin. *Malay Courtesy: A Narrative Account of Malay Manners and Customs in Everyday Use in Peninsular Malaysia*. Kuala Lumpur: Eastern Universities Press, 1981.

Siaw, Laurence K.L. "The Legacy of Malaysian Chinese Social Structure," *Journal of Southeast Asian Studies*, Vol. 12, No. 2, 1981: 395–402.

Skeat, Walter William. *Malay Magic: Being an introduction to the folklore and popular religion of the Malay Peninsula*. Introduction by Hood Salleh. Singapore: Oxford University Press, 1984. (Originally 1900)

——— and Charles Otto Blagden. *Pagan Races of the Malay Peninsula*. London: Macmillan, 1906.

Skinner, G. William. (Selected and Introduced). *The Study of Chinese Society: Essays by Maurice Freedman*. Stanford: Stanford University Press, 1979.

Swettenham, F.A. *The Real Malay*. London: Lane, 1900.

Swift, Michael Godfrey. *Malay Peasant Society in Jelebu*. London: Athlone Press, 1965. (London School of Economics Monograph on Social Anthropology No. 29)

Tan Chee Beng. *The Development and Distribution of Dejiao Associations in Malaysia and Singapore: A Study on a Chinese Religious Organisation*. Singapore: Institute of Southeast Asian Studies, 1985.

Tillema, H.F. *A Journey Among the Peoples of Central Borneo in Word and Picture*, Victor T. King (ed and introd.). Singapore: Oxford University Press, 1989.

Vaughan, J.D. *Manners and Customs of the Chinese in the Straits Settlements*. Kuala Lumpur: Oxford University Press, 1971. (Originally 1879)

Wagner, Ulla. *Colonialism and Iban Warfare*. Stockholm: OBE-Tryck Sthlm, 1972.

Wazir Jahan Karim (ed). *Emotions of Culture: A Malay Perspective*. Singapore: Oxford University Press, 1989.

Werner, Roland. *Jah-het of Malaysia: Art and Culture*. Kuala Lumpur: University of Malaya Press, 1975.

Wilkinson, R.J. *Papers on Malay Subjects 1907–16*. Selected and Introduced by P.L. Burns. Kuala Lumpur: Oxford University Press, 1971.

Williams, Thomas Rhys. *The Dusun: A North Borneo Society*. New York: Holt, Rinehart & Winston, 1965.

Winstedt, Richard. *The Malay Magician, Being Shaman, Saiva and Sufi*. Kuala Lumpur: Oxford University Press, 1982.

B. Education

Awang Had bin Salleh, Afrah Abdul Aziz, Abdul Rahmin Mohd. Yusoff, Fatimah Hamid Don, and Khoo Phon Sai. *A Critical Review of Research in Malaysia on Effectiveness of Teachers*. Kuala Lumpur: University of Malaya Press, 1978.

Bock, John C. *Education in a Plural Society*. Stanford: Stanford University Press, 1978.

Chang, Min Phang, Paul. *Educational Development in a Plural Society*. Singapore: Academia Publications, 1973.

Handbook: Southeast Asian Institutions of Higher Learning, 1983–1985. Bangkok: Association of Southeast Asian Institutions of Higher Learning, Thammasat University, 1982.

Harrison, Brian. *Waiting for China: The Anglo-Chinese College at Malacca, 1818–1843, and early nineteenth century missions*. Hong Kong: Hong Kong University Press, 1979.

Inglis, Christine. "Educational Policy and Occupational Structures in Peninsular Malaysia," in: *Issues in Malaysian Development*, James C. Jackson and Martin Rudner (eds). Singapore: Heinemann Educational Books (Asia) for the Asian Studies Association of Australia, 1979.

Kanagasabai, Chew Sing Buan, Koh Boh Boon, Leong Yin Ching. (eds). *Studies on Malaysian Education: An Annotated Bibliography*. Kuala Lumpur: Faculty of Education, University of Malaya, 1980.

Key Questions on Malaysian Education. Penang: Consumers' Association of Penang, 1984.

Khoo Siew Mun (co-ordinator). *Higher Education in Malaysia: A Bibliography*. Singapore: Regional Institute of Higher Education and Development, 1983.

Lee, Eddy. *Educational Planning in West Malaysia*. Kuala Lumpur: Oxford University Press, 1972.

Loh Fook Seng, Philip. *Seeds of Separatism: Educational Policy in Malaya 1874–1940*. Kuala Lumpur: Oxford University Press, 1975.

Marimuthu, Thangavelu. *Student Development in Malaysian Universities*. Singapore: Regional Institute of Higher Education and Development, 1984. (RIHED Occasional Paper No. 19)

McMeekin, Robert W. Jr. *Educational planning and expenditure decisions in developing countries with a Malaysian case study*. New York: Praeger Publishers, 1975.

Stevenson, Rex. *Cultivators and Administrators: British Educational Policy Towards the Malays 1875–1906*. Kuala Lumpur: Oxford University Press, 1975.

Tham Seong Chee. "Issues in Malaysian Education: Past, Present, and Future," *Journal of Southeast Asian Studies*, Vol. 10, No. 2, 1979: 321–50.

Wong, Francis H.K. and Gwee Yee Hean. *Perspectives: The Development of Education in Malaysia and Singapore*. Kuala Lumpur: Heinemann Educational Books (Asia), 1972.

——— and Ee Tiang Hong. *Education in Malaysia*. Kuala Lumpur: Heinemann Educational Books (Asia), 1975.

C. Religion

Ackerman, S.R. and Raymond L.M. Lee. *Heaven in Transition: Non-Muslim Religious Innovation and Ethnic Identity in Malaysia*. Honolulu: University of Hawaii Press, 1988.

Cheeseman, Harold A.R. "The Presbyterian Church in Malaya," *British Malaya*, October 1947: 276–77.

Comber, Leon. *Chinese Ancestor Worship in Malaya*. Singapore: Donald Moore, 1954.

Evans, I.H.N. *Studies in Religion, Folklore, and Custom in British North Borneo and the Malay Peninsula*. London: Frank Cass, 1970. (Originally 1923)

Hooker, M.B. "Adat and Islam in Malaya," *Bijdragen tot de Taal-, Land-en Volkenkunde*, Vol. 130, Part 1, 1974: 69–90.

——— (ed). *Islam in Southeast Asia*. Leiden: E.J. Brill, 1983.

Kessler, Clive S. "Malaysia: Islamic Revivalism and Political Disaffection in a Divided Society," *Southeast Asia Chronicle*, No. 75, 1980: 3–11.

Lee, Felix George. *The Catholic Church in Malaya*. Singapore: Donald Moore for Eastern Universities Press, 1963.

Lee, Raymond L.M. "Sai Baba salvation and syncretism: religious change in a Hindu movement in urban Malaysia," *Contributions to Indian Sociology*, (NS), Vol. 16, No. 1, 1982: 125–40.

McDougall, Colin. *Buddhism in Malaya*. Singapore: Donald Moore, 1956.

McLeish, A. *A racial melting pot: religion in Malaya*. London: World Dominion Press, 1940.

Means, Gordon P. "The Role of Islam in the Political Development of Malaysia," *Comparative Politics*, Vol. 1, No. 2, 1969: 264–84.

———. "Public Policy Towards Religion in Malaysia," *Pacific Affairs*, Vol. 51, No. 2, 1978: 384–405.

Means, Nathalie Toms. *Malayan Mosaic*. Singapore: Methodist Book Room, 1935.

Mohamed Abu Bakar. "Islamic Revivalism and the Political Process in Malaysia," *Asian Survey*, Vol. 21, No. 10, 1981: 1040–59.

Nagata, Judith. "Religious Ideology and Social Change: The Islamic Revival in Malaysia," *Pacific Affairs*, Vol. 53, No. 3, 1980: 405–39.

———. "The New Fundamentalism: Islam in Contemporary Malaysia," *Asian Thought and Society: An International Review*, Vol. 5, No. 14, 1980: 128–41.

———. *The Reflowering of Malaysian Islam: Modern Religious Radicals and their Roots*. Vancouver: University of British Columbia Press, 1984.

O'Sullivan, Leona. "The London Missionary Society: A Written Record of Missionaries and Printing Presses in the Straits Settlements 1815–1847," *Journal of the Malaysian Branch Royal Asiatic Society*, Vol. 57, Part 2, 1984: 61–104.

Persatuan Sejarah Malaysia. *Islam di Malaysia*. Kuala Lumpur: Persatuan Sejarah Malaysia, 1980.

Roff, William R. "The Malayo-Muslim World of Singapore in the Late Nineteenth Century," *Journal of Asian Studies*, Vol. 24, No. 1, 1964: 75–90.

Rooney, John. *Khabar Gembira (the good news): A History of the Catholic Church in East Malaysia and Brunei (1880–1976)*. London: Burns & Oates with Mill Hill Missionaries, 1981.

Sakai, Tadao. "Some Aspects of Chinese Religious Practices and Customs in Singapore and Malaysia," *Journal of Southeast Asian Studies*, Vol. 12, No. 1, 1981: 133–41.

S.Q. Fatimi. *Islam Comes to Malaysia*. Singapore: Malaysian Sociological Research Institute, 1963.

Syed Naguib Alatas. *Some aspects of Sufism as understood and practised among the Malays*, Shirle Gordon (ed). Singapore: Malaysian Sociological Research Institute, 1963.

———. *Preliminary Statement on a General Theory of Islamization of the Malay-Indonesian Archipelago*. Kuala Lumpur: Dewan Bahasa dan Pustaka, 1969.

———. *Islam Dalam Sejarah dan Kebudayaan Melayu*. Bangi: Universiti Kebangsaan Malaysia Press, 1972.

Teixeira, Manual. *The Portuguese Missions in Malacca and Singapore (1951–1958)*. Lisbon: Agencia Geral do Ultramar, 1963.

Tunku Abdul Rahman Putra, Tan Sri Dr. Tan Chee Khoon, Dr. Chandra Muzaffar, Lim Kit Siang. *Contemporary Issues on Malaysian Religions*. Petaling Jaya: Pelanduk Publications, 1984.

Yegar, Moshe. *Islam and Islamic Institutions in British Malaya, 1874–1941: Policies and Implementation*. Jerusalem: Magnes Press, 1979.

D. Sociology

Aliran. *Aliran Speaks: A Collection of Writings on Social Issues*. Penang: Aliran Kesedaran Malaysia, 1981.

———. *Corruption: A Collection of Papers Presented by Aliran Officials and Guest Speakers at an Aliran Seminar on Corruption*. Penang: Aliran Kesedaran Negara, 1981.

Bailey, Conner. *The Sociology of Production in Rural Malay Society*. Singapore: Oxford University Press, 1983.

Bisch, Jorgen. *Ulu: The World's End*. Translated from the Danish by Reginald Spink. London: Allen & Unwin, 1961.

Blythe, W. *The Impact of Chinese Secret Societies in Malaya*. London: Oxford University Press, 1969.

Chandra Muzaffar. *The Protector: An Analysis of the Concept and Practice of Loyalty and Leader-led Relationships within Malay Society*. Penang: Aliran Kesedaran Negara, 1979.

———. *Islamic Resurgence in Malaysia*. Petaling Jaya: Penerbit Fajar Bakti, 1987.

Comber, Leon. *An Introduction to Chinese Secret Societies in Malaya*. Singapore: Donald Moore, 1957.

———. *Chinese Secret Societies in Malaya*. Locust Valley: J.J. Augustin, 1959.

Craig, Joann. *Culture Shock! What not to do in Malaysia and Singapore: How and Why not to do it*. Singapore: Times Books International, 1979.

Cushman, Jennifer and Wang Gungwu (eds). *Changing Identities of the Southeast Asian Chinese Since World War II*. Hong Kong: Hong Kong University Press, 1988.

Dahlan, H.M. "Micro-Analyses of Village Communities: A Study of Underdevelopment," in: *The Nascent Malaysian Society: Developments, Trends and Problems*, H.M. Dahlan (ed). Siri Monograf Jabatan Antropologi dan Sosiologi, Universiti Kebangsaan Malaysia No. 3, 1976.

Endicott, Kirk. "The Impact of Economic Modernization on the *Orang Asli* (Aborigines) of Northern Peninsular Malaysia," in: *Issues in Malaysian Development*, James C. Jackson and Martin Rudner (eds). Singapore: Heinemann Educational Books (Asia) for the Asian Studies Association of Australia, 1979.

Freeman, Derek. *Report on the Iban*. London: Athlone Press; New York: Humanities Press, 1970.

Grijpstra, B.G. *Common Efforts in the Development of Rural Sarawak: Malaysia*. Amsterdam: Van Gorcum, 1976.

Hing Ai Yun, Nik Safiah Karim and Rokiah Talib. *Women in Malaysia*. Petaling Jaya: Pelanduk Publications, 1984.

Hirschman, Charles. *Ethnic and Social Stratification in Peninsular Malaysia*. Washington, DC: American Sociological Association, 1975. (The Arnold and Caroline Rose Monograph Series)

Hong, Evelyn. *Malaysian Women: Problems and Issues*. Penang: Consumers' Association of Penang, 1983.

Jones, Alun. "The Orang Asli: An Outline of their Progress in Modern Malaya," *Journal of Southeast Asian History*, Vol. 9, No. 2, 1968: 286–305.

Kedit, Peter Mulok. *Modernization among the Iban of Sarawak*. Kuala Lumpur: Dewan Bahasa dan Pustaka, 1980.

Kessler, Clive Samuel. *Islam and Politics in a Malay State: Kelantan 1838–1969*. Ithaca: Cornell University Press, 1978.

King, Victor T. (ed). *Essays on Borneo Societies*. Oxford: Oxford University Press for the University of Hull, 1978. (Monographs on South-East Asia, No. 7)

Kuchiba, Matsuo, Yoshihiro Tsubouchi and Narifumi Maeda. *Three Malay Villages: A Sociology of Paddy Growers in West Malaysia.* Honolulu: University of Hawaii Press, 1979. (Monograph of the Center for Southeast Asian Studies, Kyoto University, English Language Series, No. 14)

Laderman, Carol. *Wives and Midwives: Childbirth and Nutrition in Rural Malaysia.* Berkeley: University of California Press, 1983.

Loh Kok Wah, Francis. *Beyond the Tin Mines: Coolies, Squatters and New Villagers in the Kinta Valley, Malaysia, 1880–1980.* Singapore: Oxford University Press, 1988.

Mahathir Mohamad. *The Malay Dilemma.* Singapore: Asia Pacific Press, 1970.

Mak Lau Fong. *The Sociology of Secret Societies: A Study of Chinese Secret Societies in Singapore and Peninsular Malaysia.* Kuala Lumpur: Oxford University Press, 1981.

Manderson, L. (ed). *Women's Work and Women's Roles: Economics and Everyday Life in Indonesia, Malaysia and Singapore.* Canberra: Australian National University Press, 1983. (Development Studies Centre Monograph No. 32)

Nagata, Judith (ed). *Pluralism in Malaysia: Myth and Reality. A Symposium on Singapore and Malaysia.* Leiden: E.J. Brill, 1975.

———. *Malaysian Mosaic: Perspectives from a Poly-ethnic Society.* Vancouver: University of British Columbia Press, 1979.

———. "Perceptions of Social Inequality in a 'Plural Society': Malaysia," in: *Sociology of South-East Asia: Readings on Social Change and Development*, Hans Dieter Evers (ed). Kuala Lumpur: Oxford University Press, 1980.

Nash, Manning. *Peasant Citizens: Politics, Religion and Modernization in Kelantan, Malaysia.* Athens: Ohio University Center for International Studies, 1947. (Papers in International Studies, Southeast Asia Series No. 31)

Peletz, M.G. *A Share of the Harvest: Kinship, Property and Social History among the Malays of Rembau.* Berkeley: University of California Press, 1988.

Roff, W.R. (ed). *Kelantan: Religion, Society and Politics in a Malay State*. Kuala Lumpur: Oxford University Press, 1974.

Scott, James C. *Political Ideology in Malaysia: Reality and the Beliefs of an Elite*. New Haven: Yale University Press, 1968.

Shaharuddin bin Maaruf. *Concept of a Hero in Malay Society*. Singapore: Eastern Universities Press, 1984.

Shamsul, Amri Baharuddin. "The Development of Underdevelopment of the Malaysian Peasantry," *Journal of Contemporary Asia*, Vol. 9, 1979: 434–54.

———. "Patron-client Relations as an Aspect of Peasant Ideology: A Note with Reference to Malay Peasant Society," *Akademika*, Vols. 20 & 21, 1982. Special Issue on *Peasantry and Modernization in Southeast Asia*, Hairi Abdullah and H.M. Dahlan (eds). Bangi: Universiti Kebangsaan Malaysia, 1982.

———. *From British to Bumiputera Rule*. Singapore: Institute of Southeast Asian Studies, 1986.

Siaw, Lawrence K.L. *Chinese Society in Rural Malaysia: A Local History of the Chinese in Titi, Jelebu*. Kuala Lumpur: Oxford University Press, 1983.

Strange, Heather. *Rural Malay Women in Tradition and Transition*. New York: Praeger, 1981.

Swift, Michael Godfrey. "Economic Concentration and Malay Peasant Society," in: *Social Organization: Essays Presented to Raymond Firth*, Maurice Freedman (ed). London: Frank Cass, 1967: 241–69.

Syed Husin Ali. *Social Stratification in Kampong Bagan: A Study of Class, Status, Conflict and Mobility*. Kuala Lumpur: Malaysian Branch Royal Asiatic Society, 1964. (Monograph No. 1)

———. "Patterns of Rural Leadership in Malaya," *Journal of the Malaysian Branch Royal Asiatic Society*, Vol. 41, Part 1, 1968: 95–45.

———. *Malay Peasant Society and Leadership*. Kuala Lumpur: Oxford University Press, 1975.

———. *Apa Erti Pembangunan?* Kuala Lumpur: Dewan Bahasa dan Pustaka, 1976.

Syed Hussein Alatas. "The Grading of Occupational Prestige Amongst the Malays in Malaysia," *Journal of the Malaysian Branch Royal Asiatic Society*, Vol. 41, Part 1, 1968: 146–70.

———. *Modernization and Social Change*. Sydney: Angus and Robertson, 1972.

———. *The Myth of the Lazy Native: A study of the image of the Malays, Filipinos and Javenese from the 16th to the 20th century and its function in the ideology of colonial capitalism*. London: Frank Cass, 1977.

Tan Chee Beng. *The Baba of Melaka: Culture and Identity of a Chinese Peranakan Community in Malaya*. Petaling Jaya: Pelanduk Publications, 1988.

Tan Loong-Hoe. *Malnutrition, Health Resources and Education in Peninsular Malaysia*. Singapore: Maruzeen Asia, under the auspices of the Institute of Southeast Asian Studies, 1982. (Occasional Paper No. 69)

Taufik Abdullah and Sharon Siddique (eds). *Islam and Society in Southeast Asia*. Singapore: Institute of Southeast Asian Studies, 1987.

Tham Seong Chee. "Ideology, Politics and Economic Modernization: The Case of the Malays in Malaysia," *Southeast Asian Journal of Social Sciences*, Vol. 1, No. 1, 1973: 41–59.

———. *Malays and Modernization: A Sociological Interpretation*. Singapore: University of Singapore Press, 1977.

T'ien, Ju-k'an. *The Chinese in Sarawak: A Study of Social Structure*. London: London School of Economics, 1956.

Tsubouchi, Yoshihiro. "Marriage and Divorce Among Malay Peasants in Kelantan," *Journal of Southeast Asian Studies*, Vol. 6, No. 2, 1975: 135–50.

Wilder, William D. *Communication, Social Structure and Development in Rural Malaysia: A Study of Kampung Kuala Bera*. London:

Athlone Press, 1982. (London School of Economics, Monograph on Social Anthropology, No. 56)

Wilson, Peter J. *A Malay Village and Malaysia: Social Values and Rural Development*. New Haven: Human Relations Area Files Press, 1967.

Winstedt, R.O. *The Malays: A Cultural History*. (Revised and Updated by Tham Seong Chee). Singapore: Graham Brash, 1981.

Winzeler, Rober L. "The Social Organization of Islam in Kelantan," in: *Kelantan: Religion, Society and Politics in a Malay State*, William R. Roff (ed). Kuala Lumpur: Oxford University Press, 1974.

Wolters, O.W. *History, Culture and Religion in Southeast Asian Perspectives*. Singapore: Institute of Southeast Asian Studies, 1982.

Zawawi Ibrahim. "Perspectives Towards Investigating Malay Peasant Ideology and the Bases of its Production in Contemporary Malaysia," *Journal of Contemporary Asia*, Vol. 13, No. 2, 1983: 198–209.

APPENDIX 1

PARAMOUNT RULERS

1. Tuanku Abdul Rahman ibni Al-Marhum Tuanku Muhammad, the Yang di Pertuan Besar of Negeri Sembilan. 3 August 1957–1 April 1960. Died in office.
2. Tuanku Hishamuddin Alam Shah Al-Haj ibni Al-Marhum Sultan Alaiddin Sulaiman Shah, the Sultan of Selangor. 14 April 1960–1 September 1960. Died in office.
3. Tuanku Syed Putra Al-Haj ibni Al-Marhum Syed Hassan Jamalullail, the Raja of Perlis. 21 September 1960–20 September 1965.
4. Tuanku Ismail Nasiruddin Shah ibni Al-Marhum Sultan Zainal Abidin, the Sultan of Trengganu. 21 September 1965–20 September 1970.
5. Tuanku Abdul Halim Mu'adzam Shah ibni Al-Marhum Sultan Badlishah, the Sultan of Kedah. 21 September 1970–20 September 1975.
6. Tuanku Yahya Petra ibni Al-Marhum Sultan Ibrahim, the Sultan of Kelantan. 21 September 1975–30 March 1979. Died in office.
7. Tuanku Haji Ahmad Shah Al-Musta'in Billah ibni Al-Marhum Sultan Abu Bakar Ri'ayatuddin Al-Mu'adzam Shah, the Sultan of Pahang. 26 April 1979–25 April 1984.
8. Sultan Mahmood Iskandar al-Haj ibni al-Marhum Sultan Ismail, the Sultan of Johor. 26 April 1984–25 April 1989.
9. Sultan Azlan Muhibbuddin Shah ibni Al-Marhum Sultan Yusuff Izzuddin Ghafarullahulahu Shah, the Sultan of Perak. 26 April 1989–

APPENDIX 2

PRIME MINISTERS

1. Tunku Abdul Rahman Putra Al-Haj, 28 July 1955–22 September 1970.

2. Tun Abdul Razak bin Datuk Hussein Al-Haj, 22 September 1970–14 January 1976.

3. Tun Hussein Onn, 15 January 1976–16 July 1981.

4. Dato' Seri Dr. Mahathir Mohamad, 16 July 1981–

APPENDIX 3

THE CABINET LINE-UP 1991

Prime Minister	Honourable Dato' Seri Dr. Mahathir Mohamad
Deputy Prime Minister	Honourable Mr. Abdul Ghafar Baba

PRIME MINISTER'S DEPARTMENT

Ministers	Honourable Datuk Abang Abu Bakar bin Datu Bandar Abang Haji Mustapha
	Honourable Mr Syed Hamid bin Syed Jaafar Albar
Deputy Ministers	Honourable Raja Dato' Ariffin bin Raja Sulaiman
	Honourable Dato' Drs Suleiman bin Mohamed
	Honourable Dato' Wong See Wah
	Honourable Dr Haji Abdul Hamid bin Haji Othman
Parliamentary Secretaries	Honourable Haji Othman bin Abdul
	Honourable Mr Douglas Uggah Embas

MINISTRY OF HOME AFFAIRS

Minister	Honourable Dato' Seri Dr Mahathir Mohamad
Deputy Minister	Honourable Dato' Megat Junid bin Megat Ayob
Parliamentary Secretary	Honourable Mr Ong Ka Ting

MINISTRY OF RURAL DEVELOPMENT

Minister	Honourable Mr Abdul Ghafar Baba
Deputy Minister	Honourable Mr Mohd Yassin bin Kamari
Parliamentary Secretary	Honourable Dato' Mohamed bin Jamrah

Deputy Minister	Honourable Mr Mohd Yassin bin Kamari
Parliamentary Secretary	Honourable Dato' Mohamed bin Jamrah

MINISTRY OF TRANSPORT

Minister	Honourable Dato' Seri Dr Ling Liong Sik
Deputy Minister	Honourable Datin Paduka Hajah Zaleha binti Ismail

MINISTRY OF ENERGY, TELECOMMUNICATIONS AND POST

Minister	Honourable Dato' Seri S. Samy Vellu
Deputy Minister	Honourable Dato' Mohd. Tajol Rosli bin Mohd. Ghazali

MINISTRY OF PRIMARY INDUSTRIES

Minister	Honourable Dato' Seri Dr Lim Keng Yaik
Deputy Minister	Honourable Haji Tengku Mahmud bin Mansor

MINISTRY OF WORKS

Minister	Honourable Datuk Leo Moggie Anak Irok
Deputy Ministers	Honourable Mr Kerk Choo Ting
	Honourable Datuk Peter Tinggom Anak Kamarau

MINISTRY OF INTERNATIONAL TRADE AND INDUSTRY

Minister	Honourable Dato' Seri Rafidah Aziz
Deputy Minister	Honourable Mr Chua Jui Meng
Parliamentary Secretary	Honourable Dato' Dr K.S. Nijhar

MINISTRY OF EDUCATION

Minister	Honourable Dato' Dr Haji Sulaiman bin Haji Daud
Deputy Ministers	Honourable Dr Leo Michael Toyad
	Honourable Dr Fong Chan Onn

MINISTRY OF AGRICULTURE

Minister	Honourable Datuk Seri Sanusi bin Junid
Deputy Minister	Honourable Dato' S. Subramaniam
Parliamentary Secretary	Honourable Haji Mohd. Shariff bin Haji Omar

MINISTRY OF FINANCE

Minister	Honourable Dato' Seri Anwar bin Ibrahim
Deputy Ministers	Honourable Dato' Loke Yuen Yow
	Honourable Mr Abdul Ghani bin Othman

MINISTRY OF DOMESTIC TRADE AND CONSUMER AFFAIRS

Deputy Minister	Honourable Dato' Abdul Kadir bin Haji Sheikh Fadzir
Parliamentary Secretary	Honourable Dr Sak Cheng Lum

MINISTRY OF HEALTH

Minister	Honourable Dato' Lee Kim Sai
Deputy Minister	Honourable Mohd. Farid bin Ariffin
Parliamentary Secretary	Honourable Datuk K. Kumaran

MINISTRY OF FOREIGN AFFAIRS

Minister	Honourable Dato' Abdullah bin Haji Ahmad Badawi
Deputy Minister	Honourable Dato' Dr Abdullah Fadzil bin Che Wan

MINISTRY OF DEFENCE

Minister	Honourable Dato' Sri Haji Mohd Najib bin Tun Haji Abdul Razak
Deputy Minister	Honourable Dato' Wan Abu Bakar bin Wan Mohamed

MINISTRY OF INFORMATION

Minister	Honourable Dato' Mohamed bin Rahmat
Deputy Minister	Honourable Mr Railey bin Haji Jaffrey
Parliamentary Secretary	Honourable Dato' Fauzi bin Abdul Rahman

MINISTRY OF CULTURE, ARTS AND TOURISM

Minister	Honourable Dato' Sabbaruddin bin Chik
Deputy Minister	Honourable Mr Chan Kong Choy
Parliamentary Secretary	Honourable Dato' Haji Abdul Rahman bin Sulaiman

MINISTRY OF NATIONAL UNITY AND COMMUNITY DEVELOPMENT

Minister	Honourable Dato' Napsiah binti Omar
Deputy Minister	Honourable Dato' Alexander Yu Lung Lee
Parliamentary Secretary	Honourable Mr Yong Khoon Seng

MINISTRY OF PUBLIC ENTERPRISES

Minister	Honourable Dato' Dr Mohammad Yusof bin Haji Mohamed Nor
Deputy Minister	Honourable Dato' Dr Siti Zaharah binti Sulaiman

MINISTRY OF HUMAN RESOURCES

Minister	Honourable Dato' Lim Ah Lek
Deputy Minister	Honourable Dato' M. Mahalingam

MINISTRY OF SCIENCE, TECHNOLOGY AND ENVIRONMENT

Minister	Honourable Mr Law Hieng Ding
Deputy Minister	Honourable Mr Peter Chin Fah Kui

MINISTRY OF HOUSING AND LOCAL GOVERNMENT

Minister	Honourable Dr Ting Chew Peh
Deputy Ministers	Honourable Mr Osu bin Haji Sukam
	Honourable Haji Daud bin Dato' Haji Taha

MINISTRY OF LAND AND CO-OPERATIVE DEVELOPMENT

Minister	Honourable Tan Sri Datuk Haji Sakaran bin Dandai
Deputy Minister	Honourable Dato' Mohd. Khalid bin Mohd Yunus
Parliamentary Secretary	Honourable Mr Mohd Noh bin Rajab

MINISTRY OF JUSTICE

Minister	Honourable Mr Syed Hamid bin Syed Jaafar Albar (He is also Minister in the Prime Minister's Department)

MINISTRY OF YOUTH AND SPORTS

Minister	Honourable Haji Annuar bin Musa (Senator)
Deputy Minister	Honourable Ms Teng Gaik Kwan
Parliamentary Secretary	Honourable Dato' Ismail bin Said

APPENDIX 4

DETAILED CLASSIFICATION OF ETHNIC GROUPS BY REGION, MALAYSIA, 1970 AND 1980

Peninsular Malaysia			
1970 Census		**1980 Census**	
Malay:	Malay	Malay:	Malay
	Indonesian		Indonesian
	Negrito		Negrito
	Jakun		Jakun
	Semai		Semai
	Semelai		Semelai
	Temiar		Temiar
	Other Indigenous		Other Indigenous
	Other Malay race		Other Malay race
Chinese:	Hokkien	Chinese:	Hokkien
	Cantonese		Cantonese
	Khek (Hakka)		Khek (Hakka)
	Teochew		Teochew
	Hainanese		Hainanese
	Kwongsai		Kwongsai
	Hokchiu		Hokchiu
	Hokchia		Hokchia
	Henghua		Henghua
	Other Chinese		Other Chinese
Indian:	Indian Tamil	Indian:	Indian Tamil
	Telegu		Malayali
	Malayali		Telegu
	Punjabi		Sikh
	Other Indian		Other Punjabi
	Pakistani		Other Indian
	Ceylon Tamil		Pakistani
	Other Ceylonese		Bangladeshi
			Sri Lankan Tamil
			Other Sri Lankan

1970 Census		1980 Census	
Others:	Thai	Others:	Thai
	Other Asian		Vietnamese
	European		Other Asian
	Eurasian		Eurasian
	Others		European
			Others

Sabah

1970 Census		1980 Census	
Kadazan:	Kadazan	Pribumi:	Kadazan
	Kwijau		Kwijau
Murut:	Murut		Murut
Bajau:	Bajau		Bajau
	Illanun		Illanun
Malay:	Malay		Lotud
Indonesian:	Indonesian		Rungus
Other Indigenous:	Lotud		Tambanuo
	Rungus		Dumpas
	Tambanuo		Maragang
	Dumpas		Paitan
	Maragang		Idahan
	Paitan		Minokok
	Idahan		Rumanau
	Minokok		Mangka'ak
	Rumanau		Sulu
	Mangka'ak		Orang Sungei
	Sulu		Brunei
	Orang Sungei		Kedayan
	Brunei		Bisaya
	Kadayan		Tidong
	Bisaya		Other Indigenous
	Tidong		Malay
	Sino-native		Indonesian
	Others		Sino-native
Chinese:	Hakka		Native of Sarawak
	Cantonese		Native of Philippines
	Hokkien		Cocos Islander
	Teochew	Chinese:	Hokkien
	Hainanese		Cantonese
	Other Chinese		Khek (Hakka)
			Teochew
			Hainanese
			Other Chinese
		Indian:	Indian/Pakistani/Bangladeshi/Sri Lankan

1970 Census		1980 Census	
Others:	Native of Sarawak	Others:	Vietnamese
	Native of Philippines		Other Asian
	European		Eurasian
	Eurasian		European
	Indian		Others
	Cocos Islander		
	Others		

Sarawak

1970 Census		1980 Census	
Malay:	Malay	Malay:	Malay
Melanau:	Melanau	Melanau:	Melanau
Sea Dayak: (Iban)	Sea Dayak	Iban:	Iban
Land Dayak: (Bidayuh)	Land Dayak	Bidayuh:	Bidayuh
Other Indigenous:		Other Indigenous:	
	Bisayah		Bisayah (of Sarawak)
	Kadayan		Kedayan (of Sarawak)
	Kayan		Kayan
	Kenyah		Kenyah
	Kelabit		Kelabit
	Murut		Murut (of Sarawak)
	Punan		Punan
	Others		Other Indigenous
Chinese:	Cantonese	Chinese:	Hokkien
	Foochow		Cantonese
	Hakka		Khek (Hakka)
	Henghua		Teochew
	Hokkien		Hainanese
	Hainanese		Henghua
	Teochew		Foochow
	Other Chinese		Other Chinese
Others:	Indian	Indian:	Indian/Pakistani/Bangladeshi/Sri Lankan
	Indonesian		
	European		
	Eurasian	Others:	Indonesian
	Others		Vietnamese
			Other Asian
			Eurasian
			European
			Others

Table 1: Population—Ethnic composition of the population by region, Malaysia, census years between 1957 and 1980

Region	Ethnic group				
Peninsular Malaysia	Malays	Chinese	Indians	Others*	Total
		Number ('000)			
1957	3,125.5	2,333.8	696.2	123.3	6,278.8
1970	4,671.9	3,131.3	936.3	70.0	8,809.5
1980	6,131.6	3,651.2	1,093.1	68.9	10,944.8
1970 (revised)	4,841.3	3,286.0	981.4	73.0	9,181.7
1980 (revised)	6,315.6	3,865.4	1,171.1	74.5	11,426.6
		Average annual growth rate (%)			
1957–1970	3.1	2.3	2.3	−4.3	2.6
1970–1980	2.7	1.5	1.5	−0.2	2.2
1970–1980 (revised)	2.7	1.6	1.8	0.2	2.2
Sabah	Pribumi	Chinese	Indians	Others	Total
		Number ('000)			
1960	344.2	104.5	3.2	2.5	454.4
1970	500.0	139.2	7.1	7.3+	653.6
1980	792.0	155.3	5.3	3.1	955.7
1980 (revised)	838.1	164.0	5.6	3.3	1,011.0

Table 1: Population—Ethnic composition of the population by region, Malaysia, census years between 1957 and 1980 *(continued)*

Region	Ethnic group				
Sabah	Pribumi	Chinese	Indians	Others	Total
	Average annual growth rate (%)				
1960–1970	3.7	2.9	8.0	10.7	3.6
1970–1980	4.6	1.1	– 2.9	–8.6	3.8

Sarawak	Malays	Melanaus	Ibans	Bidayuhs	Other Indi-genous	Chinese	Others	Total
	Number ('000)							
1960	129.3	44.7	237.7	57.6	37.9	229.1	8.1	744.5
1970	181.4	53.4	303.5	83.6	50.7	293.9	9.7	976.3
1980	248.8	69.8	368.5	104.9	67.1	360.6	15.9	1,235.6
1980 (revised)	257.8	75.1	396.3	107.5	69.1	385.2	16.6	1,307.6
	Average annual growth rate (%)							
1960–1970	3.4	1.8	2.4	3.7	2.9	2.5	1.8	2.7
1970–1980	3.2	2.7	1.9	2.3	2.8	2.0	4.9	2.4

*This figure includes a total of 300 persons enumerated on self-enumeration forms who were not classified by detailed ethnic group.
Source: Banci Penduduk dan Perumahan Malaysia 1980 (Population and Housing Census of Malaysia), *Laporan Am Banci Penduduk* (General Report of the Population Census). Vol.1 (Kuala Lumpur: Jabatan Perangkaan Malaysia, 1983), p.17.

Table 2: Population Size and Rates of Change*, Malaysia, 1947–1980

Year	Malaysia	Peninsular Malaysia	Sabah	Sarawak
		Population size ('000)		
1947	5,775.0	4,908.1	320.5	546.4
1957	7,382.5	6,278.8	410.5	693.2
1960	8,035.6	6,836.7	454.4	744.5
1970	10,439.4	8,809.5	653.6	976.3
1980	13,136.1	10,944.8	955.7	1,235.6
1980 (revised)	13,745.2	11,426.6	1,011.0	1,307.6
		Average annual growth rate (%)		
1947–1957	2.5	2.5	2.5	2.4
1957–1960	2.8	2.8	3.4	2.4
1960–1970	2.6	2.5	3.6	2.7
1970–1980	2.3	2.2	3.8	2.4

*The figures for the years prior to the formation of Malaysia in 1963 are aggregates of the census figures for Peninsular Malaysia, Sabah and Sarawak. For years where no census figures were available, the estimates were derived by using the intercensal growth rates of the region.
Source: Banci Penduduk dan Perumahan Malaysia 1980, *Laporan Am Banci Penduduk*, p. 13.

Table 3: Education

Figures in '000	1970	1980	1985	1986	1987	1988(e)
Primary school enrollment	1,680	2,008	2,191	2,232	2,270	2,332
Primary school[1] enrollment ratio (%)	88.2	94.5	95.0	96.59	97.1	99.0
Secondary school[2] enrollment	545	1,084	1,293	1,321	1,339	1,345
University enrollment	8	23	43	49	48	51
Number of teachers—Total	58	103	150	156	169	174
Non-graduates	56	83	132	138	—	—
Graduates	2	9	17	18	—	—
Number of teachers in primary schools[1]	54	73	91	98	105	109
Number of teachers in secondary schools[2]	20	26.5	23.4	—	64	64.8
Pupil/teacher ratio (primary and secondary)	28.9	30.5	26.5	23.4	21.5	21.3

[1]Primary school enrollment as a percentage of total primary school-age population (i.e. children aged 6–11 years).
[2]Including secondary technical and vocational schools.
(e) estimates
Source: Ministry of Education, Malaysia.

Table 4: Federal Parliamentary Elections: 1955–1982
Total valid votes cast for party in terms of percentages

Party	1955	1959	1964	1969	1974	1978	1982
Alliance/BN	79.6	51.5	58.5	48.8	60.7	57.5	60.5
PAS	3.9	21.2	14.6	23*	—**	15.5	17.3
DAP	—	—	—	—	18.3	19.2	16.7
Other Opposition Parties	13.6	27.3	26.9	28.2	21	7.8	3.5

*estimates
**PAS at this stage was part of the Barisan Nasional

Table 5: Seats Contested and Won by Party

Party	1955 (a)	1955 (b)	1959 (a)	1959 (b)	1964 (a)	1964 (b)	1969 (a)	1969 (b)	1974 (a)	1974 (b)	1978 (a)	1978 (b)	1982 (a)	1982 (b)	1986 (a)	1986 (b)
Alliance/BN	52	51	104	74	104	89	118	68	154	135	153	131	142	132	176	148
Berjasa													2	0		
Berjaya (SBH)											10	9	11	10	4	0
DAP							24	13	46	9	53	16	63	9	64	24
Gerakan							14	8	8	5	6	4	7	5	9	5
Hamin															2	1
KITA											1	0				
Labour	4	0														
MCA	15	15	31	19	33	27	33	13	23	19	27	17	28	24	32	17
MIC	2	2	4	4	3	3	3	2	4	4	4	3	4	4	6	
Malayan Party			2	1												
NAP	9	0														
NasMa											4	0				
PAS	11	1	58	13	53	9	62	12	14	4	89	5	82	5	98	1
PBB (SK)							24	5	16	9	8	8	8	8	8	8
Pekemas									36	1	1	0	1	0		
PN	30	0	10	1	4	0										
PPM											1	0				
PUSAKA													2	0		
Pesaka (SK)							15	3								
Parti Rakyat							6	0								
PAJAR (SK)													1	0		
PBS															20	15
PBDS															4	4
PSRM													4	0	4	0
PAP							11	1								
PPP	2	0	19	4	9	2	6	4	4	1	1	0				
Perak Malay League	3	0														

PASOK (SBH)													7	0		
PLUS (SK)											2	0				
PW Labour			1	0												
SCA (SBH)							3	3	3	3	2	0	2	0		
SCA (SK)							3	2								
SNAP (SK)							23	8	24	9	9	9	9	6	5	5
Sapo											31	1	1	0		
SUPP (SK)							19	5	8	6	7	6	7	5	7	4
Semangat Pemuda Melayu	1	0														
SDP											1	0	1	0		
SF			38	8	63	2										
UDP					27	1										
UMCO							3	0								
UMNO	35	34	70	51	68	59	68	52	61	61	74	69	74	70	83	83
USNO (SBH)					13	12	13	13	7	5	5	0				
Independents	18	0	26	3	8	0	35	1	56	0	94	2	61	8	40	4
Total Seats	52		104		144		154		154		154		379		177	

Please see notes below:

1. Following the outbreak of disturbances of 13 May, 1969 and the proclamation of the state of emergency throughout Malaysia on 15 May, all elections which remained uncompleted on that date were suspended. This suspension affected Sabah and Sarawak and the parliamentary constituencies of Tuaran in Sabah and Kanowit in Sarawak where in each of the constituencies a candidate had died. In the case of Tuaran a fresh nomination was filed but the papers were rejected as invalid. This resulted in the only other candidate being unopposed. In the case of the parliamentary constituency of Kanowit one new nomination was received and the election was contested.

2. One of the independents elected for 1987 was in fact a non-party supporter of the BN and should therefore be counted as such.

Note:

(a) refers to number of seats contested; (b) refers to number of seats won. The figures underlined indicate that the party referred to is a member of the Alliance/Barisan Nasional for the election (therefore the total have been subsumed under the Alliance/BN total and should not be added separately in computing total number of seats for that electoral year). The figures above for 1969 refer to the composition of Parliament and the state of the parties when Parliament was reconvened in 1971.

SBH–Sabah; SK–Sarawak

Table 6: The 1990 General Elections (Facts and Figures)

	Barisan (%)	Opposition (%)
STATE		
Perlis	65	35
Kedah	62	38
Kelantan	33	67
Trengganu	54	46
Penang	51	49
Perak	56	44
Pahang	63	37
Selangor	58	42
Federal Territory	43	57
Negeri Sembilan	60	40
Melaka	62	38
Johor	61	39
Labuan	60	40
Sabah	32	68
Sarawak	58	42
STATE CAPITAL		
Kangar	69	31
Alor Setar	56	44
Kota Baru	31	69
Kuala Trengganu	47	53
Georgetown	30	70
Ipoh	42	58
Kuantan	57	43
Shah Alam	62	38
Seremban	50	50
Melaka	36	64
Johor Baru	58	42
Kota Kinabalu	47	53
Kuching	43	57

Source: *Aliran Monthly*, Vol. 10, No. 10, 1990, p. 41.

Parliamentary Seats by Party 1990 (1986 figures in brackets)

Barisan		Opposition	
UMNO	71 (83)	DAP	20 (24)
MCA	18 (17)	Semangat '46	8 (—)*
Gerakan	5 (5)	PAS	7 (1)
MIC	6 (6)	PBS	14 (10)**
PBB	10 (8)	Ind./Others	4 (4)
SUPP	4 (4)		53 (29)
PBDS	4 (4)		
SNAP	3 (5)		
USNO	6 (5)		
Others	0 (1)		
	127 (148) (including PBS' 10 seats)		

*In 1986, Semangat '46 had not been formed yet.
**In 1986, PBS was a member of the BN coalition.
Source: *Far Eastern Economic Review*, 1 November 1990.

Table 7: Economy—The Leading Commercial Crops

Crop	hectares 1988	hectares 1989
Rubber	1,870,000	1,848,600
Oil Palm	1,746,000	1,845,700
Padi	596,000	631,000
Cocoa	357,000	360,000
Coconut	267,900	n.a.
Tobacco	9,700	12,707
Pepper	8,622	9,400
Pineapple	7,000	n.a.

Source: Ministry of Finance, *Economic Report 1988/89, 1989/90.*
Figures are estimates and derived from the above source.

Table 8: Rubber—Area, Yield and Production (Peninsular Malaysia)

	1985	1986	1987	1988	1989(e)	1990(f)
Planted area ('000 ha)*	1,959.8	1,702	1,883	1,861	1,849	1,836
Yield (kg/ha):						
Smallholdings	933	1,072	1,107	1,191	1,193	1,194
Estates	1,419	1,497	1,531	1,496	1,503	1,549
Production ('000 tonnes)	1,469.4	1,539	1,581	1,660	1,580	1,590
Smallholdings**	965.1	1,042	1,083	1,186	1,116	1,128
Estates	504	497	498	474	464	462
% of World Production	33.9	34.7	33.8	32.9	30.9	30.1

(e) = estimates
(f) = forecasts

**Planted area in 1989(e):*
Estates: 35%
Smallholdings: 65%

***Distribution of smallholdings 1988:*
Peninsular Malaysia—84.4%
Sabah—11.2%
Sarawak—4.2%

Source: Ministry of Finance, *Economic Report 1988/89, 1989/90.*

Table 9: Oil Palm—Area and Palm Oil Production

	1985	1986	1987	1988	1989(e)	1990(f)
Planted area ('000 ha)[1]	1,482	1,543	1,685	1,785	1,845	1,905
Production ('000 tonnes)[2]						
Crude Palm Oil (CPO)	4,133	4,544	4,532	5,027	5,515	5,800
Palm kernel oil	512	590	610	621	743	789
CPO % of world production	60.0	60.7	59.0	58.1	57.4	55.8

(e) = estimates
(f) = forecasts

[1]*Planted area in 1989(e):*
Estates: 47%
Public sector: 44.7%
Smallholders: 8.3%

Distribution of area:
Peninsular Malaysia—86.2%
Sabah/Sarawak—13.8%

[2]*Production by area:*
Peninsular Malaysia—91.3%
Sabah/Sarawak—13.8%

Source: Ministry of Finance, *Economic Report, 1988/89, 1989/90.*

Table 10: Pepper—Area and Production

	1985	1986	1987	1988	1989(e)	1990(f)
Planted area ('000 ha)	5.3	5.9	7.7	8.7	9.4	—
Total production (million kg)	15.3	13.8	25.1	19.4	23.2	26.8

(e) = estimates
(f) = forecasts

Distribution of area:
Sarawak—97.3%
Sabah—1.7%
Peninsula—1.0%

Production:
Sarawak—99%
Sabah—0.7%
Peninsula—0.3%

Source: Ministry of Finance, *Economic Report 1988/89, 1989/90.*

Table 11: Cocoa—Area and Production

	1986	1987	1988	1989(e)	1990(f)
Planted area ('000 ha)	332	339	357	360	—
Peninsular Malaysia	32.8%				
Sabah	55.5%				
Sarawak	11.7%				
Production ('000 tonnes)	78.4	183	204	250	260
Peninsular Malaysia	28.0%				
Sabah	66.8%				
Sarawak	5.2%				

(e) = estimates
(f) = forecasts
Source: Ministry of Finance, *Economic Report 1988/89, 1989/90.*

Table 12: Padi—Area and Production

	1985	1986	1987	1988	1989(e)	1990(f)
Planted area ('000 ha)	663.3	711.1	609.6	641.6	631	627.7
Total production ('000 tonnes)	1,963.1	1,721.6	1,662.9	1,742.9	1,718.9	1,700.2
MADA production ('000 tonnes)	805.6	803.1	644.7	698.4	640	650
KADA production ('000 tonnes)	133.7	142.9	127.2	131.1	127.4	162.8

(e) = estimates
(f) = forecasts
Source: Ministry of Finance, *Economic Report 1988/89, 1989/90.*

Table 13: Forestry Areas

	1987	1988	1989(e)	1990(f)
Total area under forest (million ha)	20.3	20.2	20.1	—
Distribution:				
Sarawak: 46.8%				
Peninsula: 31.3%				
Sabah: 21.9%				
Permanent Forest Estate (PFE) in 1988 (million ha):				
Peninsula Malaysia		4.8		
Sabah		2.8		
Sarawak		4.6		
Total		**12.2**		
Productive:				
Peninsula Malaysia		2.9		
Sabah		2.7		
Sarawak		3.2		
Total		**8.8**		
Compensatory Forest Project (CFP) in Pen. Malaysia (ha)	7,090 ('85)	20,000 ('88)		

(e) = estimates
(f) = forecasts
Source: Ministry of Finance, *Economic Report 1988/89, 1989/90.*

Table 14: Timber Production

	1986	1987	1988	1989(e)	1990(f)
Sawlogs (million cu.m)*	29.7	35.9	36.4	35.4	35.1
Sawn timber (million cu.m)	5.5	6.1	6.5	6.87	6.81

(e) = estimates
(f) = forecasts
*rubberwood logs = 3.9% of saw log production (in 1988, 2.7%)

Distribution Sawlogs:	*Distribution Sawn Timber:*
Pen. Malaysia—29.9%	Pen. Malaysia—77.2%
Sabah—26.6%	Sabah—16.7%
Sarawak—43.5%	Sarawak—6.3%

Source: Ministry of Finance, *Economic Report 1989/90.*

Table 15: Tin—Production, Number of Mines and Employment

	1985	1986	1987	1988	1989(e)	1990(f)
Production ('000 tonnes)	36.9	29.1	30.4	28.9	30.0	31.0
Number of Mines	279	197	221	219	253	
Dredges	29	31	30	32	34	
Gravel pumps	207	122	146	144	176	
Other	43	44	45	43	43	
Workers employed	16,829	10,855	10,049	11,445	12,400	

(e) = estimates
(f) = forecasts
Source: Ministry of Finance, *Economic Report, 1989/90.*

Table 16: Crude Petroleum Production Figures

	1985	1986	1987	1988	1989(e)	1990(f)
Total production ('000 bpd)[1]	446.4	523.0	497.9	522.3	563.0	570.0
Processed ('000 bpd)[2]			146.8	155.8	164.6	
Free World total prod. (mbpd)		47.4	46.6	48.8	49.3	

[1]*Domestic production 1988:*

Oilfields: Sarawak—24
Sabah—12
Pen.Malaysia—17
Total—53

Oilwells: Sarawak—229
Sabah—130
Pen.Malaysia—257
Total—616

% Total Sarawak—26%
Sabah—17%
Pen. Malaysia—62%
Total—100%

[2]*Crude oil processed:*
Domestic—75%
Kerteh, Trengganu—21.6% calculated on basis new field, Seligi, coming onstream in December 1988.

(bpd) = barrels per day
(mbpd) = million barrels per day
Source: Ministry of Finance, *Economic Report 1988/89, 1989/90.*

Table 17: Natural Gas

	1985	1986	1987	1988(e)	1989(f)
Total gross prod. (mscf/d)	—	1,525	1,560	1,700	—
Liquefied Natural Gas (LNG) (million tonnes)	4.6	5.5	5.91	6.2	6.44
Liquefied Petroleum Gas (LPG) ('000 tonnes)	—	277.6	296.7	298.0	—

(e) = estimates (mscf/d) = million cubic feet per day
(f) = forecasts
Source: Ministry of Finance, *Economic Report 1988/89*.

Table 18: Commerce—Balance of Trade

Year	Exports		Imports		Balance of Trade
	$ ('000,000)	growth (%)	$ ('000,000)	growth (%)	$ ('000,000)
1989(e)	66.4	+20.2	57.7	+33.3	8.7
1988	55.2	+22.2	43.3	+35.9	11.9
1987	45.1	+26.4	31.9	+14.4	13.2
1986	35.7	− 6.0	27.9	− 8.3	3.8
1985	38.0	− 1.6	30.4	− 7.6	7.5

(e) = estimates
Source: Ministry of Finance, *Economic Report 1988/89, 1989/90.*

ASEAN Countries: Balance of Trade 1987 and 1988 (US$ million)

Year	Brunei	Indonesia	Malaysia	Philippines	Singapore	Thailand
1988	n.a.	5,973.0	4,383.5	−1,090.0	−4,600.0	−3,800.0
1987	n.a.	4,623.0	5,337.7	−1,495.0	−3,870.0	−1,643.0

Source: Ministry of Finance, *Economic Report 1989/90.*

Table 19: Exports—By Commodity
(1) The Six Leading Commodities (i.e. in 1989)

Commodity	Year	Volume ('000 tonnes)	Value $ ('000,000)	Growth (Value) (%)	Share of total exports (Value) (%)	Position
Electrical &	1989**	—	10,164	—	28.4	1
Electronic	1988	—	14,039	+36.9	21.1	1
Products	1987	—	10,251	+28.7	22.7	1
	1985	—	6,028	− 4.5	15.8	2
Crude	1989*	20,747	7,312	+19.3	11.0	2
Petroleum/	1988	19,899	6,128	− 2.6	11.1	2
Petroleum	1987	18,039	6,290	+16.5	13.9	2
	1985	16,701	8,697	− 0.4	22.8	1
Palm Oil	1989*	4,650	4,473	− 1.2	6.7	3
	1988	4,150	4,528	+39.1	8.2	4
	1987	4,044	3,250	+ 8.0	7.2	5
	1985	3,215	3,951	−12.8	10.4	3
Natural	1989*	1,520	4,320	−17.8	6.5	4
Rubber	1988	1,610	5,256	+34.2	9.5	3
	1987	1,662	3,917	+23.1	8.6	4
	1985	1,497	2,872	−21.8	7.5	4
Timber	1989*	20,000	4,200	+ 4.7	6.3	5
(Sawlogs)	1988	20,562	4,010	− 6.3	7.3	5
(production	1987	23,001	4,280	+48.8	9.5	3
in '000 cu.m)	1985	19,360	2,771	− 1.3	7.3	5
Liquid	1989*	6,400	1,952	+ 3.6	3.0	6
Natural Gas	1988	6,266	1,885	+ 8.2	3.4	6
(LNG)	1987	6,014	1,742	− 8.1	3.8	—
	1985	4,389	2,300	−29.6	6.0	6

* estimates ** first six months
Source: Ministry of Finance, *Economic Report, 1989/90.*

Table 20: Other Principal Exports

Commodity	Year	Volume ('000 tonnes)	Growth (Volume) (%)	Value $ ('000,000)	Growth (Value) (%)
Agriculture	1989*	180.0	− 5.0	547.2	−22.7
Cocoa ('000 tonnes)	1988	189.4	+20.4	708.3	+ 3.6
	1987	157.3	+48.1	684	+37.9
	1985	81.5	+23.3	409.5	+21.1
Pepper ('000 tonnes)	1989*	23.2	+14.2	161.9	− 1.9
	1988	19.4	+28.6	158.7	+30.6
	1987	14.2	− 7.0	110.0	−32.5
	1985	18.6	+12.0	139.0	+75.0
Minerals	1989*	51.0	+ 4.2	1,173.0	+28.7
Tin ('000 tonnes)	1988	48.9	− 1.4	911.2	+ 8.6
	1987	49.6	+22.8	839	+29.1
	1985	57.4	+44.9	1,648	+41.8
Manufactures	1989**	—	—	1,261	+14.4
Chemical & Petroleum	1988	—		1,912	22.4
Products	1987	—		1,583	+19.7
	1985	—		1,412	+ 4.6
Food, Beverages & Tobacco	1989**	—	—	736	+29.2
Products	1988	—		1,043	+15.6
	1987	—		880	+16.9
	1985	—		594	− 9.5
Iron & Steel Products	1989**	—	—	782	+43.5
	1988	—		1,000	+30.6
	1987	—		694	+56.3
	1985	—		300	+20.9

Table 20: Other Principal Exports *(continued)*

Commodity	Year	Volume ('000 tonnes)	Growth (Volume) (%)	Value $ ('000,000)	Growth (Value) (%)
Machinery & Transport	1989*	—	—	1,308	+57.5
Equipment Products	1988	—		1,625	+10.9
	1987	—		1,447	+40.0
	1985	—		1,031	+ 2.0
Rubber Products	1989*	—	—	213	+26.6
	1988	—		326	+25.4
	1987	—		243	+56.7
	1985	—		113	+ 6.5
Textiles	1989**	—	—	2,032	+36.5
	1988	—		2,958	+22.8
	1987	—		2,285	+39.0
	1985	—		1,289	+12.8
Wood-based Products	1989*	—	—	582	+14.6
	1988	—		918	+ 7.5
	1987	—		849	+59.0
	1985	—		363	−14.4

* estimates ** first six months

Source: Ministry of Finance, *Economic Report, 1989/90.*

Table 21: Exports by Sector (in terms of value percentages)

Year	Agriculture	Mineral	Manufacturing
1989*	29.5	15.8	54.7
1988	35	16.6	48.4
1987	35.5	19.6	44.9
1985	34.7	32.8	32.0
1965	54.5	30.0	12.2

* estimates
Source: Ministry of Finance, *Economic Report, 1989/90.*

Table 22: Exports—By Direction

The Primary Products (in terms of total values of export per commodity)

	Year	S'pore	Japan	USA	France (European Ec. Community City)	Italy (European Ec. Community City)	U.K. (European Ec. Community City)	W.G'ny Neths (European Ec. Community City)	Asean	S.K.	China	USSR	India	Rest of World
Overall % (value)	1989	19.2	16.5	17.8		14.9			5.4	4.9				2.2
Commodity:														
Rubber	1989*	9.5	5.9	10.9	—	6.0	4.4	6.4			3.9			53.0
	1988	11.7	6.3	8.8	2.7	4.8	4.4	5.5			7.6	4.5		43.7
	1985	11.6	6.2	9.9	4.0	5.3	5.2	7.5			5.5	6.2		38.1
Tin	1989*		26.9	10.1				28.0N						35.0
	1988		31.3	10.8				19.0N						38.9
	1985		17.1	0.8				71.1						11.0
Crude Petroleum	1989*	28.3	17.8	6.5					6.1T					41.3
	1988	32.4	19.8	5.3					6.4T					36.1
	1985	25.9	33.7	0.6					11.5					28.3
Palm Oil	1989*	15.3		2.4				2.6N					4.2	75.5
	1988	13.8		4.0				4.7N					17.8	60.7
	1985	30.1	6.3	4.0			1.2	3.9N					20.8	33.9
Sawn Logs	1989*	21.4			7.8		4.9	25.0	12.8					17.7
	1988	19.5			7.5		4.9	21.8	8.3T					24.7
	1985		65.8							14.6	11.8TW			7.9

Abbrev.: W.G'ny = West Germany; S.K. = South Korea; N = Netherlands; T = Thailand; TW = Taiwan
* first six months of 1989.
Source: Derived from Ministry of Finance, *Economic Report 1988/89*.

Table 23: Imports—By Source

	1985		1987		1988		1989[1]	
	'000 tonnes	$ million	'000 tonnes	$ million	'000 tonnes	$ million	'000 tonnes	$ million
Machinery & Transport Equipment—SITC *								
Total		13,262		14,356		19,539		12,644
France		436		223		294		122
Japan		4,372		4,263		6,309		4,377
U.K.		480		586		756		431
U.S.A.		3,178		4,340		5,476		3,125
W. Germany		767		705		859		555
Manufactured Goods SITC—6 + 8								
Total		6,095		6,946		9,816		6,048
Australia		229		232		366		224
China		194		293		348		199
Hong Kong		290		437		543		297
Japan		2,031		1,882		2,691		1,711
Singapore		449		530		895		525
U.K.		296		381		550		303
U.S.A.		474		593		823		385
Crude Petroleum								
Total	2,252	1,126	1,549	487	1,508	410	427	134
Kuwait	996	497	989	212	418	111	101	34
Saudi Arabia	1,256	629	516	158	766	218	185	57
Food—SITC 0								
Total Food		3,064		2,996		3,839		2,228
Australia		655		673		848		383
China		235		260		366		351
Thailand		791		648		713		530
U.S.A.		222		232		302		118

Table 23: Imports—By Source *(continued)*

	1985		1987		1988		1989[1]	
	'000 tonnes	$ million	'000 tonnes	$ million	'000 tonnes	$ million	'000 tonnes	$ million
Rice—								
Total	428	257	198	105	184	212	120	90
Burma	45	27	14	7	—	—	—	—
Thailand	334	200	178	92	272	203	120	89
Wheat—								
Total	599	242	617	214	758	320	331	185
Australia	346	140	483	167	482	204	219	122
U.S.A.	66	29	75	28	51	22	13	8
Raw Sugar—								
Total	593	313	639	334	723	4,393	22	220
Australia	415	232	409	214	520	317	141	95
Thailand	74	21	101	47	37	21	125	86
Dairy Products—								
Total		237		282		378		303
Australia		67		81		102		68
Denmark		34		38		34		19
Netherlands		9		14		—		—
New Zealand		98		126		229		160

* Standard International Trade Classification; [1] = January to July
Source: Ministry of Finance, *Economic Report, 1989/90.*

Table 24: Imports by Country (in terms of value percentage and position)

Year	Japan		ASEAN*		U.S.A.		EEC**		Aust.		W.Asia		Rest of World
	%	P	%	P	%	P	%	P	%	P	%	P	%
1989*	24.3	1	19.1	2	16.5	3	13.7	4	—	—	—	—	26.4
1988	23.5	1	18.8	2	17.7	3	13.4	4	—	—	—	—	26.6
1987	21	2	22	1	18	3	13	4	4	5	2	6	21
1985	21	2	22	1	19	3	13	4	4	5	3	6	18

P = position
* Singapore: 1989 = 13.7%; 1988 = 13.2%; 1987 = 15%; 1986 = 15%
** West Germany & Netherlands: 1988 = 4.8%; 1987 = 5%; 1986 = 5%

Table 25: Imports by Function (for first 7 months of 1989)

	Intermediate	Investment	Consumption
Overall %	44.9 • manufacturing (75.3%) • electronic components (45%): textiles, plastics, food, machine parts, metallic ores • agricultural (6.1%): fertilisers, pesticides, crude petroleum	32.4 • machinery (28.8%) • metal products (21.3%): transport equipment, electronic fittings, heavy machinery, telecoms equipment	21.6 • motorcycles, bicycles, fans • jewelry & precious stones • food—rice, cereals, beverages, tobacco

Tables 24 and 25—Source: Ministry of Finance, *Economic Report, 1989/90.*

Table 26: Overall Trade—Trading Partners, 1988

	Value ($ million)	% of total trade
ASEAN*	12,033	22.3
JAPAN	10,699	19.8
U.S.A.	9,327	17.3
EEC	7,402	13.7

* Singapore = 16.8% of Malaysia's trade
= 75.3% of Malaysia's trade with ASEAN

Source: Ministry of Finance, *Economic Report, 1988/89.*

Table 27: Balance of Payments

	$ million, Malaysia		
	1988	1989[2]	1990[2]
A. Merchandise Account Balance	+14,557	+11,220	+11,616
Exports (f.o.b.)	+14,557	+11,220	+11,616
Imports (f.o.b.)	40,039	54,557	62,325
B. Freight and Insurance	−10,265	−11,087	−11,591
C. Other transportation	− 2,108	− 2,592	− 2,787
D. Travel	− 21	+ 65	+ 37
E. Investment income	− 1,552	− 1,462	− 1,348
F. Government transactions	− 4,941	− 5,337	− 5,665
G. Other services	− 245	− 276	− 270
H. Balance on services	− 1,398	− 1,485	− 1,558
I. Balance on goods and services (I = A + H)	+ 4,292	+ 133	+ 25
J. Transfers (net)	+ 48	+ 90	+ 90
K. Balance on current account (K = I + J)	+ 4,720	+ 223	+ 115
L. Balance on long-term capital	− 3,279	− 1,282	—
M. Basic balance (M = K + L)	+ 1,441	+ 1,505	—
N. Private capital[1] (net)	− 2,893	− 1,000	—
O. Errors and omissions	+ 348	− 1,000	—
P. Overall balance (surplus +/deficit −) (P = M + N + O)	− 1,104	+ 1,505	—

Notes:
[1]A negative symbol indicates a build-up in reserves.
[2]Estimates by Ministry of Finance.
Source: Statistics Department.

Table 28: Federal Government Expenditure/Revenue

Year	Total		Operating Expenditure		Development Expenditure		Revenue Increase		Balance
	M$	%	M$	%	M$	%	M$	%	+/–
1985	20,066	73.3	7,142	26.3	27,208	100	21,144	1.5	–6,408
1986[1]	20,075	72.6	7,559	27.4	27,634	100	19,518	7.5	–3,116
1987[1]	20,186	80.98	4,741	19.02	24,927	100	18,143	– 7.0	–6,784
1988[2]	21,340	77.99	6,021	22.01	27,361	100	21,448	+18.2	–5,913
1989[3]	22,286	74.8	7,479	25.2	29,765	100	22,742	+ 6.0	–7,023

[1]Estimated action
[2]Latest estimate
[3]Budget estimate
*Tables 3 to 5 and 7 to 28 are taken from *Information Malaysia 1989 Yearbook* (Kuala Lumpur: Berita Publishers, 1989), pp. 282–502; *Information Malaysia 1990–91 Yearbook* (Kuala Lumpur: Berita Publishers, 1990), pp. 117–131, 240–245.

GLOSSARY

adat	customs, language
bahasa	language
Bendahara	the principal official in a kingdom, often likened to a Prime Minister
dakwah	to "call" or "invite", i.e. the duty of Moslems to call all mankind to Islam. In Malaysia the term is associated with a fundamentalist Islamic revival movement
Dato' or Datuk	a title often associated with a great non royal chief; in modern Malaysia the term "Datuk" is conferred in recognition of outstanding service to the nation
Durbar	Conference of Rulers, referring to the periodical meeting of the Rulers of the Malay States
hikayat	narrative, story, tale in prose
jihad	the Holy War, which is an Islamic concept referring essentially to the spread of the faith through force of arms, but used commonly in the Moslem areas of Southeast Asia in earlier centuries as a cry for unity among fellow Moslems to destroy the Christian Europeans in the area
kampung	a village; a compound of houses usually under the authority of an important individual
kongsi	Chinese business co-operative
kuala	estuary
Menteri	Minister

Min Yuen	civilian support units for the Malayan Communist Party during the Emergency
negeri	settlement, state, country
orang asli	indigenous groups living on the Malay peninsula excluding ethnic Malays
padi	rice
penghulu	headman; head of a village; district head
sungai	river
syariah	Islamic law
Temenggung	Malay Minister in charge of defence, justice, and palace affairs
umat or ummat or ummah	the world community of Moslems
Yan diPertuan Agung	Paramount Ruler

ABOUT THE AUTHOR

AMARJIT KAUR (B.A., M.A., Dip.Ed. University of Malaya; Cert. in Southeast Asian Studies, M.Phil., Ph.D. Columbia University, New York) was born in Kuala Lumpur where she received her school and undergraduate education. She is currently Senior Lecturer in the Department of Economic History at the University of New England, Armidale, N.S.W., Australia. Prior to joining the University of New England, Dr Kaur was an Associate Professor in the History Department at the University of Malaya in Kuala Lumpur, where she taught Southeast Asian and Malaysian History/ Economic History. She has researched extensively in this field and her publications include two sole-authored books, three edited books, book chapters and articles in professional journals. In 1983–84, she held an American Council of Learned Societies Fellowship at the Economics Department, Harvard University. She was also a Senior Associate Member at St Antony's College, Oxford University in 1989–90. Dr Kaur is currently writing a book on the economic history of East Malaysia and has also embarked on a general economic history of Malaysia.